HOW EXTREME IS GRACE?

Paid in Full

Deon Stevens

Contents

PREFACE

"Grace, yes please! Extreme grace, no thank you!"

A dear friend of mine has been watching the development of the message of grace with a jaundiced eye. I am not at all surprised at his misgivings—I believe his views are fairly widely shared by much of the church—some more vocal in their disapproval of it than others. Should we be concerned? How well do our grace paradigms stack up in terms of scripture?

My friend strongly objects to something he calls "extreme grace". He is convinced that it is the great end-time deception. He cautions believers to steer clear of this new-fangled gospel.

It is true to say that all believers embrace grace, but some are only prepared to go along with it to a point. To them freedom is scary—bordering on licenced disobedience and permissive ungodliness. If this is true, then we have good reason to reject it.

Well, let's check it out. Obviously, if it is not fully supported by scripture, it is heresy! If it equals licence, then it should not be touched; not even with a barge pole! More than that, it should be rejected with contempt! As believers, we aspire to live uprightly, and have every right to resist anything that invites anything less!

Believers often feel threatened by doctrinal views that do not fit neatly into their particular denominational boxes. But not a single church constitution was drafted by Jesus. The issues that are irksome to us, are not in the least bit irksome to Him. He loves us for who we are; not for how rigidly we tow the "company line". Different perspectives should be welcomed—they are a healthy sign of deeper thinking—it shows that we are not mindlessly led by our noses, as with so many cults moonlighting as Christianity. I think I understand why grace is resisted—after all, I was of the same opinion for most of my Christian journey.

Four people sitting around a table looking at a Cola bottle would each describe the detail of it differently. One may see the familiar Coca Cola logo, while each of the others may see something different, such as the bar code or nutritional value on the section of label facing them. The fact that each of them come up with different descriptions does not make one description more right than the others. In fact, the complete depiction cannot be known until all four have given their input. If one of them were to be excluded from the discussion, the conclusions of the group would be incomplete and in danger of being inaccurate. This point is clearly illustrated by the varying viewpoints of the four writers of the Gospels. The fact that each of them described the same events differently does not invalidate their accounts; to the contrary, it gives us a more complete picture of events.

If we have taken a particular stand on something as crucial as our relationship with God, we should welcome, and even invite debate. We should be open to having our convictions tested as fresh illumination of old truths is forthcoming. Failure to do so has divided the body of Christ; resulting in denominationally divided persuasions, each believing their particular version of the creed to be complete in itself.

I will endeavour to add a fresh perspective. I trust my contribution will reveal a little more of our Father's love.

In my experience, we do not necessarily hold to dogma because of its correctness. If that were the case, the whole Christian community would concur on every doctrine. Rather, we are apt to adopt the conclusions of our early mentors, often holding to them without question. Usually our current perspectives rigidly follow the pre-dogmatised opinions of our particular religious stream. But herein lies a danger—our beliefs become sacrosanct—an inflexible framework upon which all other conclusions must hang. We are apt to reject, often without due consideration, any ideas that clash with what we have already settled upon. To us, our denominational perspective is the only perspective—some may even be prepared to die in a shootout for what they believe, as is the case with Northern Ireland's Protestants and Catholics. They were prepared to die for doctrine that neither side may have interpreted correctly.

Is it possible that nobody has the complete picture, and that without the rest of the story being told, we have stopped short of understanding all that the blood covenant embraces? With this in mind, I would like to express my thoughts in a way that is respectful to those of contrary persuasion, yet open enough to be honest. Please forgive me if I fail to keep to this delicate balance.

On my journey of discovering the depths of God's love, I have often been cautioned by well-meaning friends to steer clear of anything that smacks of extremism. But are there degrees to grace? I have since discovered that His love is so extreme that it is beyond reason, as is clearly demonstrated by the extreme lengths He went to to express His love to us. What could be more convincing than dying for us? Surely, nothing could be more extreme?

I am grateful to my church for helping me to understand the basics of grace, but unless I experience His love first-hand, I simply forgo the joy of absorbing His affections for me. As with salt on steak, grace brings out the flavour of the gospel—without it the gospel is bland—in fact without it, the gospel doesn't even exist. Grace is not a necessary evil like medicine—it is the very essence of the good news of the gospel!

Do we really grasp just how dearly we are loved and cherished by our heavenly Dad? I have discovered that no matter how enlightened I am, there is always more of His affection to be discovered. Grace is a never ending journey marked with the thoughtfulness of an attentive Lover. In unveiling more and more of Himself, more and more of His love is unveiled. Be prepared to be enthralled throughout eternity!

Paul said that we will never fully understand the enormity of His love—its sheer magnanimity exceeds our sense of fairness. We tend to withhold favour from those, who in our estimation, are not worthy of it. But not God!

Although God has only one measure of grace, the same cannot be said for believers—we are divided—one religious persuasion labelling another "the error of extreme grace". For simplicity sake I will refer to the two schools of thought as "extreme grace" and "un-extreme grace". The measure of grace that we personally experience is often limited to the insights of our mentors.

When love is graciously dispensed without conditions, it is enormously liberating, yet enormously scary for those standing on the side lines. Are these fears justified? Let's take a closer look.

Fruit of the Spirit is a perfect description of God's character. For example, the reason that love is a fruit of the Spirit is plain and simply because God is love (1John 4:8).

Just as a megaphone amplifies a voice, our capacity to love others is divinely amplified by His love for us—it awakens our love for Him, and in the process, everybody benefits from our awakening—love begetting love!

What we discover in the pages of our Bibles about His love is only the introduction to a divine romance—romance simply cannot be scripted—it must be experienced to be real. In Ephesians 3:14-21, Paul urged us to put our roots down *"deep"* into His love in order to experience its riches. In this way, we become filled with the fullness of life—the same life that Jesus called abundant life. But we can only benefit from this promise if we have not reduced His love to our denomination's small concept of His grace. In the same passage, Paul went on to say that His love is so limitless that it can never be fully comprehended.

While the Holy Spirit is producing His gorgeous fruit through us, there is no need for our behaviour to be restrained. When we are being changed by the perfect love of God, as vested in His grace, the law has nothing further to add. After all, the fruit of His Spirit is a flawless manifestation of godliness. Law cannot impart even the tiniest molecule of grace to us, but the Spirit is different—He dispenses love and life with great dollops of mercy and grace!

It does not follow, that just because we are Christians, we will extend grace to others. But when we are bearing His fruit, it is different—graciousness exudes from us!

Love has a unique way of getting our attention—it speaks to the very core of who we are. We are more likely to allow lovers, rather than accusers into the guarded places of our hearts. When our actions are motivated by love, we don't need to be compelled to walk uprightly; it is something we do with eagerness!

Paul knew that we would have trouble getting our minds around the generosity of grace, and that's why he said that we will need special help to understand it (Eph 3:14-21). The Holy Spirit offers that help.

I believe that our Father wants us never to stop growing in our understanding of His magnificent love for us, and with this in mind, I trust that the words of this book will be useful to you.

If nothing else is achieved through these pages, then at the very least, by the time you turn the last page, I trust that you will be even more convinced that your heavenly Dad greatly values your friendship and cherishes your company! *"God is love"* (1Jn 4:8)—not merely in an academic sense, but like a besotted lover, He is in love, and it is you with whom He is in love!

REPENTANCE

Does being under grace make repentance unnecessary?

It was rumoured that a prominent pastor had declared that his church was not into repentance. "Repentance is for the unsaved. We are into grace".

Dr Martin Lloyd Jones said, "If you are not being misquoted and misunderstood, you are probably not preaching the Gospel".

Firstly, I suspect that this story may well be hearsay—did the pastor actually say it this way? Did the bearer of this tale take the trouble to explain the context in which it was said? Stories have a habit of changing with the telling. If, however, it was accurately conveyed, then consider the following:

Just because some misguided leaders have misunderstood what "extreme grace" is, is not a good reason to be sceptical of it. There is always a risk that a wonderful gospel concept can be misunderstood and these misunderstandings be adopted as non-negotiable dogma.

Let's set the record straight—repentance is part and parcel of everyday living. We are to renew our minds daily, and in this process, we often find that we have taken a wrong turn. The act of turning towards God, is an act of repentance—it is the part we play in God's character shaping process of bringing our actions into line with our sanctification. Let's settle this question once and for all: Repentance is vital for the spiritual health and wellbeing of all believers.

The question I deal with in this book, is the purpose for repenting and where it fits into the *"finished"* work of the cross.

According to Matthew 4:17, Jesus' opening words in His first sermon were, *"Repent, for the kingdom of heaven is at hand."* Notice that Jesus didn't simply call people to turn from something negative, He called them to awaken to something enormously positive—nothing less than *"the kingdom of heaven"*. He didn't resort to law bashing to motivate repentance; He used a higher motivation—enticing people to reach out for better things—nothing less than divine royalty—the high privilege of kingdom citizenship! Repentance is heart preparation. Although it cannot earn us more grace, it sure does keep us focused on grace—a free gift that cannot be deserved.

Compared to God's perfect holiness, we are all deficient, self-centred and sinful. When we turn in repentance, we do so in order to embrace something that is so much higher and better than anything sin can offer—there is nothing higher than a life of grace—that's because there is nobody higher than the God of grace. Repentance involves a change of attitude. And with right attitudes, right behaviour soon follows.

When we repent, we are turning away from wrong thinking to adopt kingdom thinking. With kingdom thinking comes kingdom living! *"Your kingdom come. Your will be done on earth as it is in heaven"* (Mat 6:10). Imagine that! As citizens of the kingdom, we have the privilege of living abundant lives, potentially devoid of worry, sickness and lack, similar to the way it is in heaven!

We cannot simply confine repentance to the day we came to know Jesus as Saviour for the first time. After all, in the book of Revelation, when Jesus called the churches to repentance, He was addressing believers.

Repenting should be as natural to every believer as his or her daily ablutions. There are wonderful benefits to this practise, but one of them is not to secure something that Jesus has already secured for us. Something as lovely as repentance can so easily flip over into nothing more than empty ritual.

The very reason for the existence of religion is abominable to God. It replaces intimate fellowship with ritualism and red tape. Although meant to mimic reality, official procedures serve only to put distance into romance. No matter how religion may package it, formalities are formalities, and intimacy is intimacy—romance simply cannot be scripted.

When the supernatural ceases to be experienced, believers may seek meaningfulness in the teachings of recognised reformers and revivalists—but to live by their experiences is not the same as feeding directly from the hand of God. Each believer is invited to develop a first-hand romance with Jesus!

The truth is that even distinguished reformers and revivalists were not entirely free of superfluous religious routines. As humans, they were every bit as fallible as you and me. The bottom line is that we are not to take their word above that of the Word of God. The relationship we have with our loving Father is unique—it is not mass produced on a religious assembly line. Although we love our children dearly, we relate to each of them differently, and so it is with God.

So, is repentance actually required of people of grace? Think of it this way: For every believer, a spiritual battle rages. The enemy cannot afford for us to accomplish our divinely ordained assignments. We are confronted at every turn with choices. As with finding our way through the tangled maze of city streets when travelling to an intended destination, each intersection requires yet another choice—should we turn left or right, or keep on going straight. We don't always make good choices, and at times find ourselves heading in the wrong direction. Our poor navigation skills sometimes land us in cul-de-sacs. When we find that we have come to a dead end, we have a decision to make—either to stay lost, or to retrace our steps. Making a 180° turn is what repentance is.

Life in the kingdom is no different; it's all about making choices—some good and some not so good. God, in His grace, has provided a way of escape from the perilous predicaments that our wrong choices often get us into; it's called repentance. Despite the fact that repentance is not difficult, believers often have difficulty getting around to it. Sadly, if we say that repentance is not necessary, we have chosen to stay lost.

When I say lost, there is a distinct difference between losing our salvation and losing our victory over life's challengers. In these writings, I shall endeavour to make this plain. The point to consider is: once we are saved, are we still looking for salvation—trying for dear life to hold onto it, or are we already traveling in the city called salvation, and attempting to navigate through the potholes and deviations on our way to obtaining the promises that accompany salvation?

"But we all, with unveiled face, beholding as in a mirror the glory of the Lord, are being transformed into the same image from glory to glory, just as by the Spirit of the Lord" (2Co 3:18).

Some teachers instruct us to go to God's mirror to reveal our sinfulness, but Paul's instruction is different; he instructs us to see the glory of the Lord in our reflection. To do this, we need to look beyond the obvious reflection of our sinfulness and see our Christlikeness. The strange anomaly about humanity is, that the discovery of sin in our lives does not cause us to sin less; to the contrary, it drags us into more sin. By the same token, seeing our righteousness does not cause us to sin more; it causes us to become more like the righteous person we visualise ourselves to be *"in Christ"*.

It is interesting to note that this scripture does not put the onus on us to change from glory to glory; it puts it on *"the Spirit of the Lord"*. Religion often places the burden of change upon its members; expecting them to shape up. Big mistake! While they are doing their level best to please their pastor, *"the Spirit of the Lord"* looks on, unable to play His sanctifying role.

What is this mirror? Is it the Bible? No! At the time that this instruction was given, the Bible, as we know it, had not yet been compiled. It wasn't the Torah either. The Torah was a hallowed scroll jealously guarded and available to Jews in Synagogues. The mirror is Jesus himself. Of course, now-a-days, we have the privilege of owning our own copies of the Bible, and can find Jesus described throughout its inspired pages. In His reflection, we see ourselves in the form of redeemed sons and daughters of the most-high God. When we look at Him, we are not merely looking at His divinity; we are staring straight into the eyes of the divine model of ourselves.

Having been reborn of the same Spirit as Jesus, we are of the same family and species as Him. We even share the same Father. If Jesus is royalty, then so are we. If Jesus is a prince, then so are we. If Jesus is loved of the Father, then so are we. If Jesus is one with the Father, then so are we. If Jesus is an overcomer, then so are we. After all, we are the very tangible body of Jesus here on earth. If everything is under His feet, then we, being His body, have everything under our feet. If He is the head and not the tail, blessed in the city and blessed in the country, blessed when He enters and blessed when He leaves, then so are we; not because we have fulfilled the law to qualify for it, but because He fulfilled the law on our behalf, thus qualifying us. If He is gracious, then it is time for us to be gracious; not only towards the comely and affable, or those who hold to our persuasions, but to all, whether they're nasty or nice. This is the divine lifestyle that Jesus modelled for us—we are Jesus personified—His very body here on earth.

Although this scripture invites us to see Jesus in the mirror so that we can be changed from glory to glory, many believers get it back to front. Instead of expecting His glory to change them, they assume that they will only see His glory if they manage to change themselves. Big mistake! This is how easy it is to fall into the trap of meaningless religious performance!

James has a different take on the mirror; he tells us to see who we are in Christ as seen through the perspective of *"the perfect law of liberty"*; it's not in the least bit like the law of sin and death (James 1:23-25). Another word for the perfect law of liberty is "grace". The mirror reveals our blood washed redeemed identity—sinless, entirely righteous, and without the slightest hint of condemnation. Sadly, most believers don't find this reassurance from the mirror. How can they when they have been taught to approach the mirror to have their faults revealed? That's all that the law of sin and death can do for them. But it is our likeness to Christ that we are meant to discover in the mirror—our identity is found in His identity!

Why the mirror? Visualisation is an extremely powerful force for change—it steers our lives towards the picture that we form of ourselves, and with this image, change follows without conscious effort. Jesus used visualisation to get His points across—His parables were pictures painted in words. If we visualise ourselves as defeated, we tend to act as though we are defeated; if we visualise ourselves as sinful, we tend to act sinfully. However, if we visualise ourselves to be righteous, righteousness becomes evident in our actions without effort. Whether we are prepared to admit it or not, we become exactly what we think of ourselves. *"For as he thinks in his heart, so is he"* (Pro 23:7).

We can be quite certain that James was not wanting us to discover our sin in the mirror, because he went on to say, that upon leaving the mirror, we should *"continue in it"*. Obviously, he would not instruct us to continue in sin, if that is what we saw in the mirror; he wants us to continue in the righteous character of Jesus as revealed by the mirror.

Light dispels darkness. Fighting darkness does not make darkness disappear—only light can do that. Our "righteous" indignation and religious criticism do not give light to the world; they are dark, and darkness is a killer. Let's face it—unless His graciousness is emitting from us, we have no light to offer.

When the early church drifted away from the reality of grace into a formalised relationship with God called religion, personal communication with God became a third party relationship through the clergy. Grace was labelled heresy—it was seen to be a threat to the misplaced power that religion had conferred upon the clergy. Religion had given the clergy the right to manipulate their flocks into submission. If they had allowed their followers to discover grace, they would have lost their right to rule. Their ungodly practises led to the abolishment of the "priesthood of the believer", and that was enough to ring the death knell to the vibrancy of spiritual life.

Reformers were commissioned by God to restore what had been lost to religiosity. Each of them arrived in history with a piece of a giant jigsaw puzzle, which when added to the other pieces, began to form a picture of the victorious believer. None of them arrived on the scene with all the pieces, yet each piece brought the church a little closer to God's dream for humanity.

Sadly, when subsequent reformers arrived on the scene, their message was shunned by those who had bought into the messages of previous reformations, and this shunning is still going on in our day and age. Many religious groups are prepared to grant grace to unbelievers, but fail to extend the same privilege to fellow believers. Such freedom is looked upon with suspicion—seen to be too extreme to be godly. Sadly, the "liberty" of the cross is not easily accommodated within religious paradigms.

Thank God! He has not stopped reforming the church, but sadly, believers have not stopped shunning modern day reformers. The jigsaw puzzle is not yet complete, but a beautiful picture of "Christ within the believer" is emerging, as God continues to reveal more of Himself to His beloved church. In this process, it is not only His identity that becomes clearer, but ours—His glory revealing our glory!

A CHANGE OF MIND

Is repentance a matter of changing our
actions or changing our thinking?

The word repentance is translated from the Greek word *metanoeō*. It means a change of mind that leads to a change of conduct, a turning from sin and a turning to God, involving a person's intellect, emotions and will. Repentance is not just a paradigm shift; it is a paradigm U-turn.

There are two chief motivations given to us for repenting: The first is in response to the favour of God, and the second is to avoid the unfortunate consequences of sin. The one appeals to our best interests, while the other appeals to our worst dreads. Without question, human nature is more likely to be influenced by the positive, than by the negative, and that's why Paul said, *"The goodness of God leads you to repentance?"* (Rom 2:4). Please note that it is not repentance that leads to the goodness of God—it is the other way around. In God's graciousness, He reversed the Old Covenant sequence which required repentance before blessings could be conferred. Now instead of repenting to get God's goodness, we repent because we have His goodness. No longer do we perform to obtain His favour; rather we perform because we are favoured.

Resolving to stop doing something bad is commendable, but the execution of our noble intension is often problematic. But we are not expected to go it alone. God has a clearly scripted solution. He has switched the emphasis from a matter of turning from sin, to a matter of turning towards Him. *"Repentance toward God, and faith toward our Lord Jesus Christ"* (Act 20:21). God wants us to leave matters in His hands. When He has dealt with our appetite for sin, our desire for it simply fades. Conversely, when we try to live up to the law's requirements, we don't defeat sin; we empower sin. *"But sin, taking opportunity by the commandment, produced in me all manner of evil desire"* (Rom 7:8). Only by giving up the struggle and repenting towards God do we put an end to the struggle. If we can accept, that despite our obvious undeservedness, we are nevertheless deeply loved, His love will change the way we compute life. Loved people see life differently—interpret life differently—react to life's challenges differently—not because they try to be godly, but because their perspectives of themselves and others have been adjusted and indelibly encoded into the way they process life. God's undying love presses all the right buttons, and nothing can be more influential than a divine romance! What we think of ourselves has an enormous bearing upon the way we treat others. It's a strange quirk of humanity—loved people have less trouble loving people—to them love comes naturally.

By and large, religion has demonstrated a foreign form of God's love. It gives accolades to deserving saints—the rest must earn approval, or suffer the disapproval of the religious elite. But love that must be earned or deserved is not love at all—it is diametrically opposite to grace.

It is so easy to lose sight of the reason for the church's existence. The church is an institution that exists for the benefit of non-members—those who do not deserve anything but outright contempt—people who do not necessarily even have the time of day for God.

Often the Church does a great job of bringing the lost to salvation, but not such a great job of revolutionising the way they behave. Why is this? Maybe it has to do with its emphasis. Could it be that performance has become more important than people? Often believers are so busy keeping the wheels of religion turning that they lose sight of the church's real purpose. When the emphasis flips over from people to programmes, lives cease to change for the better.

A change of behaviour does not necessarily signify a change of heart. Rules do not have the power to make meaningful change at heart level. We only know how effective our religion is when it is tested by adversity. That's when we discover what we are made of.

Love has a way of inspiring personal value. And with self-esteem, we have all the more reason to choose the high road when challenged by spiteful humanity. Without question, humanity thrives on love. Adversities lose their ominous-ness as they become opportunities for bridge building and reconciliation. The church does not exist for those who have earned the approval of the guardians of religion; it exists for those who have difficulty with godliness.

Conditional love, given in response to a person's affableness or favour is likely to fail the moment that person's affableness or favour fades. I am sure that I don't have to convince anybody that this is not God's kind of love; it is nothing more than the shallow practise of "selective selfishness". This practise says, "I love you as long as you fulfil my plans" or, "I love you as long as you agree with my doctrines" or, "I love you as long as you admire me" etc. If the moment that we no longer agree on a doctrine, becomes the moment that we can no longer relate to each other, then we have proved beyond any shadow of doubt that we are practitioners of the superficiality of "selective selfishness". There is nothing genuine about it!

There is a practise that Paul came down on more harshly than he did on sin. He warned against the practise of trying to find justification for ourselves through law keeping and good behaviour. Of course, good behaviour is commendable, but trying to find justification for ourselves in this way is the one and only way that can cause us to fall from grace. *"You have become estranged from Christ, you who attempt to be justified by law; you have fallen from grace"* (Gal 5:4). We dare not risk it. Once we have fallen from grace, we are done for—there is nothing other than grace to hold our salvation together (Heb

10:26). And no amount of good works can make up for the grace we reject, even if our rejection is based on the supposed pious grounds of not giving licence to sin.

> By what are we saved? Is it by our good living or by faith
> in the blood of Jesus, or could it be a little of each?

Salvation is not something that is secured by behaving right; it is secured by believing right—it's called spiritual rebirth—the only credentials required by passport control at the Pearly Gates. The officer in charge is not impressed with our résumés of religious achievements; he asks only for our kingdom of God birth certificates.

According to Hebrews 10:26, *"If we sin willfully after we have received the knowledge of the truth, there no longer remains a sacrifice for sins"* (Heb 10:26). At first glance, this is one scary scripture! It is a verse often misused to scare believers into holiness. But nothing could be further from holiness than fear—it's the wrong motivator.

Some believe this verse to mean that sin can only be forgiven if it was not wilfully done. But New Testament writers made it perfectly clear that sin is sin—when we are guilty of one, we are guilty of all (Jas 2:10). Besides, none of us can say that we have never wilfully sinned. If we have broken the speed limit, we have done it on purpose. If we have bickered, we have done it on purpose. Every believer that has ever lived sins on purpose. Do legalists understand that their view on this point applies equally to their own sins? Their distorted view would exclude any possibility of them finding forgiveness for their own sins! After all, their sins are just as wilful as anybody else's. We simply cannot have it both ways.

What can be said of legalism? Consider for a moment—if per chance religion was right, nobody, but nobody could go to heaven. If there is no longer a sacrifice for wilful sin, then there is no longer a sacrifice for any sin, and therefore salvation is a myth. There would be no way out of eternal damnation—everybody would be destined for hell!

This is how easily scripture can be misused by legalists to enforce their ideas of holiness. But if we understand the context of this verse, it takes on a very different meaning. Who was the writer of Hebrews addressing? Gentiles or Hebrews? Seeing it was addressed to Hebrews, we can safely say that it bears significance for Jews and their customs. Up to then, what were Jews sacrificing for their sins? Was it not bulls, goats and birds? When was *"the knowledge of the truth"* revealed? Was it not when Jesus became the final sacrifice? This is when their animal sacrifices ceased to hold any further spiritual significance? So, the writer of Hebrews was not saying that wilful sin cannot be forgiven by Jesus; He was saying that the animal sacrifices *"no longer remains a sacrifice for sins",* and therefore it is this kind of sacrifice that cannot atone for wilful sin. Rest assured, Jesus has fully dealt with all sin, including wilful sin on the cross.

Fortunately, it's not our sin that cancels our salvation; it's our efforts to make ourselves right that cause us to fall from grace *"You have become estranged from Christ, you who attempt to be justified by law; you have fallen from grace"* (Gal 5:4). But we are not to despair for He has given us a more sure way to remain in right standing with Him.

If we believe that on-going and timely repentances are required to keep us saved, then all believers are headed for hell. There is always a time lag between sinning and repenting. We may sin in the morning and only come to repent of it in the evening—for us to believe this way, we would be damned if we were to die at noon. If this were so, all saints would be damned, because one thing is certain; all saints think wrong thoughts, and wrong thoughts are no less sinful than wrong deeds (Mat 5:28).

Repentance is what keeps us on track with God's process of bringing our actions into line with our sanctification. Repentance has many other wonderful spinoffs, such as keeping our consciences clear.

When our consciences don't condemn us, we can exercise the kind of uncompromising faith that gets results (1Jn 3:21).

Times of repentance are also times of facing up to our frailties. Being confronted with our weaknesses is humbling, yet infinitely empowering, as we discover anew, God's love and willingness to show mercy and grace. Times of repentance become joyful times as sorrow quickly turns to gladness. Repentance doesn't only bring us to acknowledge our inadequacies; it also reminds us that we are connected to something far more adequate than our paltry self-sufficiencies. When we adopt His all-sufficiency, His all-sufficiency becomes our all-sufficiency! How amazing is that! He has committed Himself by covenant to bless us. And of one thing we can be certain—God is not a covenant breaker! (Psa 89:34)

God does not hide from us when we sin; it is we who hide from Him, much in the same way that Adam and Eve hid after they had sinned in the Garden of Eden. Their sin did not cause God to desert them. To the contrary, He came looking for them, wanting to continue fellowshipping with them in the cool of the day. But Adam and Eve no longer saw themselves worthy of God's company, and so hid from Him. There is no getting around it; sin spelt spiritual death to mankind. But as awful as their sinful blunder was, it was not their sin that severed their fellowship with God; it was their sense of shame—shame ruined the innocence of intimacy with God.

This does not make sin any less abominable—the whole human race continues to suffer the consequences of Adam's folly. By their disobedience, Adam and Eve were responsible for causing the painful torture and agonizing death of the Son of God—it took a sacrifice on God's part, of unthinkable extremes, to undo the catastrophic blunder brought about by their disobedience. Praise God for such a gracious Saviour as ours, who at enormous cost to Himself, not only restored us to Adam's former glory, but exalted us over and beyond, to the glorious privilege of being sons and daughters of the most high God.

Interestingly, before their blunder, Adam and Eve were not in the least bit sin conscious—God had shielded this awareness from them. It was only much later, when through their disobedience, they were exposed to the diabolical *"knowledge of good and evil"* for the very first time. They were righteous without trying to act righteously. Although we, as believers, have come to know and understand the concept of sin, we can have the same innocent sense of sinlessness that Adam and Eve once knew. We are the *"righteousness of God in Christ"*, not because we do not sin, but because Jesus imputed His righteousness to us.

David experienced the darkness of a guilt ridden conscience and only found relief in confession (Psa 66:18). Nothing can separate us from the love of God, but the weight of shame and self-accusation for disappointing the Person who loves us so completely, is enough to shipwreck our faith—confidence does not fare well in uncertainty.

But we have something that David never had. In the words of John, *"For if our heart condemns us, God is greater than our heart, and knows all things"* (1Jn 3:20). We have the indwelling Holy Spirit who is able to bypass our self-condemnation, and continue an unbroken relationship with us, as though nothing ungodly had taken place. While sin was an issue, a relationship with God was simply not possible. First God had to render sin a nonissue through the application of the blood of the sinless Lamb of God. Only then was a matrimonial union with Him possible.

Condemnation comes to us through many voices—amongst them are unbelievers, fellow believers, and even church leaders, but most of all from our own self-denigrating sense of guilt. God is not the author of any of these; for that *"the accuser of the brethren"* must take all the credit. He takes every opportunity to ensure that we nurture our guilt for his own diabolical purposes.

Satan entices us into sin, but instead of congratulating us for falling in with his wicked schemes, he points a reproving finger in our faces and accuses us of being flawed Christians. Sounds wrong, doesn't it? But then again, everything about that twisted confidence trickster is warped.

But doesn't mercy and grace let us off the hook without us having to suffer sin's punitive consequences? Yes! Halleluiah! That is exactly what the good news is all about. But surely God would want us to feel the guilt and shame of it. No, no, no! He knows that we will feel guilt and shame, but he also knows that these self-destructive emotions do nothing to cleanse us—they succeed only in dragging us under, deeper into the doldrums of sin. Self-denigration is the tactic of the accuser! God takes the high road—He lifts us out of self-condemnation with a love that is entirely unconditional.

Jesus said, *"I did not come to judge the world, but to save the world"* (Joh 12:47). But surely that opens the door to all kinds of abuse? That's the risk that God was willing to take to make an entirely pure and honest loving relationship with sinful humanity possible. This relationship is one that cannot be contaminated by sin, not because we do not sin, but because He has dealt with the whole sin issue, and brought its power to contaminate and condemn to a decisive and final end.

If the Word says that love never fails, then we can be quite certain that the same applies to God's love—it never fails (1Cor 13:8). God encourages us to love in a complete way that has no limits—it's the way He loves. If there is one certainty in life, it is that, *"Jesus loves me this I know, for the Bible tells me so"*.

"Extreme grace" is extremely unconditional. Isn't that rather risky on God's part? It is reasonable to think that way, but in reality, when we find complete love, it has a profound effect upon our thinking. The more extreme we come to accept that we are loved by God, the less likely we are to respond with ungracious behaviour to those around us.

People tend to respond defensively and retaliatory when accused, but lovingly and respectfully when loved and accepted in their less than perfect condition. Contrary to expectation, the freedom that comes with "extreme grace" does not promote sin; it has precisely the opposite affect—in the light of such all-encompassing love, sin becomes even more abhorrent to contemplate, and less likely to be carried out.

In a marriage, it is not the marriage contract that holds the marriage together; contracts can be rescinded. It is the degree to which their loving commitment is unconditional—it is this that keeps the marriage glued together. Love begets love in much the same way that mistrust begets infidelity.

Todays' radio news featured the unfortunate story of a bloodied new born baby, with its umbilical cord still attached, found in a trash can in Philippi, Cape Town. When this child grows up and gets to understand her mother's rejection, it could lead to all manner of damaging feelings of worthlessness and low self-esteem—the perfect breeding ground for all kinds of sinful anti-social behaviour. Often drug taking, self-mutilation, prostitution, pornography and the like, incubate in these self-despising emotions.

We all have very different concepts of what we believe love to be. Our particular concept is formed and seared into our subconscious minds by the kind of love that we have personally experienced from others, more especially from our parents. God's concept of love is very different to ours. We tend to love people provided they are kind to us. This is not so with God—He doesn't base His love on anything that we have or have not done. There is stability in being loved in the way God loves—it bears no relationship to our behaviour. Unless we have an anchor in knowing that we are still dearly loved, even when we have foolishly fallen into sin, sin will suck us into a dark hole from which we will have difficulty escaping.

A relationship with God, defined by His love towards us, has far greater potential for intimacy, than a relationship mistakenly defined by His anger towards us. When we misunderstand His attitude towards us, we end up evaluating ourselves poorly. How we evaluate ourselves has a knock-on effect. It affects the way we relate to each other. Instead of with kindness and consideration, we respond with cynicism and relationship damaging acid kneejerk reactions.

The way we perceive God's attitude towards us, plays a vital role in determining the way we personally develop, either for the better or for the worse. In many cases, instead of religion drawing us into a divine romance established on unconditional love, marked with encouragement and edification; it accuses us, casting aspersions upon our personal value, and this disparagement perpetuates sin in our lives. Sadly, when religion assumes the role of moral policeman, instead of curbing sin, it inadvertently promotes sin. The law of Moses was a moral policeman, and guess what? Instead of promoting holiness, it promoted sin. *"But sin took advantage of this law and aroused all kinds of forbidden desires within me! If there were no law, sin would not have that power"* (Rom 7:8 NLT).

If we don't get to know that we serve a God who will *"never leave us nor forsake us"*, we will live in a state faith debilitating fear. When we are led to believe that our divine relationship is held together by our actions, we are insecure, never quite sure of whether or not we have done enough. But our God is not a child abuser; certainly not a child deserter. He has promised never ever to abandon His children. He would never do what the mother in this story did to her baby—He is a perfect parent. When we really understand this, we get to realise that the reason we are in safe hands has nothing to do with our faithfulness, which is usually fickle, and everything to do with His faithfulness, which is never fickle. *"If we are faithless, He remains faithful; He cannot deny himself"* (2Tim 2:13). In this kind of loving family environment, we find healthy self-esteem for ourselves and this self-worth translates into healthy behaviour towards others. Believer's attitudes and behaviour, whether good or bad, stem from how they perceive themselves to be loved and accepted by their heavenly Father despite their sins, or judged and shunned by Him because of them. Although negative concepts of Him may be wildly offbeat, and seriously unfounded, yet our personal misperceptions carry enough weight to steer us off course.

The concept that we have of God translates into the concept that we have of ourselves. If we can see Him as gracious, and accept that we are every bit like Him in nature—it awakens something beautiful within us. We begin to see His magnificence portrayed in our actions. Whatever discovery we make of His glory, becomes a discovery of our glory. When we begin to understand how loving, merciful and gracious He is towards us, our perceptions of ourselves change—we find our actions becoming more loving, more merciful and more gracious towards others without trying.

If we could get the briefest of glimpses into how glorious we are right now in our redeemed yet seemingly imperfect state, it would change everything about what we think of ourselves, and these thoughts would translate into healthy behaviour. The need for one-upmanship would disappear—servant-hood would become more appealing to us, and sin would lose its allure. We can obtain all of this from God's mirror. But not everybody gets it right—it all depends on what we have been instructed by our mentors to see in the mirror.

Seeing that the mirror is not the Bible, but the Jesus of the Bible; how should we discover our identity in Him? We certainly do find Jesus in the pages of our Bibles, but He is so much more than words on a page. The story of His life is the story of our lives. When we look into the spiritual mirror, we look directly into Jesus' eyes as though they are our own. He is the prototype of every believer. In the same way that all motor cars are manufactured to be precise replicas of their prototypes, so every believer is a replica of Jesus, our prototype. Whatever we admire in Him is something to be admired in ourselves. As we delve into the beauty of who He is, we are actually delving into the beauty of who we are. Whatever magnificent attributes we find in Him, we begin to accept about ourselves. Is He worried and depressed? No! Neither are we. Is He defeated? No! Neither are we. Is He sick? No! Neither are we. Is He poor? No! Neither are we. Is He at peace? Yes! So are we. Is He filled with faith? Yes! So are we. Is He an overcomer? Yes! So are we. Is He a conqueror? Yes! So are we. Is He compassionate? Yes! So are we. Is He merciful? Yes! So are we. Is He loving and kind? Yes! So are we. Is He righteous? Yes! So are we. And so we can go on and on naming the magnificent character traits that we share with the Lover of our souls, for *"As He is so are we in this world"* (1Jn 4:17).

Jesus is the original and we are carbon copies of Him. The only distinctive difference in a carbon copy is in the texture of the paper. And so it is with us; the texture of our individual personalities distinguish us one from another. Although our personalities make us unique, the essence of the message of the original is nevertheless the essence of the message of the copy. Copies require authentication, and for us it is the same. As the fruit of His Spirit becomes evident in our actions, it serves as His signature of authentication.

This is all well and good, but if we have been conditioned to see our faults in the mirror, the mirror will destroy us with self-condemnation and shame. Nobody is immune from shame—every last one of us have enough skeletons in our closets, capable of destroying our self-worth, and therewith bankrupting our faith. It is *"the accuser of the brethren's"* business to drag our skeletons out and to rub our noses in the shame of our faux pas. We must guard against falling in with his diabolical agenda—he is out to trick us into seeing ourselves as worthless—our most holy faith is at stake.

In the room of crazy mirrors at the fair, we get to laugh at the distorted reflections of ourselves. Different curves showing us up in different ways—grotesque heads on small bodies etc.

It is important to have a right perspective of God's character before going to the mirror. After all, we can only get what we believe the mirror to be showing us. If we believe God to be angry and judgemental, we obtain anger and judgementalism from the mirror. If we believe Him to be loving, merciful and gracious, we obtain love, mercy and graciousness from the mirror. We become what we see of ourselves in Him. If we get it wrong, our perspective of our right standing with Him will be distorted. If we believe that we are loved any less when we sin than when we don't, we will never know where we stand with Him.

Religion has done a fine job of getting us to lose sight of the reality of His unconditional love, and has side tracked us into performing for favours. More meetings, more courses, more church corporate ladder climbing, more toe kissing, more giving, more praying, more bowing to religious politics, more serving, less sinning. Perform, perform, perform! Some of these activities would be good if they were done for the right reasons. But we are not favoured because we are righteous; we are favoured because Christ is righteous. Besides, God is our beloved Papa, and we are His dearly loved children! That alone should be enough to reassure us.

Can repentance restore our salvation once it is lost?

Is our salvation held together by our latest repentance and right living, or by the blood of the lamb? The way repentance is often portrayed, one might think that we are only saved to the extent that we have repented. But this would switch our security from God's dependability to our undependability, making our salvation tenuous and insecure. Paul found security in God through faith rather than through his most commendable works of the flesh. He said, *"I no longer count on my own goodness or my ability to keep the law, but I trust Christ to save me. For God's way of making us right depends on faith"* (Phi 3:9 NLT).

The writer to the Hebrews clearly states, *"It is impossible ... to renew them again to repentance"*. This scripture refutes the notion that we can regain salvation once it is lost. But thank God, we do not breach the point of no return through sinning.

To infer that this scripture makes sin out to be the reason for not being able to return to God, is to infer that every single believer throughout the ages has breached this scripture and consequently lost their salvation without any recourse to regain it. Seeing that sin is the blight of all believers, this would have to be the outcome for everybody. As John put it, we would be liars if we were to say that we have no sin (1 John 1:8). Some believers are brave enough to admit that they sin every day. No, it is not sin; rather it is our efforts at trying to find justification through good behaviour—it is this that cancels grace (Rom 4:14-15). Galatians 5:4 is clear—to depend on our good behaviour for our justification, is to fall from grace.

I have been in business for 46 years, and as sad as it is to admit, I have encountered many Christians who are no different to unbelievers when it comes to ethics. By and large, "un-extreme grace" has failed in its quest to bring about moral change to its followers. Many believers are just as likely to let one down in business as unbelievers. This being the case, we can safely say that religion's version of repentance has done precious little to change the hearts of believers; it has only forced them to give the appearance of holiness for the sake of finding acceptance in their pious circles. It causes believers to play pious games with each other—hiding behind polite masks while keeping their ungracious thoughts to themselves. Tragically, holiness, in the way that "un-extreme grace" has promoted it, has failed to bring about change at heart level.

The world out there is not for one moment fooled by righteous posturing. They are tired of hearing pious words when these words are trashed by un-pious actions—flip-flop piety makes nonsense of religion.

When grace is leached out of the gospel, the shallowness of charm slips in as congregants do their best to mimic grace. Insincerity may escape our notice, but it certainly does not escape the notice of those who get hurt in the process. When we are backed into a corner, unbelievers get to see exactly how real our religion really is.

Only grace has the power to change hearts, and only changed hearts are able to bring about behavioural change that is not contrived. Behavioural change flows from hearts that have been touched by a love that is not in the least bit deserved. When the penny finally drops, we awake to God's love for us. Then it is only a matter of time for this awareness to translate into godly actions—it happens almost as if by accident.

If holiness could be gained by behaving well, then Buddhists are holy. When the electricity failed in Japan after the tsunami, supermarket shoppers simply unpacked their shopping trollies in semidarkness, making sure that every item was put back onto the shelves. It seems to be very different in a Christian country like ours where shops are looted and ransacked under similar circumstances. This is a sad indictment on a predominantly Christian country. Regretfully, when "extreme grace" is religiously forbidden, it is prevented from carrying out its sanctifying work and consequently cannot influence Christians' to behave any better.

It takes extreme love to lift us out of the doldrums of guilt and shame. The value that we find in God's love is enough to engender healthy self-esteem. We play the game of life so much better when we see ourselves the way God sees us. He sees us as sinless and never imputes our sins to our accounts. He imputed them to Jesus' account long before we committed them (2Cor 5:19). Thank God! We are not expected to earn right standing with Him through behaving right.

Twelve spies were sent to spy out the land of Canaan. Ten of them were intimidated by the giants, but two of them were convinced that the land could be conquered. Not surprisingly, these two were the only ones to survive forty years of aimless wanderings—the doubters perished in the desert. These two went on to lead the Israelites into Canaan, and they did so with overwhelming victory. What was the difference? It all came down to perspectives—how they saw themselves, how they saw their opposition, and how they perceived God's love for them. When we realise how unconditionally we are loved, our opinions of ourselves change for the better. And better self-esteem leads to better behaviour. Sin has a hard time competing for the affections of a person inspired by love.

When we discover the depth of His love for us, it becomes a lot easier to take Him at His word. All ships rise on the tide. Our faith rises on the incoming tide of His love. The dependability of His love gives us all the assurance we need to launch out in faith. His steadfast love never fails, nor does it cease—not even when we foolishly slip into sin. With this knowledge, we are assured that He can be relied upon to provide for us, keep us in health, and keep us saved.

On another occasion, the entire Israelite army was intimidated by a singular Philistine soldier. They allowed his size to frighten them. But there was a shepherd boy who could not be intimidated, and not surprisingly, he just happened to be a prolific author of myriads of love poems dedicated to the Lover of his soul. His name was David and he wrote more verse extolling God's love than anybody else. His intimate relationship with God had given him an insight into the extent of God's love for him, and that's all it took to embolden him. The question in His mind was, "How could an uncircumcised Philistine intimidate an agape inspired individual?"

When we, like David, begin to understand God's love for us, it makes a huge difference to our perspectives—our confidence rises and temptations lose their appeal. That does not mean that we will never sin again. David did. And his sin was no ordinary sin. He did the unthinkable when he murdered his most loyal of loyal subjects for no other reason than to steal his wife. Even so, his sin was not too great for God's grace. If grace is sufficient to cover an abomination of this magnitude, then there is hope for all of us!

Jesus was known as the son of David. Imagine that! This illustrious privilege was granted to an unfaithful philanderer and dastardly murderer! The child born of this disgraceful union became the ancestor of the Saviour of the world. What kind of grace is that? The very act that should have sent him to the gallows, was the act that honoured him as the father of our Saviour. Can there be any greater honour than to have God's son known as your son? Isn't God's grace simply amazing? Think about it! He could have chosen a prophet known for his piety, but he chose a disgraced ruler known for his thuggery. God chose to have His son be the offspring of an adulterous affair facilitated by murder.

For us it is decidedly different. David's sins were counted against him; ours are not. The writer of Hebrews quotes Jeremiah's prophecy about the coming New Testament age: *"their sins and their lawless deeds I will remember no more"* (Heb 10:17). In saying *"no more"*, he was inferring that Old Covenant saints did not have this privilege. Jeremiah was prophesying of a time to come—that time is now; it is made possible by the blood of Jesus.

A love affair cannot be taught: it can only be caught. The Holy Spirit is our romantic matchmaker, connecting us to our bridegroom. There is no end to God's loving kindness—He takes pleasure in caring for us with deep love, infinite patience and understanding. Just knowing that He enjoys our company is enough to ignite our joy at being in His company. Being appreciated is enormously edifying! Our worship ceases to need the formalised worship framework that religion has invented. Rather, our worship becomes a romantically entwined love affair. Earthly romances are mutually edifying, but nothing inspires love like a divine romance!

Worship existed long before church organs, grand pianos and gospel bands. We don't need the pizzazz of an enthusiastic worship leader to rouse us to worship. We are in love! With our every breath we adore Him! It is not something that only happens when the atmosphere is conducive. If our hearts are beating, we are enthralled with our Lover—adoration comes naturally—it surges through our veins. His love is intoxicating—we crave more! *"As the deer pants for the water brooks, So pants my soul for You, O God"* (Psa 42:1).

But if we have made up our minds as to the limits of His love and grace, we have curtailed our transformation. In drawing the line on grace, we have consigned our divine romance to shallowness. But for those who set no limits to His love and grace, the romance is all consuming—sin simply cannot survive the fulfilment we have in God's goodness.

His love trumps sin's allurements. When our deepest desires are completely satisfied with His love, there is no need to look for satisfaction elsewhere—how can sin possibly compete with divine fulfilment? When we are convinced that we are loved, despite our most deplorable sins, a God-assuredness arises within us. While the Holy Spirit is wooing us with divine love, there is no need for legalistic restraints to keep us out of sin. Once awakened to God's unconditional love for us, we are not conscious of being restrained—we are only conscious of being loved—nothing else is necessary—nothing else matters—love is enough!

Grace does not give license to sin; we don't need a license; sinning comes naturally, whether licensed or not. The most self-disciplined monk living on a diet of thistles, stale bread and water, with a lifetime vow of silence and self-imposed isolation in a cave in the middle of the Kalahari Desert, cannot attain anything remotely close to sinlessness. Try as we may, our best behaviour is often tainted with skewed motives. In God's sight, the very best that we are capable of is nothing better than the stench of *"filthy rags"*. If we want right standing with God, we must seek it from a source that bears no relationship to our behaviour. Jesus has provided that source—He calls it grace. *"But now God has shown us a different way of being right in His sight—not by obeying the law..."* (Rom 3:21 NLT).

Grace is not license; it is diametrically opposite to license; it is the empowering force granted to enable mankind to overcome sin. In the fight against sin, grace is immeasurably more effective than self-effort.

In fact, grace of the most extreme kind is the only solution that has any hope of truly conquering our propensity to sin. Anything less is too superficial; it cannot deal with what is buried deep within our less than perfect hearts. If we insist on striving to make ourselves right, we are ignoring the work of grace, and without grace, there is nothing else for the believer except the cold darkness of nothingness in the lost emptiness of outer space. The stone cold reality of the matter is that no relationship with God can exist outside of the *"abundance of grace"*.

What must we do to be rewarded with eternal life?

Have you heard of the "reward" of eternal life? It is sometimes preached by well-meaning clergymen, but to this day, no person on the face of the planet has ever managed to do enough to be rewarded with eternal life. *"Can we boast then that we have done anything to be accepted by God? No, because our acquittal is not based on our good deeds. It is based on our faith"* (Rom 3:27 NLT).

The truth of the matter is that nobody is capable of doing enough to attain the high standard that God would have to require of us if it were not for grace. Yes, there is broad agreement that rebirth cannot take place without grace; but the question is, "Do we accept that the same measure of grace continues to apply to us after rebirth?"

Whether before rebirth or after, we are hopelessly incapable of achieving anything remotely holy enough to be rewarded with eternal life. This is where religion has taken a wrong turn and misled Christendom. Religion motivates us to perform for rewards, but this is not how the New Covenant works. Rewards belong to the Old Covenant where blessings had to be earned. For New Covenant believers, God's favour is all at Christ's expense. And when it comes to eternal life, the Bible describes it as the *"gift"* of eternal life; not the "reward" of eternal life (Rom 6:23).

It is imperative to understand that salvation is entirely a *"gift"* that cannot be rewarded for anything we have or have not done. *"When people work, their wages are not a gift"* (Rom 4:4 NLT). If we were to insist that we have been "rewarded" with eternal life, then in the light of this scripture, it stands to reason that our reward did not emanate from God—His salvation is a gift, and gifts cannot be rewarded.

Only two requirements must be met in order to qualify to be *"declared"* righteous: (a) we must be unrighteous and admit it and (b) we must turn to God, believe, and accept that Jesus has atoned for our sins, period! Pretty simple isn't it? *"Anyone who calls on the name of the Lord will be saved"* (Act 2:21 NLT). If you are wondering how repentance features in this process; the answer is that it takes a change of mind to turn to God and that is what repentance is.

What about sorrow? Where does it fit in? If you are sorry then you are sorry—trying to act sorry is hypocrisy—it is no different to hiring professional mourners to create an atmosphere of gloom and sadness—nothing could be flakier than that!

No promises to change are required of us—God has a lifelong sanctifying programme to bring about change—it's all His doing and none of ours. Only unrighteous people qualify to receive God's righteousness. And it is not by reward; it's by divine *"declaration"*. *"People are declared righteous because of their faith, not because of their work"* (Rom 4:5 NLT). To base our righteousness on anything else is to *"fall from grace"* and to be *"cut off from Christ"* (Gal 5:4).

SELF-RETRIBUTION

Does grace excuse us from feeling godly sorrow for our failings, shortcomings and wilful disobedience?

This is only a question in the minds of those who have not grasped what God's grace encompasses. "Extreme grace" does not play down the importance of repentance; to the contrary, it draws us into repentance. *"The goodness of God leads you to repentance."* (Rom 2:4). When God uses His grace, favour, goodness and love to beckon us into repentance, it becomes "willing" repentance rather than "reluctant" repentance.

Grace is how God expresses His love to us, and His love has a way of drawing the very best out of us. Conversely, religion, fearing that grace may be mistaken for licence, is likely to proceed with caution, preaching the negative ramifications of sin, rather than the positive enticements of God's goodness. But enslavement to fear is certainly not the good news of the gospel of our Lord Jesus.

If at some time in our pasts, we were frightened into repenting, we are unlikely to repent in the future unless we are scared enough into doing it again—we will need repeated doses of fear to keep us on the straight and narrow. If however, God's love drew us into a romance, we will repent with eagerness—love will be enough to keep us on the straight and narrow. The most well used invitation to salvation, John 3:16, has a lot to say about God's love and nothing at all to say about His wrath. Jesus made His intentions patently clear when He said, *"I have come to save the world and not to judge it"* (John 12:47 NLT).

Paul reinforced this thought when he wrote, *"Who dares accuse us whom God has chosen for his own? Will God? No! He is the one who has given us right standing with himself. Who then will condemn us? Will Christ Jesus? No, for he is the one who died for us and was raised to life for us and is sitting at the place of highest honour, pleading for us"* (Rom 8:33-34 NLT). We have no accusers in heaven—both God the Father and God the Son have given us their word on this.

Also, fear motivated repentance does not make for intimacy with God—intimacy wilts and withers in an atmosphere of fear, but blossoms and blooms in an atmosphere of unconditional love. We simply cannot enjoy intimacy with someone who we believe to be angry with us. If we perceive that we are accused, or that God is angry with us, it is like throwing a wet blanket on a fire—it smothers every last ember of intimacy out of divine romance. Fortunately, God has already disposed of His anger towards us; He took it out on Jesus!

"Of how much worse punishment, do you suppose, will he be thought worthy who has trampled the Son of God underfoot, counted the blood of the covenant by which he was sanctified a common thing, and insulted the Spirit of grace?" (Heb 10:29). How do we cheapen the Spirit of grace? From this verse it is patently clear that we do not cheapen grace by sinning; we cheapen it by adding requirements to what is already given unconditionally. Additional requirements do not reinforce grace; they dismantle grace. According to this scripture, to add requirements to grace would *"insult"* the Spirit of grace, and anybody who *"insults"* the Spirit of grace is headed for *"worse punishment"* (Heb 10:29). Need I say more?

In this verse we also see that *"the blood of the covenant"* sanctifies us from sin. Again, it is all His doing and none of ours. This covenant is a one sided covenant, in that Jesus, being the son of man, fulfilled all of mankind's obligations to the law without any help from mankind. He did it on our behalf and left nothing undone for us to complete, except that we believe in Him, turn to Him and call on His name. Seeing that both parties to the Covenant, being God the Father and God the Son of man, are entirely trustworthy, we can rest assured that the covenant is in safe hands—in fact it is watertight. To suggest that our efforts can reinforce it to make it any more secure than it already is, would at best be presumptuous, and at worst be arrogant.

The Company that I worked for paid for our annual overseas holidays. The company made all the arrangements with the travel agent and paid the bill in full. All Sue and I had to do was to pitch up on time for our flight. Five star accommodation, fine dining and tours were included. It is the same for believers. All the arrangements have already been made between God the Father and God the Son of man. A price was determined and Jesus made a payment that settled the bill in full. All that we have to do is to pitch up, and by faith, receive all that Jesus purchased for us with His blood.

In the same way that Sue and I could have forfeited our holidays by not pitching up to receive them; believers forfeit their grace privileges by not pitching up to receive them. In the same way that it would be senseless for me to try to pay for something that the company had already paid for; any attempt to deserve grace would be just as senseless.

Even so, grace is not something that happens without us playing our part, but our part is not in making ourselves right by law-keeping or by remembering the details of what must be confessed. Grace requires us to receive what has already been achieved for us. It is ours without cost, purely in response to our faith. The question is, "faith in what?" The answer is, "In knowing that our redemption is complete and all conditions to inherit have been met in full—there is no further need to prove that we are worthy". Unless we are convinced that we already have the entire redemption package, we will in all likelihood do our best to gain what we mistakenly believe to be lacking. Such striving will not achieve anything—grace is only obtainable by those who are convinced that it has already been signed over to them—this is enough to embolden them to claim ownership of the promises.

It almost seems audacious to claim entitlement, especially in view of the fact that we have not made a single contribution towards its purchase. We get it horribly wrong when we come to feel that we must do our best to impress God to make up for what we lack. But God is not impressed with what we can boastfully say that we have or have not done. In our efforts to earn brownie points to trade at the convenience store in the sky, we end up window dressing our behaviour. But this leaves our hearts unchanged. Unless behavioural change starts with a change of heart, it is not holiness. Any right making effort on our part to earn right standing is simply grace annulling.

But without works, faith is dead—right? The works that James was referring to were certainly not works of good behaviour or repentance; they were works that demonstrate our emphatic resolve and immovable conviction of belief. James substantiates his argument by quoting Abraham's willingness to sacrifice Isaac. This bears no relationship to behaving well, or for that matter repenting much— rather his obedience was evidence of what he emphatically believed.

Interestingly, Abraham was not granted righteous standing with God for being willing to sacrifice his son. Righteous standing was granted to him much earlier when he believed that he would become the father of many nations at a time when his wife was way beyond child bearing age. This being the case, it becomes even clearer that the point that James was making, was that Abraham's willingness to sacrifice Isaac was not done to earn righteousness; it was merely done to demonstrate how uncompromising and emphatic his faith was.

> Now that we are under grace, is sin any less abominable?

Certainly not! Sin is sin, and it remains deplorable! Grace does not change the fact that sin is abominable, but grace does change the fact that God no longer imputes or credits sin to our account. He credited all of it, whether past, present or future, to Jesus' account. *"... God was in Christ, reconciling the world to Himself, not imputing their trespasses to them ..."* (2Co 5:19). Please take special note of the emphatic tone of this verse. If He says that He does not impute sin to our account, then it would be incorrect of us to assume that He temporarily imputes it when we sin, and then later un-imputes it when we finally decide to repent of it. If this were true, then the sins that we neglectfully fail to repent of would remain imputed to us forever—we would be none the wiser as to why we were headed for hell! But this kind of thinking would make God out to be a liar—especially in view of His unbreakable promise to not impute trespasses to our account.

God treats our sins in the same way that He treated the sins of those who lived before the introduction of the law. *"For until the law sin was in the world: but sin is not imputed when there is no law"* (Rom 5:13). Not a single sin was imputed to Old Testament believers who lived before the introduction of the law. And since the blood of Jesus has made the law obsolete, the same applies to New Testament believers—He no longer imputes sin to our account. In removing the covenant that condemned, He removed the basis upon which accusations can be levelled against us. *"He has made the first obsolete"* (Heb 8:13). When God makes something obsolete, it is over and done with! The covenant of law has nothing on us—it can no longer be used to accuse believers. God laid all our sins on Jesus—in Him we have an eternal scapegoat!

The fact of the matter is that transgressions can only take place when there is a standing law that can be transgressed. Jesus fulfilled the Law of Moses on our behalf, thereby nullified its accusations (Rom 8:4). Once a law has been annulled, it can no longer be transgressed.

Obviously, that does not make sin any more acceptable—God didn't do this because He has come to like sin; He did it because He hates what sin does to us. Besides, He desired intimacy with his children, but could not fellowship with anybody tarnished with sin.

So, seeing that there is no law to break, is it okay to sin? *"All things are lawful for me, but all things are not helpful. All things are lawful for me, but I will not be brought under the power of any"* (1Co 6:12). All things are lawful? Wow! Pretty wide, isn't it? But just because there is no law to prohibit something, it doesn't make doing it anymore acceptable to God. Besides, we don't need the law to tell us that something is harmful; we have a brain, and more than that, we are Spirit led.

Jesus gave us the whole Bible in a nutshell when He said, "Love God; love people" (paraphrased). When this principle is etched into the very essence of who we are, our hearts produce godly behaviour without any assistance from laws etched in stone. Grace has a way of winning our affections. Just knowing that we don't deserve the love we get, has a profound effect on our conduct.

If we have come to think that we have done something good enough to give God reason to love us, then we have missed grace by a country mile. No! Because God's love is given for no apparent reason at all, we have good reason to feel secure. If His love was based on something that we had done, then we would have good reason to feel insecure, not knowing whether or not we have done something else that would give Him reason to change His mind about us. How fortunate we are to be loved without reason!

Grace is how God expresses His undying love to us. When we really understand the extreme lengths He went to to put pay to our sins—preventing any possibility of them blemishing our relationship, then we find ourselves instinctively responding in like manner to Him. Love has a wonderful way of arousing love in the hardest of hearts.

There is something enchanting about love; it has a way of invoking a desire to be in one another's company. Young lovers cannot bear the thought of being out of each other's sight for more than a moment, and so it is with our divine romance. God is ever present and intensely intimate in the person of His Holy Spirit. His love gives us good reason to "want" to walk by the Spirit.

Without the help of grace, we are left to meet religion's required standard of behaviour by our own strength. Sadly, the very effort of striving to behave better is what "walking in the flesh" is—flesh simply cannot produce fruit of the Spirit. The Spirit's fruit has got to be His doing and His doing alone. Just knowing that we are so deeply loved by our heavenly Father is reason enough to draw us into a closer walk with Him. And when we allow His Spirit to guide us, we are walking in the Spirit, and the fruit He produces through our actions is nothing short of godly behaviour.

"The law gives sin its power" (1Cor 15: 56 NTL). By trying to keep the law, we simply empower sin to control us. When law is preached, flesh responds. But when grace is preached, faith responds!

It is quite understandable to want to be close to the One who is so gracious—a safe refuge from accusations (Rom 8:33, 34).

The law requires us to live up to its dictates. Sadly, what we manage to achieve in the flesh, more often than not, leads to religious pride. But with grace, we have nought to boast of. To walk by grace is to walk by the virtues of Jesus as conveyed to us by the Spirit. It is a matter of allowing Him to produce His fruit through our actions. We cannot take any credit for it—all the glory belongs to Him alone!

God's way of achieving holiness is very different to the religious way. Striving for holiness is striving for superficiality—we can only hope to change our actions—sadly, inwardly we remain the same. And anything less than inner change bears no eternal significance. But when we turn in repentance *"towards God"* it allows Him to deal with our hearts. In yielded-ness, we give the reins of our lives to the Holy Spirit. Real godliness is only possible in His hands. His work is always a work of grace—it is done without our help—yielded-ness and trust is enough.

With Him producing His fruit through us, we find ourselves behaving progressively more like the righteousness imputed to us. But we cannot demonstrate true righteousness in our actions unless we have first embraced it in our hearts. For as long as we remain sceptical—unconvinced that our imputed righteous standing is forever established, we will not draw holiness from within, and consequently not transpose our latent holiness into holy actions.

"For to me to live is Christ" (Php 1:21). For "us to live" is not supposed to be about what we can do, but about what Christ can do in and through us. Imagine that! Christ, behaving in the godly way that He always does, but now He is doing it through our actions. The moment I take over and try to live godlier, becomes the moment that "for me to live is Deon"—I leave no room for Paul's experience of *"for to me to live is Christ"*.

There is a power that keeps our hearts soft; it's the power of being loved—the most influential force for change known to mankind. Just knowing that we are loved in such an extreme way is life transforming in itself.

A parent's attitude towards his or her child has a direct bearing on the child's attitudes. A child may reluctantly submit in fear while under the supervision of an overbearing parent, but rebel the moment he or she is not controlled. Conversely, a child under the guidance of a nurturing parent has no reason to rebel when not under supervision— there simply isn't anything to rebel against. When love has removed fear from the relationship, submission becomes all the more appealing. Love inspires love and openness, while fear inspires closed-ness and secret sinning.

Obviously, we don't endure to the end because we are sinless or up to date with repentance; we endure to the end because we hold fast to grace, for it is grace and grace alone that assures salvation.

Is grace at loggerheads with holiness?

There is a misguided notion that with "extreme grace", there is no need to repent. But nothing could be further from the truth. *"...I gave her time to repent ... and she did not repent"* (Rev 2:21). "Extreme grace" would never set out to disagree with God's instruction.

"Extreme grace" is so convinced about repentance that it takes it to higher level—it purports that the need to strive for change is unnecessary when the Holy Spirit is given charge of our lives. After all, the Holy Spirit's behaviour is never less than perfect—He is just as much "God" as Jesus and our heavenly Father—totally incapable of anything less than holiness.

Religion may insist that we do what Jesus would do in any given situation. A lofty, yet daunting ideal! Anybody who has tried it has discovered the impossibility of achieving it. What a relief to discover that God does not expect this of us. I have not met a single believer who has got it right, but I have met many who are hard on themselves for getting it wrong. Sadly, their reward is not holiness; just a sense of defeat. But praise the Lord! God has a better way! Jesus doesn't have to strive to be like Himself; He always behaves like himself. When we allow Him the privilege of being Himself and living His life through our actions, our actions become Christ's way of living. Problem solved!

Also, no amount of missing the mark can cancel grace—after all, grace can only be granted when it is "not" deserved—in fact it is only available to those who miss the mark—where there is more sin, more grace abounds (Rom 5:20). Of course, all humanity, including the most pious amongst us continue to miss the mark, and that's why God provided grace in the first place.

Churches are bulging with Christians who continually repent of the same brand of sin without the slightest hope of ever conquering these sins—many take their hang-ups with them to the grave.

Clearly religion is incapable of bringing about meaningful change. Sadly, its high expectations are more likely to induce a sense of shame and rejection—the fuel that ignites sin—rather than a sense of love and acceptance—the fuel that ignites righteous living!

Law plays directly into the hands of *"the accuser of the brethren"*. This scoundrel welcomes our sincere striving for holiness— he knows that it will lead to self-blame, shame and unworthiness— enough to immobilise our faith. More than this, these debilitating emotions make it even more difficult to stop sinning. If Satan can convince us that we are weak and useless, because our best efforts to keep the law are failing, he can keep us enslaved to the very sins we are struggling to overcome. He knows that if we come to discover who we actually are in Christ, that he will lose the battle against us. Believers, who are convinced of their right standing with Christ, have less chance of accepting Satan's disparagements. They are not easily tricked into falling for his life sapping ways of guilt and shame.

Satan does his level best to convince us that we have an "on again, off again" relationship with God—he cannot afford for us to discover stability in our eternal state of righteousness. By keeping us focused on our weaknesses, he is able to block our faith, and this allows him to wreak havoc on us with supposed impunity. When we are made to feel unworthy, we are unlikely to believe that God would favour us, and consequently, fail to claim covenant privileges that are already ours by inheritance. Also, he knows that for as long as he can keep us focused on our failures, he can keep our gaze off Jesus. In our weakened sense of unworthiness, we find it difficult to believe that God would want to favour us. But God's grace assures us that He is not looking for worthiness. Faith, trust and belief are enough!

FILTHY RAGS

As believers, are we expected to change our ways?

"Self-effort change" is ineffective—it has been the misguided way of religion for countless centuries. We are only truly changed when our hearts are changed. Anything less is superficial and therefore hypocritical—our actions saying one thing while our hearts say the opposite. We can only hold this kind of pretence together to a point, but have great difficulty keeping our composure when pushed too far. This is when our holy appearances falter, and ultimately let us down, sometimes in caustic sarcasm or angry retorts. Suddenly the intolerance of our hearts show through. At times we come away with our Christian witness in tatters.

Whether we are prepared to admit it or not, we all have our own brand of quirks and hang-ups, and if we are not careful, they can so easily drag us into a defeatist attitude. Sometimes we may wish we could withdraw ill-chosen words spoken in the heat of the moment. The world expects better from Christians, and are quick to notice when it is not forthcoming.

We cannot afford to trim the leaves. We must allow God to go to the root of the problem, and the root exists in our less than perfect hearts. Once the roots have been attended to, the leaves need no further attention. But we don't open our hearts to just anybody. The key to the door of our hearts is called love and acceptance—the language of our hearts. Nothing can change our hearts the way love does. Sincerity can't do it. Religious instructions can't do it. Law keeping can't do it. Love is needed—the only power capable of changing the way we think and therefore live.

Humanly speaking, we do not easily respond graciously when confronted with ungraciousness, but we seem to find oodles of patience and grace for people who are gracious to us. The Holy Spirit is not only gracious to us; He is the *"Spirit of grace"* (Heb 10:29). Just knowing this makes the prospect of yielding to Him appealing—obedience follows with eagerness.

As we yield to Him, He is able to direct our paths. There is no need to fear that a Holy Spirit guided life will be any less fulfilling. After all, He knows how to do life a whole lot better than we do. When we attempt to change ourselves, all we get for our troubles are works of the flesh. They may look like fruit of the Spirit, but counterfeits are only illusions. Our flesh simply cannot manufacture fruit of the Spirit, period!

When personal change is not grace initiated, it is self-effort initiated, and that is a gazillion miles short of godliness. For example, while religion expects us to be more loving; in all innocence we respond, but our best efforts are nothing better than "selective selfishness"—it's the best that we are capable of. But it is not our business to change ourselves—it is the Spirit's business—our business is to yield to Him in obedience.

Trees do not produce fruit—they can't—they are made of wood. However the sap within them produces gorgeous fruit. In the same way, we are incapable of producing fruit of the Spirit; however, the Holy Spirit within us is well able to produce gorgeous fruit. His fruit is precisely the same fruit that Jesus produced while walking this planet. *"May you always be filled with the fruit of your salvation—the righteous character produced in your life by Jesus Christ—for this will bring much glory and praise to God* (Php 1:11 NLT). Please take special note that *"righteous character"* is not something that we are expected to produce; it is *"produced in* (our lives) *by Jesus Christ"* within us. Religion would have us produce righteous character, but whenever we attempt it, it becomes a work of the flesh—a country mile short of godliness. Better that we stop striving, and simply allow Jesus the freedom to guide us by His Holy Spirit from within.

So many sermons from respected pulpits do no more than commission sincere believers to strive to produce fruit of the Spirit. But self-effort is not how it is done. Plastic smiles and plastic charm is not holiness, it is *"filthy rags"*. I can only imagine that "holier than thou" attitudes are just as nauseating to God as they are to us.

In the lists of works of the flesh and fruit of the Spirit, as recorded in the fifth chapter of Galatians, it is obvious that works of the flesh concern "conduct", whereas fruit of the Spirit concerns "attitudes". And attitudes stem from our hearts—the very place where both love and hatred are nurtured.

The Spirit of God does not work with reasoning; He works with passions! Our passions feed our appetites! It is as though we are driven to fulfil them—at times for good, and other times, not so good.

We have a two way switch within us. When in the down position, we connect with our flesh and must jump to its demands; whereas in the up position, we connect to the Spirit who guides us from within. It is not difficult to surrender when it is love that we are surrendering to. When the switch is in this position, it is no longer our efforts and strivings, but the life of the Spirit that manifests in our conduct. And because the Spirit always behaves like Jesus, we find the attitudes of Jesus effortlessly showing up in our actions. Now we can relax and be ourselves—there is no need to put up fronts—His gracious attitudes shine through. What could be more satisfying than having His conduct flowing through our conduct in an unforced way? It is the unforced rhythm of grace!

The question is: "What would motivate believers to surrender control of their lives to the Holy Spirit? Would finger pointing, fault finding and the dread of falling foul of the curses of the law do it, or would the kind of love that is accepting, supportive and unconditional have a better chance?" In grace, we find a God who is understanding and compassionate. One whose love bears no relationship to our personal degree of holiness. It is not difficult to surrender to someone who knows our frailties yet loves us regardless of them.

That's all well and good, but nothing will happen unless we have a desire for it. Do not despair; God has got that one covered too. *"For God is working in you, giving you the desire and the power to do what pleases Him"* (Php 2:13 NLT). God is not slack—He knows that we need all the help we can get, and He has not left it up to us to conjure up a desire to do what pleases Him. The desire for it comes from Him in the form of grace! And grace cannot be earned; it can only be received—faith is enough!

What must we do to ensure that our
justification continues uninterruptedly?

However commendable our contribution may be, it adds nought to the finished work of the cross. Self-help to godliness and the payment of penance are diametrically opposite to grace.

Sadly, penance has crept into modern day religion in the form of "churchified" demands for holier living, and when we fail to meet these expectations, we are in danger of seeing ourselves as lesser Christians. When shame is taken to the next level, we end up with self-condemnation which becomes penance by another name. How can shame be penance? We mistakenly think that God will look more favourably upon us if we can show him how ashamed we are. With this rationale we beat ourselves half to death with shame. Shame seems so pious and noble, yet so self-destructive and contrary to redemption.

Believers tend to hold their spiritual leaders in such awe that they willingly give them the right to define them. If they are defined as anything less than God's dearly loved children, who are every bit as righteous as Jesus, they are likely to take on a defeatist persona that drags them under—is it any wonder that so many live less than overcoming lives?

One sometimes hears a Christian comparing himself to another in feigned humility saying, "He is a better Christian than me". But there is only one kind of Christian and that is a blood bought one.

In attempting to find acceptance within a congregation, believers often resort to living double lives. Sadly, once duplicity is accepted as the norm, religion falls into fraudulence.

Jesus didn't usher in grace only to hide it from us for 2000 years. When religion becomes an unattainable moral code, people are likely to fake it. And then, when they are labelled as anything less than the righteousness of God in Christ, they will in all likelihood live up to the definition handed down to them. Sadly, giving a dog a bad name can be profoundly prophetic.

The reality of their perpetual right standing with God is simply overlooked and a lesser identity adopted. Once this happens, it is only a matter of time before lesser conduct is produced. But if we start out by accepting that we are perpetually in right standing, it impacts positively on our relationships with Him and with those with whom we rub shoulders. As surely as day follows night, right actions follow right thinking. It is essential to our spiritual health and wellbeing that we define ourselves as *"the righteousness of God in Christ"*. It is better to live up to our right standing, than to live up to our religiously defined weaknesses and wrong standing.

Our position as the *"righteousness of God in Christ"* does not expire when next we sin. We are entirely *"without spot or wrinkle!"* If we fail to define ourselves as such, our subconscious minds will come up with a definition, and in the light of our many failings and shortcomings, we are likely to define ourselves poorly. This definition becomes a self-fulfilling, self-defeating prophecy, likely to consign us to a life sentence of needless striving for something we already have. No matter how hard we may try; no matter how sincere we may be, holiness by self-effort remains *"filthy rags"*.

But for those, who out of sheer habit, renew their minds with the reality of their perpetual right standing in Christ, they have an enviable self-fulfilling prophecy that guides them from glory to glory!

OLDER BROTHER MENTALITY

Do I have to earn the right to stay saved?

The parable of the prodigal son gives us a glimpse into how repentance relates to grace. The prodigal returned to his father in the same way that Paul explained repentance in the book of Acts. He said that it is to repent *"towards"* God (Acts 20:21). In the process of turning *"towards"* Him, sin gets abandoned in our pasts. It is God's idea that we should be more concerned with the Person we are turning towards, than with the sin that we are turning from. When we do it His way, rather than being obsessed with sin, we become obsessed with righteousness.

"For as he thinks in his heart, so is he" (Pro 23:7). We become what most predominantly preoccupies our thoughts. Holiness teaching has a lot to say about sin, but the more obsessed we become with our sin, the more inclined we are to sin. On the other hand, to be grace minded is to be obsessed with God's love and the righteousness He

granted us. And with this mind-set, we have all the more reason to stay away from sin.

Repentance is a thinking revolution—the consequence of thinking differently is different behaviour. Behavioural changes take place without any assistance from us. When it comes to living right, the be all and end all is to adopt the kingdom's way of thinking as though it is our own.

It's not our efforts that must change; it's our believing. It all starts with knowing that our state of righteousness is uninterrupted, unvarying, and everlasting. It is entirely secured by Jesus with absolutely no help from us except that we believe that it is so. When our righteousness is established and sustained by Jesus, it is rock solid. If we were expected to keep ourselves saved with good behaviour and timely repentances, we would not be at all secure. If God had left it up to us to re-establish our righteous standing with Him through repentance every time we sinned, we would be unrighteous for longer periods than righteous—sin continuously interrupting our righteous standing. Seeing that we bear His righteousness and not our own, our state of *"righteousness of God in Christ"* makes us every bit as righteous as Jesus, even though it may not always be evident in our behaviour. As unchanging and stable as His righteousness is, so is ours.

The prodigal had prepared a speech of repentance, but his father would have nothing of it; he was too busy welcoming and *restoring* him—expecting no further explanations or words of self-recrimination. Here Jesus gives us a clear picture of what repentance is. The prodigal did not repent with many words of remorse and regret, perhaps his only regret was that he had run out of money, but his shallowness did not faze his father. The prodigal simply returned to his dad in the hope of getting some help—nothing more—the rest was all his father's doing.

This parable is a perfect explanation of God's grace. During the prodigal's dreadful fall into debauchery, his father's love for him never even skipped a beat. And when he returned, he walked straight into the loving arms of grace at its best. He gets *"the best robe"* by grace. He gets a *"ring"* for his finger by grace. He gets *"shoes"* by grace. He gets *"the fatted calf"* by grace. He even gets to *"eat, and be merry"* by grace.

The older brother just couldn't come to terms with such gracious generosity and "easy" forgiveness. Where are the, "I could have told you so" speeches? Is there no lecture of retribution from his father? His father's grace irked him, in much the same way that followers of "un-extreme grace" are irked by those who have discovered "extreme grace" in our day and age. We get an idea of the older brother's ire as he disowns his brother—sarcastically referring to him as his father's son. The very thought of making merry with someone as undeserving as he, peeved him. *"But he was angry and would not go in. Therefore his father came out and pleaded with him. So he answered and said to his father, 'Lo, these many years I have been serving you; I never transgressed your commandment at any time; and yet you never gave me a young goat, that I might make merry with my friends. But as soon as this son of yours came, who has devoured your livelihood with harlots, you killed the fatted calf for him.'"* (Luk 15:28,30).

Such bitterness and un-forgiveness—what a dreadful display of gracelessness. The older brother is the perfect picture of modern day religion throwing stones at "extreme grace". If only they knew that the Father has afforded them the same measure of grace, and all of it at His Son's expense.

The older brother exposed his wrong thinking when he said, *"Lo, these many years I have been serving you"*, wrongly thinking that his father's favour could be earned with much serving. Nothing could be further from the truth. His father made this perfectly clear when he replied, *"Son, you are always with me, and all that I have is yours"* (Luk 15:31). The older brother could have killed any number of fatted calves and partied to his heart's content, but because he imagined that privileges had to be earned, he completely missed out on a life of grace and privilege. Ignorance can be very costly! So many good Christian folk innocently labour in vain—seeking favour for their much serving, when in reality God's favour is available to them purely through grace. Their part is to believe that it is so, and to rest in this truth.

Although the father extended the same measure of grace to the older brother, he could not bring himself to participate in it. In the same way that he missed out on the delights of grace, many modern day believers have been cautioned to be suspicious of "extreme grace" and consequently have excluded themselves from indulging in the delights of it. They cannot grasp the fact that they have just as much access to the privileges afforded by grace—it is what the gospel is! They feel compelled to busy themselves with religious effort in a quest to obtain the things, that unbeknown to them, are already theirs. Their scepticism of "extreme grace" can be awfully limiting—excluding them from indulging in the privileges that Jesus obtained for them at enormous personal cost.

Wherever "extreme grace" emerges, it is very quickly quashed by the religious elite. But this is nothing new; throughout the ages, religion has stoned the prophets. When Stephen addressed the Council before his stoning to death he said, *"Name one prophet your ancestors didn't persecute! They even killed the ones who predicted the coming of the righteous One—the Messiah whom you betrayed and murdered"* (Act 7:52 NLT).

Throughout Bible times, stoning the prophets was Israel's national pastime. Since Calvary, the executions have continued unabated. Through the dark ages, some reformers were executed while others were ostracised, imprisoned and labelled heretics. In hindsight we honour these courageous saints for the measure of grace they restored. In our day and age, a form of stoning God's messengers continues unabated. The methods of ostracising have changed to bad mouthing and excommunicating. This crusade continues, supposedly with impunity, and seemingly without repentance. I for one am labelled by the leaders of our previous congregation as a heretic, and the congregation is not permitted to associate with me. They cannot risk the thought of being contaminated by one who aspires to live by grace alone. Fortunately, God has given me the grace to bless, love and forgive them.

Jesus said, *"No longer do I call you servants,... but I have called you friends"* (Joh 15:15). The way that we relate to Him makes all the difference. We do not serve God to get His favour; we serve Him because we are already favoured. What a relief! What freedom! What victory! What a difference a grace mind-set makes!

WHICH SINS ARE FORGIVEN?

Are we set free to continue sinning without guilt?

"Having been set free from sin" (Rom 6:18). Interestingly, we were not set free from sinning—which no one can deny continues in all believers after their rebirth. This verse sets "extreme grace" apart from religious thinking. So if we are not set free from sinning, what is it about sin that we are set free from? We are set free from sin's right to condemn us. God promised not to remember our sins—no record of them is permitted to be kept in heaven—not only the particular sins that we have repented of; all of our past present and future sins. *"For I will be merciful to their unrighteousness, and their sins and their lawless deeds will I remember no more"* (Heb 8:12).

By using the words *"no more"* it is obvious that this was not always the case. Something dramatic must have taken place for God to stop recording believers' sins. Prior to this change, God not only remembered Old Testament believers' sins, but also visited their iniquity upon third and fourth generations (Exo 34:7). But we can take God at His word—He will never again remember a single New Covenant believer's sin, no matter how heinous. Thank God for His wonderful grace! As clear as Hebrews 8:12 is, there are many who insist that it is not so!

If we were expected to repent of each and every individual sin in order to keep our salvation afloat, but found difficulty recalling all of them, would this mean that we have lost our salvation? Of course not! Nobody can remember every wrong thought and deed—no one has perfect memory. Some may argue that the Holy Spirit will convict us of all our sins, but the Holy Spirit would never convict two people of the same crime. Jesus has already been convicted and sentenced for all our sins in advance of them being committed.

"And you, being dead in your sins and the uncircumcision of your flesh, hath he quickened together with him, having forgiven you all trespasses; Blotting out the handwriting of ordinances that was against us, which was contrary to us, and took it out of the way, nailing it to his cross" (Col 2:13-14 KJV).

If God had done no more than blot out our transgressions, one would have thought that that would have been sufficient, but in reality He didn't stop there; He did a good deal more; He blotted out the very ordinances that accused us—they no longer have jurisdiction over our actions. Once God has blotted something out, it cannot be unblotted. So there is no possibility of falling foul of these accusations at some future date. If however, we were to insist on living by the law, we would be defying God—digging up something that He has buried. Once He had blotted out every ordinance that could possibly be used against us, all accusations against us were forever invalidated! And that is final!

Isn't it wonderful? The law showed us our need for a Saviour, but the moment we turned to Him, it lost its right to accuse us. Its ordinances are no longer enforceable—they remain forever nailed to the cross.

This information is huge! It puts a completely different complexion on our good standing with God. In heaven's books, there isn't a single charge that can be laid against us. When Jesus blotted out the law's *"handwriting of ordinances that was against us"* its stringent demands were brought to a decisive and final end. What more can be said? All accusations are forever nullified! And God's word has the last say on the matter! The law has lost its authority to condemn believers, period!

Does this information cause you to want to go out there and sin yourself silly? It is a reasonable question. If we cannot be blamed for our sin, then why not let rip and make a proper job of it? Come on, let's get down and dirty and give grace something worthwhile to work with.

Well, if that's how this liberty makes you feel, then it shows that you have misunderstood the reason for your exoneration. It was not granted to you to make sinning more acceptable to you and to your heavenly Father; it was granted to you to make you, as His dearly loved child, entirely righteously acceptable, welcome and at home in His presence. Why on earth would we want to twist such a thoughtful holy making gesture into something that is so jarringly at odds with holiness? To use our liberty from sin to fall into sin, just doesn't add up! But this is most unlikely to be the way of those who have grasped the true meaning of authentic grace.

Amnesty was granted to bring you into the very righteousness that you were unable to obtain for yourself—not only for the sake of being positionally righteous before your Father, but also to empower you in your joint endeavour with His Holy Spirit to overcome temptations. Let's face it; temptations are infinitely less alluring when viewed from the lofty heights of an unblemishable state of righteousness—especially if it was imputed to us by God Himself. The bottom line is that we are untouchable in so far as the ordinances are concerned.

There is strength in looking upon temptations from an elevated position of righteousness equal to God's righteousness (we are the righteousness of God in Christ). The same cannot be said of believers who insist on living by the very ordinances that accuse and encumber them with guilt. Without the help of grace, they are left to fight temptation from a disempowered position, where guilt has the last say on the matter. They are compelled to give answer to the accuser of the brethren who conveniently misuses obsolete Bible ordinances to accuse them. For them holy making is daunting—victory over sin is elusive—righteous living is always just beyond their grasp.

John 16:8-9 is often used by well-meaning Bible teachers to convince believers that the Holy Spirit convicts them of sin, but that is not what this scripture says. In these verses, Jesus makes it perfectly clear that it is unbelievers that the Holy Spirit convicts. He spells this out very plainly: *"And when He comes, he will convince* (convict) *the world of its sin"* (NLT). When Jesus speaks of the *"world"*, He is specifically referring to unbelievers. Just in case we are not entirely convinced, Jesus makes this point even clearer by going on to specify which particular sin the Holy Spirit would convict them of. He says, *"The world's sin is unbelief in me"*. The New King James Version says, *"they do not believe in Me"*. It is clear that believers are not included in this statement—the reason that believers are called believers in the first place, is because they do believe in Him.

The conviction of conscience that we as believers experience may have a different origin. Both believers and unbelievers experience convictions of conscience. Whether saved or unsaved, everybody has a conscience, but not everybody has the Holy Spirit. Only born again individuals have His indwelling presence. That being the case, we should take care to distinguish between convictions of conscience and Holy Spirit promptings.

You have probably heard many sermons on this scripture. How many of them mentioned that the Holy Spirit also convicts the world of *"righteousness"*? Perhaps none! Yet that is what this scripture says. The way that religion often portrays conviction, makes the Holy Spirit out to be the holy accuser instead of the holy edifier.

There is another issue—each of our consciences have different values and standards, yet the Holy Spirit has only one standard. For both believers and unbelievers alike, our consciousness of *"good and evil" was* inherited from the *"knowledge of good and evil"* that Adam was tricked into gaining. This, together with the sum total of our unique life's experiences give shape to our particular world view.

That being the case, what part does the Spirit play in the spiritual development of believers? A few verses further on in the same passage of scripture, Jesus gives the answer: *"When the Spirit comes, he will guide you into all truth"*, and, *"He will bring me glory by revealing to you whatever he receives from me"* (NLT). For unbelievers there is conviction, but for believers, there is guidance from the Holy Spirit—two very different promptings. He also reveals to us what He receives from God the Father. His agenda is redemptive; not anti-redemptive—He is too holy to stoop to breaking His promise of *"no condemnation"!*

With misinformation, we unintentionally besmear the Holy Spirit's impeccable reputation. Sadly, the *"accuser of the brethren"* is quick to use this confusion to his advantage—he pretends to be an angel of light, when in reality, he is an angel of darkness.

The problem with religion is that it has a tendency to innocently pass on misinformation inherited from respected spiritual fathers. It is only right to hold these wonderful men and women in high regard, but it all goes horribly wrong when they are regarded as spiritual gurus. A problem arises when misinformation is adopted as gospel—their words quoted as though Spirit breathed. When leaders are exalted, it is easy to forget that they are mere men with similar weaknesses to our own.

Now, the accuser of the brethren has a very different agenda. He will do whatever it takes to besmear God's perfect reputation and to sow mistrust into our perfect relationship with Him. He is a dirty player—he'll stoop to anything. If he can get us to fall into guilt, condemnation and shame, and then convince us that his accusations are the convictions of the Holy Spirit, then his filthy work is done. When his accusations are mistaken for Holy Spirit convictions, he takes the opportunity to sow doubt, destroy peace and steal joy. He goes for the jugular, and once he has stolen our joy, he can steal anything else of value from us with supposed impunity.

Conversely, the Holy Spirit is our closest ally. He is in continuous communication with us, not to condemn, but to warn of danger, to comfort, to edify, lead, inform and help. One of the fruits of the Spirit is peace. The moment we lose it, we know that He is trying to get our attention. It is imperative to hear what He is telling us—He always has our best interests at heart; always leading us to something more beneficial. When we are led into godliness, we don't need to be led away from sin—we are too busy following the Holy Spirit into righteous living to be bothered with Satan's distractions. This is not an argument against repentance—to the contrary, the act of turning to God is what repentance is.

Repentance is a radical reversal. By doing our best to turn from sin, we are not likely to have the same degree of success as we would if we were to turn towards God. God is infinitely more capable of dealing with our penchant for sin than we will ever be. Besides, turning away from something towards nowhere in particular, is as good as guaranteeing a relapse into what we have turned from. When we are not heading towards a specific objective or person, we are directionless and easy pickings for the *"accuser of the brethren"*. If we haven't established a definite direction to turn to in repentance, before we know it, we will discover that we have been drawn back into our same old sinful ways. The kind of repentance that God requires of us, is a turnabout that points us directly into the loving arms of our heavenly Dad.

In reality, religion has so watered down redemption from its original potency that it now requires all kinds of other religious gymnastics to hold our salvation together. All the sin of the world was included in Christ's atonement. When He died, He left not a single sin un-atoned for, and when we accept that our redemption is complete, we are able to enter in and enjoy exactly what it means to be entirely set free from sin.

If we reject the notion that grace is extreme, we end up with a watered down gospel that lacks the gospel's fundamental power and purpose. In this way, we make the finished work of the cross out to be something that is incomplete and unfinished. It would be presumptuous of us to imagine that our puny efforts could possibly complete what Christ supposedly left undone—He does nothing by half measures. How easily we insult our Redeemer—He liberated us from sin's clutches at enormous personal cost. The gospel really is very good news—religion has reduced it to reasonably good news— certainly nothing to crow about.

In summary; to answer the question, "Are we set free to continue sinning without guilt?" We must ask what it is about sin that He has destroyed.

He came to destroy sin's power to condemn us! And He accomplished it in full! *God destroyed sin's control over us by giving his Son as a sacrifice for our sins. He did this so that the requirement of the law would be fully accomplished for us who no longer follow our sinful nature but instead follow the Spirit"* (Rom 8:3,4 NLT). A follower of the Spirit is a perfect description of a follower of "extreme grace". The converse would be a follower of the law. But the law cannot give us righteousness; it can only arouse sin and expose our sinfulness.

It is important to see that God *"destroyed sin's control over us"*. Religion is likely to jump to the conclusion that in saying this, Paul was inferring that we must stop sinning. While that goes without saying, that is not what he was referring to. He was saying that the control or power of sin to condemn us has been destroyed. God most certainly did not destroy sin's ability to lure godly saints into sinful living, as is abundantly obvious from the way that the saintliest of us continue to miss the mark.

But grace does not stop there; grace goes on to empower us to have victory over sinning. It does this by dealing with the root cause of sin, and the root cause is seated in our hearts. But for most of us, our hearts are a very guarded place—we do not easily open our hearts to accusers. But to those who love us, we readily throw our hearts' doors wide open. Thankfully the God of the gospel is not the god of accusation; He is the God of love. The One who patiently stands knocking at our hearts' doors is the Jesus of love, and the love He brings is enough to change the way our hearts operate. There is little place for sin in a heart that is enraptured with Jesus. To be enthralled by Him and His gracious ways, is to be captivated by unconditional love!

Peter deserted Jesus when He needed him most; denying that he even knew Him. Yet Jesus had no words of accusation for him; only a question, *"Do you love Me?"* As with Peter, God does not use wrath to deal with our sin; for that He uses unconditional love, mercy and grace. And it really makes a difference to the way our lives are lived! It was the same with the prodigal's father; he had not a single word of accusation for his wayward son.

Live loved! You are not accused!

DOES GRACE MAKE IT EASIER TO SIN?

If grace allows us to sin without fearing sin's consequences, how will we be restrained from sinning? Should we assume that Jesus died for the purpose of promoting sin?

To suppose for one moment that religion has succeeded in freeing its followers from sinning would require a gargantuan stretch of the imagination. The general state of Christian integrity is adequate proof that "un-extreme grace" has not done a good job of bringing about meaningful change to the behaviour of its followers. Generally speaking, in as far as ethics are concerned, the church is not much different to the world. Obviously, in light of the lengths that Jesus went to in order to make a difference, this ought not to be so. Something is amiss! What is lacking? In a word, it is "grace"! God provided grace, not only to save sinners, but to equip saints to conquer the sin that so easily besets them. How sad to see "extreme grace" shunned because, in religion's opinion, it may give rise to licence—yet it is God's idea and the church's one and only hope.

The law provides religion with enforceable restraints, but Jesus has liberated believers from its ordinances. Grace presented religion with a dilemma—how can holiness be imposed without the aid of ordinances to govern and police it? The need to govern holiness gave rise to legalism. Legalism says, "If we can't have Moses' laws, we will devise our own set of rules". Religion cannot accept, that when the ordinances were nailed to the cross, legalistic restraints on Christians were finally abolished for all time and eternity. Not a single Christian can ever be found guilty of anything in God's sight.

So in its wisdom, religion resurrected laws in a new guise. In the process of gradually phasing legalism in, ungraciousness slipped into the church unnoticed. Sadly, the re-imposition of restrains re-imposed the very guilt and shame that Jesus took so much trouble and pain to eradicate. More legalism meant less grace and less grace meant more sin and less redemption.

Contrary to what one would expect from such freedom—"extreme grace" gives a person more reason to turn from sin than any other gospel. *"But even if we, or an angel from heaven, preach any other gospel to you than what we have preached to you, let him be accursed"* (Gal 1:8). My word! Seriously? Will we be accursed for preaching anything other than grace? Makes one think, doesn't it?

Guilt is a tool of *"the accuser of the brethren"*. Guilt causes us to have an inward sin focus, instead of an upward *"righteousness of God in Christ"* focus. Guilt leads to a preoccupation with the very things that we are trying to overcome, and this preoccupation causes us to do more of what we are preoccupied with. Conversely, "extreme grace" causes us to be preoccupied with God's love and our right standing with Him. In this way, He is able to reshape our attitudes. And righteous attitudes have a natural way of transposing into righteous actions. When righteous attitudes are not contrived, they are genuine.

Besides it being a Bible truth, it is commonly known that wrong thinking leads to wrong actions. For instance, a preoccupation with sexual fantasies makes one more susceptible to infidelity when opportunity comes knocking. Or the harbouring of anger, though piously suppressed, makes one susceptible to angry outbursts when pushed too far. We are powerless to win the battle against sinful actions, unless we have first won the battle against sinful thinking.

Those, who in the commendable interests of holiness embroil themselves in an all-out battle with sin, give more prominence to sin than it deserves. An obsession with holiness becomes an obsession with eradicating sin. But sin focused-ness is a far cry from holiness. Is it any wonder that legalistic holiness is so hollow? Legalism is not the gospel of Jesus! God's standard is much holier than that!

We are instructed to renew our minds. It takes a grace empowered discipline to pull down every thought that would exalt itself above the knowledge of our right standing with God. If we must be obsessed with something, rather let it be an obsession with our righteousness and right standing with God, than with our weaknesses, flaws, failures, sins and perceived wrong standing with Him. The one obsession edifies and elevates, while the other drains, dampens, depresses and throws a wet blanket over the vibrancy of a life lived *"in Christ"*. In this weakened state, what chance is there of actually getting ahead of sin?

When it comes to living right, grace is not an excuse; it's a reason. It does not provide us with an excuse to sin; it is precisely opposite—it provides us with a reason to live righteously—a matter of living outwardly what we are inwardly. If we can accept that in Christ we are perpetually righteous, ultimately, this inner righteousness will translate into righteous actions.

Very often, believers are proud of feeling guilty. We are quick to tell others how bad we feel for what we have done—it's how we ease our consciences and let ourselves off the hook. We practise the self-retribution ethic which says, "I am okay with God as long as I can feel bad enough about my iniquities". We feel that our case is all the stronger if we can say that we've shed many a tear and had sleepless nights over our blunders. How unfortunate! With religion, it is all about me and my efforts to be holy, whereas with grace it is all about Jesus and the holiness He bestowed upon us—He did it all! And now His imputed righteousness is spilling over into our behaviour.

"Looking unto Jesus the author and finisher of our faith..." (Heb 12:2 KJV). In this scripture it is clear that our *"looking"* or our focus and obsession is not supposed to be on our paltry efforts to free ourselves from sin. Our *"looking"*, focus and obsession is meant to be squarely on Jesus. *"Looking"* at Jesus is life changing—when we go to the spiritual mirror to see ourselves reflected in Him, His image becomes indelibly imprinted on our psyche. And before we know it, His righteousness is revealed in our actions. When we are convinced of our righteous standing, righteous living becomes a synch. As with an aeroplane's autopilot, we allow the mirror, who is Christ within, to set our coordinates, and once set, our destiny is assured.

Not only is He the *"author"*; He is also the *"finisher"*. By trying to finish the job ourselves, we forego the finished work. Although we have the complete work, many have chosen to live in something that is incomplete. As the author, He began the job and as the finisher, He completed it. We weren't even there when He did it—there is no way that we could have made even the slightest contribution towards its completion. When He finished the task, all was done and dusted—absolutely nothing further is required of us, except that we believe and receive. The best that we can do is to get out of the way and let God be God.

Religion thrives on the fear ethic, but fear motivation is a poor substitute for grace motivation. Fear of each other drives us apart, while love draws us together. And it is no different with our relationship with God—with Him, we are not driven by fear; we are drawn by love.

If your wife were to tell you that she loves you unconditionally, would you take her commitment to be an invitation to be unfaithful to her? Most certainly not! To the contrary, it would cause you to be even more faithful, wouldn't it? The same goes for our relationship with God—the discovery that we are unconditionally loved, causes us to be all the more faithful to Him; not less faithful, as religion would have us believe.

May I suggest that grace is the one and only answer to sin! Love captivates our hearts—changing them from glory to glory. There is no need to strive for personal change when our hearts are losing their appetite for sin. Love is not a quick fix, but as our concept of being loved by God grows, our actions become more like His. Godliness flourishes in hearts that are infused with divine love, and this love gushes over in waves of kindness as it overflows to those around us.

With computers it is a matter of garbage in; garbage out. Fortunately, the opposite is also true—good data in; good data out. With us it is a matter of grace in; grace out! The more grace we receive, the more equipped we are to be gracious to others. The more extreme the input; the more extreme the output! With grace, the battle with stubborn sin is over! Sadly the converse is also true—law in; law out! Religion in; religion out! Accusations and finger pointing in; accusations and finger pointing out! "Un-extreme grace" in; "un-extreme grace" out!

This brings us back to the question: Did Jesus die for the purpose of promoting sin? Contrary to what one might suppose, sin does not fare well in the sunshine of God's grace; it flourishes in dark places where feelings of unworthiness are nurtured by guilt and self-condemnation. It is only unconditional love and acceptance that can lift self-loathing believers out of the doldrums of despair. Righteousness thrives in the sunshine of divine edification; sin thrives in the misery of self-blame, melancholy and gloom.

Then there is the other question: If grace allows us to sin without fearing sin's consequences, how will we be restrained to stay away from it? Restraints were at the core of the Old Covenant. In abolishing the Old Covenant to make way for the New, Jesus removed all restraints with their punitive retributions, clearing the way for a sublime relationship based on "want to", rather than on "have to". A love relationship based on "want to" is infinitely more sincere than a relationship built on "have to". Jesus is looking for a genuine romance—not one that is imposed upon us. But the question arises, "Will it result in more sin?" That possibility always exists, but only for those who have not grasped the full impact of being completely accepted and loved without reason—a concept that is immensely life changing in and of itself.

Love and acceptance carry more weight and influence than laws and accusations. Believers are more apt to want to please their Lover than to disappoint Him. When one is inspired by love, one is less likely to give way to sin. But sadly, it is distinctly different for those who are regularly brow beaten with burdensome laws.

In view of this, godly living can be described as a by-product of divine love. Sin does not fare well in loved hearts—divine love elevates one out of despair, guilt and shame. When it comes to winning the battle over sin, healthy self-esteem, inspired by divine grace, gives believers a head start on those who are encumbered with guilt, condemnation and shame—the burdensome legacy of law keeping.

Does grace leave us in a moral vacuum? Naturally speaking, one cannot be blamed for thinking it would, but Jeremiah's description of the coming New Covenant of grace was very different. He said that we would no longer need the written law, because the law would be written on our hearts. In other words, we would be led by the promptings of the Holy Spirit from His dwelling place within us. Paul put it this way in Galatians 5:18 *"But if you are led by the Spirit, you are not under the law"*. From this it is plain that it has to be one or the other—either the Spirit or the law; never both. Being led by the Spirit is the way of grace.

Paul had only one question, *"This only I want to learn from you: Did you receive the Spirit by the works of the law, or by the hearing of faith?"* (Gal 3:2). He takes them to task for attempting to live the Christian life by a lesser grace than it took to save them. We are not to scale down in grace; we are to grow in grace, which means that grace must play an ever increasing role in our living (2 Pet 3:18). It also means that the law must be abandoned for the sake of being Spirit led. This is the treasured gift of every New Covenant believer. It takes commitment to grow in grace—we are to become more and more radical in our knowledge of grace, and more and more extreme in what we choose to draw from it.

In this chapter, Paul interchangeably uses the words *"faith"* and *"the Spirit"* as the way to access grace. There is no moral vacuum in grace; it is a three stranded cord made up of the Spirit of God, our perpetual righteous standing, and God's loving grace. Seeing that it is all God's doing, we are left with only one responsibility, and that is to add our faith. When it comes to walking in godliness, this rock solid combination is infinitely more reliable than the legal restraints of the law.

We have a perfect example of how effective the law was when we read the record of the Prophets of Old Testament times. Boy, did they have a tough assignment dealing with Israel's sin! Grace was not responsible for this sad state of affairs—for that the law must take all the blame. Paul put it this way, *"The law aroused these evil desires that produced sinful deeds"* (Rom 7:5 NLT). The law did nothing to restrain sin; it served only to obstruct godliness. Contrary to what one would expect, grace does not make it easier to sin. Praise God! Grace makes it a whole lot easier to say no to sin!

"Whatever we ask we receive of Him, because we keep His commandments, and do those things that are pleasing in His sight" (1Jn 3:22). It is clear from this scripture that we do need to keep His commandments. The question arises—which commandments was John referring to? The Ten Commandments? No! *"He has made the first one obsolete"* (Heb 8:13). In the very next verse, John goes on to tell us exactly what His commandments are: *"And this is His commandment: that we should believe on the name of His Son Jesus Christ and love one another, as He gave us commandment"* (1Jn 3:23). In a nutshell: believe Him and love people, period! This positions us to walk in His undeserved favour.

Well, the first part of this commandment is a synch—all New Covenant believers believe in Jesus. It's the second part with which we have difficulty. We find it difficult to love spiteful, hateful and revengeful, tit for tat humanity—especially when we are on the receiving end of their spiteful jibes. How can we break this vengeful cycle, and bring ourselves to love undeserving humanity? The answer is; we first have to know that we are loved when we don't deserve it, before we can attempt to love others, when it is obvious that they don't deserve it. Herein lies the problem; we cannot receive such "extreme grace" if we have made up our minds that it is not so extreme.

Although grace is extended to all believers; it stands to reason that we can only indulge in the grace that we embrace. We cannot participate in what we have deemed to be too extreme. That indulgence is reserved for those who have not set limits to grace. Seeing that it takes faith to make withdrawals from grace, it follows that we will only lay claim to what we believe we are entitled to. The grace that exceeds the limits we have set will remain unclaimed.

But surely Jesus gave many more commandments than these? He sure did! But we should not lose sight of the difference between commandments that condemn, and commandments that exude life. *"For the law of the Spirit of life in Christ Jesus has made me free from the law of sin and death"* (Rom 8:2). Unlike the commandments of sin and death, Jesus' commandments are not onerous; they invite us to partake of the effervescent life of the Spirit!

Read the words of this commandment of Jesus and discern whether the law He referred to is *"the law of sin and death"* or the law of *"the Spirit of life in Christ"*. Jesus said, *"Come to Me, all you who labor and are heavy laden, and I will give you rest"* (Mat 11:28). Is this a commandment of *"death"* or of *"life"*? The answer should be obvious! He commands us to go to Him, not to do something for Him, but to get something beneficial and worthwhile from Him—something that will make our lives enormously richer.

Another commandment of Jesus, if it can be called that, tells us to give and it shall be given back to us. Here Jesus is not trying to get something out of us; He is trying to get something even better to us. In another commandment, He tells us to speak to mountains, telling them to move into the sea. When we obey this commandment, mountainous heaps of problems become subject to our words. He commands us to make disciples, heal the sick and cast out demons. None of His commandments reduce our lives in any way, shape or form—they are all a joy to fulfil. Then to top it all, He empowers us with grace to accomplish them. What kind of a Jesus is this that we serve? So gracious! So generous! So amazing!

In Romans 8:2 Paul painted a contrast between the commandments of Moses and the commandments of Jesus. He associated Moses' with *"sin and death"* while associating Jesus' with *"the Spirit of life"*. Isn't following Jesus' commandments just so edifying and fulfilling? Let us lift our glasses and sing with Tevye, the Jewish Russian milkman from the "Fiddler on the Roof":

To life, l'chaim!
L'chaim, l'chaim, to life!
A gift we seldom are wise enough
Ever to prize enough,
Drink l'chaim, to life!

God would like us to be joyful
Even though our hearts lie panting on the floor;
How much more can we be joyful,
When there's really something
To be joyful for.
To life, to life, L'chai-im!
L'chai-im, l'chai-im, to life!
It gives you something to think about,
Something to drink about,
Drink l'chai-im, to life!
l'chai-im!

Jesus is not a cosmic killjoy; He is the very essence of abundant life and joy. He didn't come to give us dreary grey one dimensional religious lives that barely scrape through; He came to give us effervescent life bursting at the seams with merriment and joy! Everything about Him is superlative! And there is nothing ordinary about the life He offers; it is abundant and overflowing with pleasure! None of His commandments subtract from the wealth of high-spirited living; they add richness to life! When He commands us to do something, He is commanding us to participate in His exuberance and cheer. Sure, He didn't promise that life would always be a bed of roses, but with His effervescent life within us, not even the worst that life can throw at us is able to rob us of our joy, unless of course, we allow it. It is a delight to obey Jesus; especially when we know that His commandments impart *"fullness of life"*.

Under normal circumstances it would be natural to think of commandments as being a drag—something that must be done to appease a demanding and egotistical god, but not so with Jesus' commandments; His commandments are uplifting, encouraging, edifying and empowering. How can we not want to follow and obey them with every ounce of our being?

Seeing that His commandments hold out so much promise, why are we so reluctant to throw our weight in with Him, and obey Him whole-heartedly? A good question! But then, who can blame anybody for being reluctant when they have been taught the law of the *"Spirit of life in Christ"*, seasoned with a sprinkling of the *"law of sin and death"?* There is nothing appealing about *"sin and death"*, but then that is certainly not what Jesus' commandments offer. When we have the *"Spirit of life in Christ"*, there is no need for seasoning or condiments—anything added would spoil what is already perfect. When we are satisfied with the gracious gift of the life of Jesus, we are completely satisfied!

—oOo—

Nobody is fooled by the emptiness of "love" that is given just because it is expected; least of all God. He desires a relationship that is far more real than that. And He knows that we are only able to give love to the extent that we have received love from Him. Receiving it is a choice—we cannot receive the fullness thereof if we have set limits to it. Sadly, our denominations small thinking can so easily put His generosity beyond our reach. Consequently, we end up with no more than the dregs when we could be drenched to the skin with a gushing shower of His goodness.

Sadly, religion has taught us to be content with only a small part of our covenant rights, and tragically we have bought this half-truth. Once we settle for less than what He has given us, we are left to survive on less of Him in our day to day living. When this happens, we turn to our puny efforts to make up for what we lack in grace. And that's when our holiness falls apart—it simply cannot be held together with *"filthy rags"*.

We have a divine Lover who intensely desires to be intimate with us. May I suggest that we break with our limitations? Let us embrace all that grace encompasses, and allow ourselves to be more deeply loved. The more that we allow ourselves to be loved, the less trouble we will have loving others, and the less trouble we will have saying no to sin!

SHOULD WE TOLERATE SIN?

If God doesn't impute our sins to us, is it okay to sin?

One can almost be excused for thinking that imputed righteousness through grace is actually divine tolerance of sin. But nothing could be further from the truth. It is God's sin destroying strategy; certainly not a sin supporting strategy. Unless we understand the purpose of grace, we are likely to turn to legalism to make us look good. This is Religion's best shot—it has come up with nothing more than a set of ineffective rules to substitute for the sin destroying power of grace. But how can manmade legalistic rules possibly measure up to God's full proof remedy for sin? The bottom line is: if sin cannot be fixed with grace, it cannot be fixed at all! Religion has not come up with anything that works. Yet, by and large, religion rejects the notion that God's grace could be a solution to sin. In its wisdom, it believes that it will lead to licence.

But sin cannot be cured by behaving better; it can only be cured by thinking better. Sin is not in actions that can be seen—actions are only the outworking of something far more terrible—it's the sinful heart of man—this is where sin is germinated, propagated and then finally disseminated in the form of unhealthy behaviour. Like a cancer, sin incubates in secret—it takes place in our hearts where nobody sees, and religion has no answers for this dastardly disease. On the other hand, grace goes directly to the heart, where it tackles the very kernel of sin with a king size dollop of love. Hearts do not respond well to accusations, but eagerly yield to love. Hearts react defensively when accused, but readily open up when loved. Loved hearts are receptive and yielding hearts. Like water softener added to the wash load, love softens the stoniest of hearts.

Grace is the only force capable of freeing us from slavery to sin. Neither Old Testament laws nor present-day denominationally devised rules can do it. Sadly, religion resurrects the very thing that Jesus took so much torture and pain to dismantle. Instead of totally embracing the grace embedded in the New Covenant, religion selectively picks and chooses what it deems to be religiously appropriate, and what it deems to be inappropriate, and then does the same with the Old Covenant. The two Covenants are then blended into a more theologically plausible doctrine than God's.

There is a problem with this—neither covenant can be invoked by a believer while any part of the other covenant is in force. In as much as unmerited favour, better known as grace, cannot be merited; favour through law keeping can only be rewarded if it is merited. The problem with the covenant of rewards is that one slipup on the most minor of transgressions, makes us guilty of the entire law. Deuteronomy 28 is clear on this: Unless we manage to keep *"all"* the law, down to the minutest detail, we are cursed. James reiterated this point when he said, *"For whoever shall keep the whole law, and yet stumble in one point, he is guilty of all"* (Jas 2:10). And Paul warned, *"CURSED IS EVERYONE WHO DOES NOT CONTINUE IN ALL THINGS WHICH ARE WRITTEN IN THE BOOK OF THE LAW, TO DO THEM"* (Gal 3:10) It is significant that the NKJV uses capital letters to express this warning. If we insist on striving to obtain God's favour by law keeping, we will be cursed for the slightest infringement thereof. If we want to go this route, we cannot pick and choose. In as much as the law promises blessings, it also promises curses. And the curses are too horrendous to contemplate. The odds are stacked against anybody actually getting it right—nobody has—yet many dare. One can only wonder if they have considered the dire consequences awaiting them.

The way of grace is very different. Jesus fulfilled the law on our behalf and took upon himself the curse for what He knew we would fail to fulfil (Rom 8:4). He did this by becoming a curse for us. *"Christ has redeemed us from the curse of the law, having become a curse for us (for it is written, "cursed is everyone who hangs on a tree")"* (Gal 3:13). God has provided a plan of escape—there is no need to put ourselves at the risk of suffering the dire penalties promised to those who would attempt to make themselves right through law keeping— the consequences are too awful to contemplate. Old Covenant law keeping ought to be forbidden territory for all New Covenant believers! Paul did his level best to warn us against this malpractice.

We may think of grace as being wishy-washy and therefore soft on sin, but this is certainly not the case. Grace can handle any amount of sin, but there is one thing that it simply cannot handle. In fact, it is something for which it has zero tolerance. It cannot accommodate the slightest compromise with Old Covenant law. *"He takes away the first that He may establish the second"* (Heb 10:9). If we dare to disagree with this scripture, our disagreement will be done at our peril—it's how we invite *"punishment"* and make our faith *"useless"* (Rom 4:14). It is sad to say, but with legalism, religion is often unwittingly caught up in the business of undoing the work of the cross.

Repentance has a vital role to play—it is the part we play in our joint endeavour with the Holy Spirit to bring our actions into line with our sanctification.

Grace is always a work of the Spirit; diametrically opposite to our dogged efforts at striving for holiness out of a sense of duty. What we manage to achieve by self-effort may give us reason to be proud, but there is nothing quite as contemptible as Mr and Mrs Christian goody-two-shoes who look down their noses in contempt; quick to say, "We don't do this or that", as though they are proud of putting their *"filthy rags"* out on public display.

Throughout the Gospels, Jesus made His feelings known; He did not appreciate super spiritual specimens of so called holiness—He called them a brood of vipers! Contrast this with His attitude towards sinning humanity—for them He never had a single word of criticism— the depravity of their sin never fazed Him. He deplored the holy man's prayer and exalted the publican's prayer. One can only imagine the sin, drunkenness and debauchery that took place in a publican's house of ill-repute. Although Jesus surrounded Himself with the dregs of society, like cursing fishermen, corrupt tax collectors and promiscuous prostitutes, there is not a single mention of Him ever accusing any of them.

Romans 8:1 says, *"There is therefore now no condemnation to those who are in Christ Jesus, who do not walk according to the flesh, but according to the Spirit."* Striving to be godly is not holiness; it is walking after the flesh. Conversely, being led by the Spirit is the heart changing process of grace at work. Changed hearts find no pleasure in sin. Once the problem with sin has been fixed in our hearts, our problem with sinful actions is fixed without us having to lift a finger. That does not mean that we will never sin again, but God's love sure does make saying no to sin a whole lot easier.

It is oh so satisfying to have our efforts at good living noticed and acknowledged. To be honest, Christian striving can be pretty good for the ego, but the accomplishments of our striving is the antithesis of the fruit of the Spirit. The Holy Spirit doesn't need our help to produce His fruit; He can do it all by Himself; all He needs from us is our willingness to yield to His guidance. Victory over sin is far more likely when empowered by love, than when disempowered by guilt, condemnation and shame.

In the watered down version of the gospel as proclaimed by those who are content with a less extreme form of grace, it is so easy to mistakenly believe that our divine relationship rests on "our" holiness. The writer of Hebrews has a very different take on this, He says that we are *"... partakers of His holiness"* (Heb 12:10). When we are urged to shape up, we end up partaking of our own form of "holiness", and in the process, miss out on the opportunity of being *"partakers of His holiness"*. Grace is not about giving us permission to sin; grace is about giving us permission to partake of His divine holiness (Heb 12:10); His divine righteousness (Ph 3:9); His divine nature (2 Pet 1:4); His Spiritual things (Rom 15:27); His promise in Christ (Eph 3:6); His inheritance (Col 1:12); His benefits (1 Ti 6:2); He Himself (Heb 3:14) and the Holy Spirit (Heb 6:4).

Our divine relationship with God has nothing to do with what we have "done" and everything to do with "receiving" what Christ has already completed doing for us. We are invited to partake and benefit from the *"gift"*. If we really want to make God's day, then we ought to step out and partake of even more of His generous *"gifts"*—the more we partake, the more we please Him.

Am I only saved if I have repented of
each and every sin individually?

We repented to be saved from perishing—it's what we did to be born again. Not only this, but repentance has become our daily routine, because life is a process of trial and error—requiring regular adjustments to our walk as we discover ever deeper levels of godly living. The Bible describes it as moving from glory to glory. The folly of believing that our salvation needs constant propping up, rescuing and patching up with repentances should be obvious—nobody but nobody is ever entirely up to date with repenting.

I was in a church where the pastor said with absolute conviction from his pulpit that we should not deal with the sickness before we have dealt with the sin in a person's life. Really! If that were true, then Jesus was out of order. He gave us a perfect pattern for repentance. He healed and delivered without making the slightest suggestion that a person first repent. When we go to Jesus, we go just as we are. In the same way that we don't clean ourselves before taking a bath; we don't have to repent before approaching Jesus. Of course, just being in His presence is profoundly life altering—repentance is likely to follow without persuasion.

We must ask ourselves the question, "Are we saved because of our efforts, or because of Jesus' efforts? Is it our blood, sweat and tears or Jesus' blood that made us righteous in God's sight?"

Believe me—repentance is not just good and right; it is essential to the spiritual wellbeing of any believer. But repentance is not the stitching that holds our salvation together—our right standing with God stands on something far more reliable than the fickleness of human stitching—it stands on the solid foundation of the blood of the lamb!

If you are thinking, "Does it really matter that I believe otherwise?" It most certainly does! "Why?" For one thing, you would be minimising the completeness of your redemption. You can only benefit from the use of a gift to the extent that you understand its uses. I have a top flight smart phone with a myriad of functions, but only use one or two. Unless I take the trouble to learn how to use the others, I cannot benefit from them. Despite the fact that these applications would be useful to me; for as long as I have an aversion for technology, they are of absolutely no value to me whatsoever. The fact that they are conveniently tucked in my pocket means absolutely nothing—they might as well be it Timbuktu. Here is the tragedy; we cannot benefit from any part of our redemption for which we have an aversion, albeit on the pious basis of "sound" religious reasoning.

For another thing, a healthy reverential fear of God is a very different concept to the disempowering scary fear of losing one's salvation. Such a fear is relationship destroying—it is not possible to enjoy intimacy with a person holding a gun to our head. This is precisely opposite to the gift we received from Jesus. He made us secure in salvation; religion has made us insecure.

Old Testament believers were not saved by law keeping—the law has never saved a single soul—it was not implemented for that purpose.

Grace is not a new concept brought into existence by the cross. Abraham was counted righteous long before the introduction of the law.

If law keeping did not save those who kept it; how did Old Testament saints get saved? They were saved purely by the blood of Jesus. Obviously, they lived and died before the coming of their Messiah. After Jesus atoned for all sins, past, present and future on the cross, He entered hell and then Paradise to preach redemption to Old Testament believers, who like Abraham had been counted righteous for believing. Their law keeping, annual sacrifices, the releasing of the scapegoat, and the sprinkling of blood on the mercy seat were merely shadows of what they would ultimately obtain through Christ. These rituals did not save them; it was grace and grace alone that did it. They had the Old Testament in which Christ is concealed in shadow and type, while we have the New Testament in which Christ is finally revealed.

Faith continues to be the only way to find righteousness. *"And this I say, that the law, which was four hundred and thirty years later, cannot annul the covenant that was confirmed before by God in Christ, that it should make the promise of no effect"* (Gal 3:17). During the reign of the law, the law did not reveal their righteousness; it revealed their sin. Nor did it make them righteous; it exposed their sinfulness. As with Abraham who lived 430 years before the law, righteousness came to them purely by faith. And so it is for us in our day and age.

Repentance is an on-going process of bringing our actions into line with our sinless born again position before God. But we are incapable of holding our salvation together with our actions—only God can do that, and He has already finished doing it. Nevertheless, the practice of repentance is a means of living in purity and godliness. In many cases, believers may take months, and even many years to finally relent and come to repent of certain sins—nobody is immune from putting matters off. To assert that that would be salvation cancelling is to imply that nobody can stay saved. It would invert salvation from a work of God to a work of the flesh. Such a notion makes a mockery of the cross—it would cease to serve any purpose. Even the thought of such a wishy-washy covenant would be an insult to the One who validated it—it brings His integrity into question and makes nonsense of His covenant promises!

To suggest that we lose our state of *"no condemnation"* through the act of sinning, and subsequently reinstate it through the act of repentance, is to suggest that the blood of Jesus is no better than the blood of bulls and goats of the Old Covenant which only gave them temporary immunity. Praise God! We do not lose and later re-obtain a state of *"no condemnation"* every time we sin and subsequently repent. We have a robust state of *"no condemnation"* and it is not based on anything that we have done or not done; it is entirely based upon what Jesus has done—He was condemned in our place. And because we got this status while we were sinning, we cannot lose it because we continue to sin—even the saintliest of us sins until the day we die. Fortunately, we have a God who is well aware of this, and in His grace, has made adequate provision to deal with our every failing and moral weakness.

WHY THE LAW?

Religion would have us believe that the law sends us to grace, and that once grace has done its work, grace sends us back to the law to frame our way of life. But is this so?

It is true that the law reveals our sin, but the law is powerless to do anything about its exposé. We must look elsewhere for a solution. God has provided the answer—it is grace in the person of His Son, Jesus!

So grace sends us back to the law, does it? Are we seriously going to ignore Paul's many warnings for saints to stay away from the law? Religious rationale can be very puzzling. *"In that He says, "A NEW COVENANT," He has made the first obsolete"* (Heb 8:13).

Jesus came to disconnect us from the law in order to connect us to the Holy Spirit's promptings from within. *"But this is the covenant I will make ... on that day, says the Lord. I will put my laws in their minds, and I will write them on their hearts"* (Jer 31:33 NLT). *"It is written not with pen and ink, but with the Spirit of the living God. It is carved not on stone, but on human hearts"* (2 Cor 3:3 NLT).

Often modern day religion affords grace to unbelievers but lays down the law as soon as they become believers. In foreseeing this error, Paul instructed us *"As you therefore have received Christ Jesus the Lord, so walk in him"* (Col 2:6). How did we receive Christ? Was it not by faith without a single good work to our credit? If so, then the same applies to the way that we should continue walking in Christ— we never get to the place where we qualify for God's favour through Old Covenant law keeping. And denominational legalism is no better—it is equally ineffective! It's only benefit is to make us scary!

Religion should be commended for calling us to live morally sound lives, yet be deplored for suggesting that it can be achieved by returning us to the very thing that arouses sin, shame and condemnation. The Holy Spirit is the executor and trustee of the testamentary Covenant of Grace. Our covenant privileges were conferred upon us by gratuitous bequest. The covenant of Law succeeds only in reversing this privilege. But praise God, it is defunct! Unconditional gifts remain entirely unconditional forever!

To turn to the law is to cold-shoulder the Holy Spirit—choosing to be policed by ordinance rather than to be graciously led by inner promptings—choosing a covenant of death in preference to a covenant of life. Religion is mystifying—a no brainer if ever there was one! We are made ministers of the New Covenant, *"not of the letter* (of the Law) *but of the Spirit; for the letter* (of the Law) *kills, but the Spirit gives life"* (2Co 3:6—text in brackets added for the sake of clarity).

We cannot have it both ways. If we have chosen to look to the law for spiritual guidance, we are not getting our guidance from the Holy Spirit. Here's the deal—if it's the law, it is not the Holy Spirit! If He is not guiding us, His fruit is not being displayed in our actions. Under the law, our flesh is forced to try to come up with conduct that resembles the fruit of the Spirit. But to trade the Spirit's genuine fruit for the flesh's counterfeit works, is to do a bad deal of calamitous proportions! *"Filthy rags"* is certainly not holiness! Besides, by invoking the Covenant of Law, we nullify the Covenant of grace!

Where did religion get the idea that grace sends us back to the law? Was it perhaps from Paul's statement in Ephesians 2:8-10.

"For by grace you have been saved through faith, and that not of yourselves; it is the gift of God, not of works, lest anyone should boast. For we are His workmanship, created in Christ Jesus for good works, which God prepared beforehand that we should walk in them." In this passage of scripture Paul says that although we are not saved by works, nevertheless our salvation empowers us to do good works. Please note that it is not the law to which we are directed; we are directed to faith! James expressed a similar idea in saying that our faith is demonstrated by the works we do.

The law is the schoolteacher to the sinner, not to the believer. This is made clear in Galatians 3:23. *"But before faith came, we were kept under guard by the law, kept for the faith which would afterward be revealed."* Once we have received our righteousness by faith, we have graduated from School—the law is no longer our schoolteacher. When we become *"the righteousness of God in Christ"*, we instantly put that teacher out of work. This is the chapter in which Paul specifically deals with the folly of reverting back to the law—it's how we fall from grace.

Religion's way of offering grace to the sinner and law to the believer is quite obviously the wrong way around. If the law is the school teacher to the unbeliever then we should be using the law to convince unbelievers of their sin. The right order is: law to the sinner and grace to the believer. Obviously, after a sinner acknowledges his sin, it opens the way for grace to do its sanctifying work within him. If we couldn't attain salvation by any means other than grace through faith, what makes us think that we can keep our salvation by any means other than grace through faith?

Although the law has lost its right to condemn, yet it is not something evil to be shunned; it is to be embraced for the purpose for which it was established, namely: to show us God's unequivocal holy standard; expose sin in the lives of unbelievers; reveal our inability to attain its high benchmark, and hopefully point us in the direction of a saviour, who can do for us what we are incapable of doing for ourselves.

Although grace releases us from having to keep the law to make us right, we still have the privilege of using the law to check that we are on course. The law is the divine ethical yard stick. But the law must never be used to establish justification—it was never intended for that purpose. Besides, any effort to do so reduces our rock solid, blood bought justification down to nothing more than a rickety boardwalk constructed of the rotten planks of our shaky attempts at living uprightly. What should be a matter of justification by faith alone, becomes a matter of hoping that we have done enough to deserve justification (Rom 4:14-15). Big mistake!

As good as the law is, it is not without fault. *"If the first covenant had been faultless, there would have been no need for a second to replace it. But God Himself found fault with the old..."* (Heb 8:7 NLT). This scripture makes it perfectly clear that the Old Covenant has been replaced, because in God's estimation, it is faulty. Verse six refers to the New Covenant as being *"superior"* and a *"better covenant with God, based on better promises"*.

No self-respecting believer would willingly wish to empower sin. Yet many readily empower sin by embracing Moses' law. *"The law gives sin its power"* (1 Cor 15:56 NLT). If the law empowers sin that leads to death, then it makes perfectly good sense to abandon any thought of living by it!

No wonder God scrapped the first one. *"When God speaks of a new covenant, it means that he has made the first one obsolete. It is now out of date and ready to be put aside"* (Heb 8:13 NLT). In the same way that food commodities have use by dates, the Old Covenant reached its use by date when Jesus announced *"it is finished"*. Not only was the work of redemption *"finished"*, but the law's authority to curse and accuse was also *"finished"*. Yes, it still has relevance, but for a very different purpose.

Even though, according to Paul, the law is sin empowering, faulty, inferior and obsolete, it still gives us a peek into God's high standard. But, we should bear in mind, that we don't reap morality simply because morality is preached from our pulpits; we reap morality when we embrace grace, because as part and parcel of grace, we get the leading of the Spirit. The Holy Spirit is as gracious as Jesus—after all, His fruit is grace in action!

When Israel received the law, they did not reap morality—they built themselves a golden calf and worshipped it. Throughout the reign of the law, the prophets had their time cut out dealing with Israel's flawed morality. The Law failed dismally to bring about meaningful change. But then again, that was not its purpose. Its purpose was, *"to show that the entire world is guilty before God"* (Rom 3:19 NLT).

Sadly, when we live with a consciousness of the law, we become more conscious of our sin than of our righteousness, and this fosters a mentality of shame and unworthiness. The Roman centurion and the Canaanite women, being non-Jews, did not have the law, and therefore the law played no part in shaping the way they lived—it could not convince them that their ungodly way of life was sinful. Not being conscious of their sinfulness, they were able to receive Jesus' favour without giving the slightest thought to their degree of worthiness or unworthiness. Interestingly, they got Jesus' highest commendations for their faith—decidedly higher than Jewish people who meticulously kept the law. It takes a lot to impress Jesus, but he *"marvelled"* at the faith of a person who made absolutely no attempt to keep the law. The law only applied to Jews—Romans were pagans. He said of the centurion, *"I have not found such great faith, not even in Israel!"* (Mat 8:10). He is not in the least bit impressed with our boast of law keeping. It takes a lot more than that to impress Him—it takes bold faced faith!

In all of Jesus' ministry, He was never selective; He healed anybody who asked for it. Their state of holiness or repentance never entered the equation—He never even broached the subject. Let's face it; a dead person cannot first repent before being raised from the dead.

After saving the woman caught in adultery from the hands of her accusers, He said "Go and sin no more". Note the sequence—first she received His favour, then His instruction. If He had done it the other way around, she may have tried to obtain His favour by self-effort, which would have been nothing other than a work of the flesh. But it was the grace He extended to her that motivated her to stop sinning. That is what grace does for a person.

"And because of their unbelief, he couldn't do any mighty miracles among them..." (Mar 6:5 NLT). It was not their lack of law

keeping that prevented the miraculous from taking place; it was their lack of faith. The bottom line is that God's favour does not rest upon our degree of holiness and timely repentances; it rests upon the covenant He made with us—we received it without a single good work to our credit. But then again, it is not difficult to put faith in something that is as rock solid and reliable as God's promise to favour us—especially when He promises not take our degree of law keeping into account. You know a covenant maker is serious about keeping a covenant when he has taken the trouble to write every promise in His very own blood.

Jesus is the same yesterday, today and forever. Just as His favour was available without regard for holiness or repentance at that time, it remains available to us without any regard for our degree of holiness and repentance. Having said that, the sheer experience of His goodness has a profound influence upon how committed we are to holiness and repentance.

Religion will tell you, that without the law, we will have nothing to restrain us from falling headlong into lawlessness. Interestingly, Joseph didn't need the law to restrain him when Potiphar's wife tried to seduce him. He lived before the law was instituted. No! The Bible makes it perfectly plain; the law has a poor record of restraining sin. Immediately after the law had been instituted, Moses had his time cut out contending with disobedience and rebellion in the camp. *"The law made nothing perfect"* (Heb 7:19).

Abraham, the father of all who believe, never had the law to restrain him. As with us, he was counted righteous purely for believing—there wasn't a single law to restrain his behaviour. To turn to the law for our restraint, is to turn away from the Holy Spirit's guidance. It was God Himself who replaced the ineffective restraints of the law with something that really works—nothing less than the guidance of His very own Spirit. God does not have a plan B—if we cannot be restrained by love, we cannot be restrained at all! He achieves His purposes by grace alone—our degree of godliness does not even enter the equation; faith is enough!

God has a way of loving us into living righteously. To rely on the law's restraints, is to rely on our flesh to make ourselves righteous—

it's a matter of exchanging God's flawless imputed righteousness for our flawed and ineffective strivings to act righteously. If ever there was a bad trade, this is it! Our righteous making efforts add nought to our holiness—righteousness simply cannot be produced by unrighteous attempts, and we are not capable of anything better.

Under grace, love is all we have to restrain us, but love is more than enough! To depend on the law for our restraint is to reject what the New Covenant stands for. And that's not clever! God found fault with the Old Covenant of law and that's why he abolished it and replaced it with something that really works—nothing less than a Covenant of Grace.

"For on the one hand there is an annulling of the former commandment because of its weakness and unprofitableness" (Heb 7:18). It couldn't be clearer; the law is weak and unprofitable! In other words, we cannot achieve anything through law keeping—it's a waste of valuable time and energy! We would do well to agree with this scripture and distance ourselves from any thought of living by the law!

When I discussed this liberating thought with a church leader, he fully agreed with me, but felt that he could not share this information with his congregation, because he felt that they would take advantage of it and fall into sin.

What does that say about the strength, or should I say the weakness of their version of holiness? Does it not show how ineffective "un-extreme" grace is? Holiness is not holiness when holy actions are not the reflection of what has taken place in our hearts. But if our hearts are in it, our actions take care of themselves.

Only favour that is given when not deserved is capable of winning our hearts and melting our inherent resistance to embracing holiness. Holiness that does not emanate from our hearts, is not holiness at all! We are merely practicing hypocrisy when our "holy" actions belie the hidden feelings of our hearts. To put it another way, holiness is not in our actions; it is in the attitudes of our hearts. But then again, holy actions flow naturally from holy attitudes, and holy attitudes are Holy Spirit inspired attitudes, known as fruit of the Spirit. It all starts with finding out that God's love for us is unwavering and undying, despite our obvious undeserved-ness. But then again, God's way of loving and accepting us just as we are, makes the thought of surrendering to Him gloriously appealing!

> Does the responsibility of establishing
> security in our salvation rest with us?

There is a rumour doing the rounds. It says that "extreme grace" advocates that there is no need for repentance. But this is certainly not the case. Romans 2:4 is an oft quoted and much loved verse in "extreme grace" circles: *"Or do you despise the riches of His goodness, forbearance, and longsuffering, not knowing that the goodness of God leads you to repentance?"* Repentance is triggered by God's goodness towards us; whereas "un-extreme grace" would have us believe that God's goodness is trigged by repentance. This is obviously putting the cart before the horse.

It seems that "un-extreme grace" will go to any lengths to discredit "extreme grace". But spreading misinformation about it is indefensible. I have heard whole sermons decrying the purported principles of "extreme grace", even though they are not anything like the principles of "extreme grace". Often "extreme grace" is mis-described and then this mis-description criticised and condemned. Frankly, in most cases, people of "extreme grace" would be just as horrified by the principles so wrongly ascribed to them. I would like to give the benefit of the doubt to "un-extreme grace" and say that these distortions are not maliciously intended. Perhaps they can be put down to one of the following more innocent motivations:

- "Un-extreme grace" does not understand that unconditional love empowers godliness.
- "Un-extreme grace" fears that the freedom afforded by grace will result in a loss of moral control of its followers.

- "Un-extreme grace" does not understand that grace works in partnership with the Holy Spirit—to walk by grace is to walk by the Spirit.
- "Un-extreme grace" honestly believes the misconception that grace equals licence.
- "Un-extreme grace" does not realise, that with the passing of time, the church has scaled down in the veracity of grace and scaled up in personal obligations—a matter of 'do' instead of 'done'. Ultimately, grace as practiced by religion, bears little resemblance to the grace that Paul so passionately championed.
- But the most likely reason is simply that "un-extreme grace" is innocently defending what has been passed down to them by highly esteemed mentors.

Perhaps "un-extreme grace" fears that its belief system is under threat, and that those in its charge are likely to fall prey to licence. But such a conclusion can only be reached if "extreme grace" is misunderstood.

THE LOVE CONNECTION

Does unconditional love open the door to sin?

Grace does not only grant us favour undeservedly, it also empowers us to live uprightly. "Extreme grace" goes to the crux of the matter—our hearts. When we realise that we are generously loved without regard for our measure of holiness, we are more inclined to open our hearts. Unrestrained love has a wonderful way of dissolving our inherent resistance to change.

The thought of being so completely loved can be pretty overwhelming. When we are satisfied with the warmth of God's affection, sin's empty promises have little chance of captivating our affections. Is it any wonder that our appetite for sin fades? Hearts enthralled with God's love soon lose their penchant for sin—inner changes soon manifest in outward actions.

Human nature does not take kindly to accusations. Accusations do not possess the power to sway a person into godliness. In fact the opposite is likely—a sure way to get a person's back up. It is difficult to surrender to accusers, but easy to surrender to lovers. There is a calming sense of rest in trusting in, and surrendering to somebody who is as gracious as our Saviour. To us, He is not a stern judge; He is a loving Father and loyal ally—our closest Friend! When we realise that we are not just tolerated, but intensely treasured—not just liked but deeply loved, it is enormously edifying! When God has honoured us in this way, there is no reason to look for honour elsewhere; least of all in sin.

Even though we are sanctified in an instant, transposing our sanctification into sanctified actions is not instantaneous. It is a continuous process that runs at the pace that we are prepared to submit to the Holy Spirit's on-going life changing process. But then again, unconditional love makes submission considerably more appealing.

The more we perceive ourselves to be loved, the easier it becomes to be submissive. And we will never encounter a more complete love than God's. Who could blame us for falling in love? Romance is perfectly understandable—divine love is irresistible! In it we find value for ourselves, and this value gives us ample reason to value others more highly.

As we stare into our loving Saviour's eyes, we are overcome with the thought that He is totally besotted with us. We are so precious to Him that not only did He give up His glory to hang despised and naked on a cruel cross to gain our affection, but also shared His glory with us. Jesus said to His Father, *"The glory which You gave Me I have given them"* (Joh 17:22).

His love awakens something beautiful within us. Although at first, we find it difficult to accept that we are like Him, He encourages us to see ourselves as He sees us (1Joh 4:17). When that happens, Christlikeness follows without trying. Christlikeness is not something that we must achieve; it is something that we already are! When we understand what it means to be *"in Christ",* we understand what it means to be Christlike! We are not merely figuratively *"in Christ"*; we are so intertwined with Him that His identity is our identity. But it is another matter for our inner Christlike beauty to show through. Before that can happen, we might have to put aside the small thinking of our religious legacies—especially if they are preventing us from participating in the extremeness of God's glorious grace. We should accept God's love, not as a nebulous ethereal concept, but as a personal reality. When the touch of God's love becomes a personal experience, rather than a theological doctrine, we take on a glow that touches others in special ways.

His sweet whispers touch us deeply—we cannot get enough—our hearts crave more—His love is intoxicating! With all that religion has to offer, it simply cannot compete with the delights of a divine romance.

He elevates us from servants to lovers. He wooed us while we were entangled in sin—He asked for our hand in marriage while we were wanton and wretched. But now we are safe in His loving embrace. He is not an abusive partner. His love enthrals us—the courtship is exciting—His wooing today is as thrilling as it was when we first met!

In as much as we adore Him, it is obvious that He adores us. His loving advances awaken something beautiful within us—we get to feel wanted and desirable. He doesn't harp on our shortcomings; He is too busy loving us. Our hearts are romanced—our minds renewed! The beauty of the One within us soon shows through—His graciousness is revealed in the spontaneity of our actions. To encounter grace inspired individuals, is to encounter the God of grace within them.

There is nothing genuine about gritting our teeth to be kind to our enemies. We are neither genuine to them nor to ourselves—our inward animosity belying our outward civility. But anger is anger, whether suppressed or vented—we have not defeated it until we have defeated it in our hearts, and so it is with all sin. Jesus is clear on this. He said, *"First cleanse the inside of the cup and dish, that the outside of them may be clean also"* (Mat 23:26).

A Christian acquaintance of mine often suggests that a bullet would be the best solution for the corruption and philandering of the politicians of our country. I know it is just frivolous talk, but the mere harbouring of such notions in his heart is sufficient evidence to find him guilty of murder in Jesus' estimation.

A lifetime is not long enough for all our wrinkles to be ironed out. No matter how many sins we may repent of, there are multitudes more that we are not even aware of—we will only become aware of them in the years that lie ahead. We are often blissfully unaware that we are rubbing people up the wrong way. It is not possible to be entirely up to date with repentance. This being the case, it should be obvious that our salvation does not rest upon our ineffective attempts at holding ourselves together with "holiness".

The aforesaid is not meant to detract from the beauty of a repentant heart—we need repentance for the purpose of being humble, transparent and sincere, and to tread in the right direction, amongst many other healthy reasons.

If repentance is a change of mind (heart) that brings about different behaviour, then once our hearts have been changed, we no longer behave the same. If we choose to go about this task by any other means, it won't be long before we revert back to our same old insensitive ways.

Nobody has access to his or her subconscious minds. When we are not purposely directing our thoughts, we simply live out the programmes that our particular life's experiences have seared into our subconscious minds. Often we are left to wonder why we instinctively behave in the same old embarrassing ways, when we ought to know better. It is as though we are entrapped in self-destruction—driven by something other than rationality.

But then again, our subconscious minds do not operate with rationale. Instead they react as though automated—much like a computer programme. The computer does not have a choice—it must carry out processes in the precise way that the programme was written.

When we manage to change our minds, we have only changed our conscious minds, and like a thermostat on a hot water system, over time we simply revert back to the thermostatically controlled behaviour set in our subconscious minds. Our innate ways are too deep seated to be changed by sheer force of will power—no amount of grit and determination can override our embedded subconscious thermostat settings. We do not control our subconscious minds—it would be more correct to say that our subconscious minds control us, especially in unguarded moments. And to make things worse, we do not have access to the settings of that part of our minds—they are subconsciously hidden from us.

Isn't it fascinating to observe how quickly we revert back to our original weight after being on a weight loss diet? It is as though we have no say in the matter. Our subconscious minds (our hearts) have settings that we are powerless to disable. It took a lifetime of personal experiences to form rigid paradigms in our subconscious thinking, and it will take much to convince our subconscious minds to override these paradigms. This is where Paul's instruction to renew our minds comes in (Rom 12:2). It is not enough to hear something once or twice from God's word; we have to devote ourselves to the mind altering process of repeatedly hearing His word over time. Only then do our minds come into alignment with His will.

God has a solution to this dilemma. He wants to be involved in our struggles. When we repent *"towards"* Him, it becomes His responsibility to change us from the inside. This is a grace discipline with glorious rewards.

Just as we dare not discard "faith" because some misguided religious charlatans have distorted and misused faith's beautiful principles to milk the public with "get rich quick" promises; we simply cannot discard "extreme grace" because some misguided individuals, seeking scriptural loopholes, have misused God's magnificent grace to give themselves licence to sin. Such distortions bear no resemblance to authentic grace!

DISPENSATIONS

The Old Covenant is a covenant of rewards,
while the New Testament is a bequest of gifts.
That being the case, where do works fit in?

Repentance is vital to the on-going process of bringing our actions into line with our sinless standing before God. But, as already mentioned, our right standing with God is neither established nor sustained by our flawed actions—it was secured by Jesus! Our right standing is in His actions, and He has completed His assignment with aplomb. What He has established is firm, unshakable and eternal.

It is unconscionable to imagine that a responsible God would risk leaving something as crucial as the eternal destiny of His beloved children in the fickle hands of a bunch of rascals who could not save themselves if they tried. As parents, we are responsible citizens—we would not hire a paedophile to take care of our children, and neither would God be irresponsible with His kids. Our salvation is secure because it is in Him—it is established by covenant, promised by a last will and testament, signed in the blood of Jesus and witnessed by our

Father, the righteous Emperor of the entire universe. Our faith in Him is not misplaced—our God is holy!

As rock solid as a pyramid, God in His grace has established our salvation on the firm foundation of His righteousness and good works; not ours. Religion has inverted the pyramid, and put the onus on us to keep it balanced on its pinnacle. But an upside down pyramid is difficult to balance. One thing is certain, it will fall over—nobody is capable of consistently keeping up the performance that religion requires.

Works is not a bad word to those who walk by grace. Faith inspired works are part and parcel of living by grace. To walk by grace is to walk by the Spirit and to walk by the Spirit is to walk by faith. These three aspects are operationally intertwined and do not function in isolation. Although grace is freely given, it cannot be unlocked without faith, and faith cannot exist without making itself visible in the form of works of faith.

Faith without works is dead in the water. Faith must be activated to be effective. We do it by declaring what we believe—our actions support our stand. When faith is spoken, it takes on physicality. Our actions are a sure give-away—they demonstrate what we believe. When we are convinced of the outcome of our prayers, we will proceed as though we have received what we have asked for. To such individuals, nothing is impossible.

Our words and actions demonstrate confidence in God's benevolence. A matter of laying claim before having sight of the answer. In fact, our actions are advanced evidence of ownership.

God cannot work with wavering faith; He requires authoritative commands, backed by strong convictions that give the enemy no room to manoeuvre.

Additionally, as we participate in God's benevolence through faith, we are able to pass on the graciousness we receive. His gracious way of dealing with us has a profound effect on how gracious we are to others. As conduits of His love and grace, we find ourselves cutting others as much slack as we believe God cuts us. God's measure of grace to us becomes our measure of grace to others.

"Extreme grace" does not avoid repentance; it encourages repentance. But to put matters into perspective, repentance does not reinstate our *"righteousness of God in Christ"* after each time we sin. We are not the righteousness of God because our actions are righteous; we are the righteousness of God because our actions are not righteous! We have obtained righteousness from God because we cannot manufacture it for ourselves. In as much as our actions could not bring us salvation, our actions cannot reinstate our salvation—at best, we are only capable of producing *"filthy rags"*. Our righteous standing is entirely a gift secured by Christ. We are left only to accept it without charge.

Throughout the ages, God has always been prepared to grant mercy and grace. Abraham's gift of righteousness is but one example—it survived Abraham's most deplorable sins. Abraham did not lose and subsequently regain His righteous standing with God in response to his sin and subsequent repentance—it survived his weakest moments, and remained unchanged and unaffected by his most deplorable blunders.

What's the point? Should we really concern ourselves with the theology of dispensational differences? Decide for yourself. Well, for starters, the Bible clearly distinguishes each dispensation from others. For instance, scripture is clear on the different treatments of sin during each dispensation. When Cain killed Abel, God did not require Abel to be put to death—it took place before the dispensation of the law. Contrast this with the first transgression of the law—it was the serious crime of picking up sticks on a Sabbath day. Clearly, it was decidedly less serious than murder, yet the penalty handed down under the law's jurisdiction required that the stick collector be put to death.

There can be no disputing the fact that there are myriads of dispensational differences. God does not count our sins against us; He has already counted them against Jesus, and God is too holy to punish two people for the same crime. Romans 5:13 says *"For until the law sin was in the world: but sin is not imputed when there is no law"*. Our sins are not imputed to us in the same way that Abraham's sins were not imputed to him.

If sin is treated so vastly differently in each dispensation, then it stands to reason that dispensations must be taken seriously, and what is said in each dispensation must be weighed up in terms of the requirements of that particular dispensation.

When Jesus taught the "Lord's prayer", He was teaching people who lived by the laws of the Old Covenant. It would have been wrong, even criminal of Him to break the very law that He had personally instituted through Moses. Therefore, it stands to reason, that while Jesus' "Mosaic law" was still in force, He would not teach people to be transgressors of it. That being the case, how do we explain Jesus defending His disciples when they were accused of transgressing the law? The answer is that it wasn't Moses' law that they had transgressed, but the pedantic Pharisaic addendums to the law, known as legalism. Jesus had very little time for Pharisaic hair-splitting. Clearly He feels the same about the religious legalism practised in our day and age.

Old Testament saints could not ignore Old Testament law; severe penalties would ensue—they certainly could not practise New Covenant precepts before they had been established by Jesus' death and resurrection. They were given a set of rules that applied specifically to the dispensation they lived in—most of which are no longer practised in our dispensation. For example: They had Levitical priests; we are the priesthood of believers. They had a temple built of stone; we are the temple of the Holy Ghost. There are far too many differences to list in one chapter.

Jesus said, *"I was not sent except to the lost sheep of the house of Israel"* (Mat 15:24). He made this statement during the dispensation of the Old Covenant. This statement is undeniably one of Jewish exclusivity. But the gospel that we know is certainly not exclusively for Jews. That being the case, why would He say that the gospel is exclusively for Jews? Clearly, this statement does not apply to the present dispensation of grace—if it did, all non-Jews would be consigned to hell—period!

Almost everything recorded in the four Gospels took place during the dispensation of the Old Covenant of law, and as such their messages were specifically directed to Old Covenant people living under its laws. As wonderful as the Gospels are, they have very little to say about the dispensation that would follow. For that we need to look beyond the Gospels. The Acts of the Apostles and the writings of the apostles disclose a very different dispensation. Having said that, we certainly cannot ignore the Gospels, or for that matter, any part of the Old Testament—all scripture is God breathed and vital to the knowledge of our Saviour. We cannot know God the Father without knowing Jesus, and there is no better place to come to know Jesus than in the pages of the Gospels.

I have heard preachers say, that where there is an apparent contradiction between what Jesus said and what the apostles said, we should go with Jesus' words, because His words carry more weight than anybody else's. This is insanity! To hold to such a view would be tantamount to denying that all scripture is Holy Spirit inspired. No! Many of these apparent discrepancies are not contradictions at all— they are simply different rules applying to different dispensations.

Interestingly, under the Old Covenant, Jesus told us to forgive in order to be forgiven; whereas Paul switched the order around when he said that we should forgive because we have already been forgiven. *"... forgiving one another, even as God in Christ forgave you"* (Eph 4:32). There is no question about it; we relate differently to God in the post Old Covenant dispensation.

Under the Old Covenant we had to earn God's forgiveness by forgiving others; under the New Covenant there is nothing to be earned—Jesus earned it all for us. Now we grant forgiveness to underserving humanity to the same extent that we receive forgiveness despite our undeserved-ness.

By reversing the sequence of forgiveness, Paul was not making light of forgiveness. In no way was he reducing the importance of its role in grace; if anything, he was emphasising its importance. Forgiveness should be at the top of the page—it is the very essence of grace!

Grace is not exclusively the province of Divinity; it behoves each and every believer to follow Christ's example by granting forgiveness and grace to the most undeserving of loathsome individuals. But then again, just being the recipient of such extravagant love and grace is enough to motivate us to want to pass it on to others—it is difficult to keep blessings of such magnitude to oneself.

Nothing is more edifying than the realisation that we are loved and accepted exactly as we are. Contrary to what one would expect—love is not proof of weakness; it is proof of strength—it is enormously influential—accomplishing so much more than can be achieved by the sternest outburst of "righteous" indignation.

When we see tears of joy welling up in the eyes of somebody that we have touched with God's grace, it makes the practise of love, grace, mercy, forgiveness and generosity enormously fulfilling.

I once attended a Sunday morning church service where one of the elders had disguised himself as a hobo. Shabbily dressed in filthy tattered clothes, his hair mattered and his face unshaven, the stench of body odour and stale beer preceded him into the church. Incognito, he found a pew and waited to see how he would be received by the pious faithful. By the wide birth that the devout made around him, their lack of grace soon became apparent.

Perhaps they thought, "If we can make something of our lives, why shouldn't he?" But is such snobbery the way of grace?

We live in a world that survives on the "reward ethic"—our wages are the reason that we are prepared to expend our labour, abilities and time at the salt mine—it's how we bring home the bacon month after month. But like so much in the kingdom of God, its principles work in reverse. For example: The world receives by taking; the kingdom receives by giving. The world obtains life by demanding it; the kingdom obtains life by dying to it. We do not forgive to be forgiven; we forgive because we have already been forgiven. The tragedy of the matter is, that while the church teaches reward for actions, even though they may be commendable actions, the church may unwittingly be robbing its members of the privilege of participating in God's grace—grace simply cannot be deserved.

If it is true that New Covenant believers should not be driven by reward, then why would God tell us to give so that it may be given to us? Surely this must be construed to be a reward and therefore a contradiction to grace? No! Giving has nothing to do with reward, and everything to do with an earlier covenant—the Covenant that He made with Noah—the covenant of seedtime and harvest. God said that as long the earth remains, that covenant will not be broken (Gen 8:22). That covenant has nothing to do with reward, and everything to do with the miraculous multiplication of seed when it is sown.

All, including Old Covenant saints, must be born again. But Old Covenant saints were not born again during their sojourn on earth. Their sacrifices only gave them temporary (one year) atonement. Their rebirth took place after the cross when Jesus preached His redemptive story to them in Paradise. That's when the reality of their long awaited Saviour was finally revealed to them.

Up to that point, they had been dealing with mysteries hidden in prophecies and sacrificial rituals. Now for the first time, they came to terms with what had been no more than rites, ceremonies and customs to them. Yes, the story of Jesus was woven into their religious observances, but as wonderful as these truths were, for the most part, they were hidden from their understanding.

If we think that the common Jewish folk had the slightest inkling that the shadows and types in the Old Testament were a depiction of Jesus, we are mistaken. The Pharisees were by far the most theologically enlightened of all Jews. If anybody had understood shadows and types it would have been them. When we see how they rejected Jesus as their Messiah, we get to see just how twisted their interpretation of shadows and types were. Despite all their learning, the story of the cross, woven into their scriptures, traditions and prophecies, remained a mystery to this clueless bunch of blind leaders of the blind. It is clear that they did not understand the underlying meaning of the rites and rituals they so meticulously observed.

After His death, Jesus entered Paradise (the place where Old Covenant departed dead were waiting to hear the gospel for the very first time). There He preached the good news to them. He gave each of them the choice to either accept or reject Him as their Saviour. They had to decide for themselves, in much the same way that we had to decide for ourselves. This was their first opportunity to be born again. Thereafter Jesus led *"captivity captive"*, ushering them into heaven (Eph 4:8).

Before the cross, it would seem that Paradise was not in Heaven. Jesus said to the thief on the cross, *"today you will be with me in Paradise"*. But Jesus did not go to Heaven on the day He died; He went to hell for our sins and thereafter to Paradise to preach redemption to the Old Testament saints who were waiting for Him. We know that He hadn't been to Heaven, because immediately after His resurrection He said to Mary, *"Do not cling to Me, for I have not yet ascended to My Father"* (Joh 20:17). Obviously, Paradise was not in Heaven where His Father lived.

Jesus was a fiction story teller of note; using parables to get His points across. One of His stories was definitely not fiction and therefore not a parable—we know this because it was the only story in which He actually named the characters. It's the story of the rich man and Lazarus the beggar (Luk 16:19-31). From Hell the rich man was able to communicate across a great gulf with people in Paradise, also known as Abraham's Bosom. Here the covenant people of God awaited their redemption. They had not yet entered Heaven—they were not yet born again. *"He also first descended into the lower parts of the earth"* (Eph 4:9). Before the time of the cross, it would seem that Paradise was situated in the lower parts of the earth adjacent to Hell.

David said, *"In the grave who will give You thanks?"* (Psa 6:5). Obviously, if as many would suppose, he would immediately enter Heaven upon his death, he would have ample opportunity to give thanks and praise in the immediate presence of God. But from David's words it is obvious that Old Testament saints did not enter Heaven immediately—at least, not before Jesus had opportunity to preach the good news to them. When they finally received their Saviour and were reborn of the Spirit of God, they were ushered from Paradise into Heaven for the very first time.

Before preaching to the Old Testament saints in Paradise, He first had to disarm the dark Powers and Principalities. *"Having disarmed principalities and powers, He made a public spectacle of them, triumphing over them in it"* (Col 2:15). It seems that this public display of triumph over the powers and principalities may have been visible from the pavilions of Paradise—after all, it was a public spectacle.

Matthew 11:11 says, *"Assuredly, I say to you, among those born of women there has not risen one greater than John the Baptist; but he who is least in the kingdom of heaven is greater than he"*. Why would Jesus exalt the weakest Christian alive today to be greater than John the Baptist? The weakest Christian is born again into the God class of being—a new kind of creature that could not have existed before Christ made it possible through His redemptive work on the cross. Old Testament believers, including John, did not have this privilege; at best, they could only partner with the Holy Spirit. Elijah had a portion and Elisha had a double portion, but neither of them were transformed into new creations. We, as New Covenant believers, do not have a portion; we have the whole Godhead merged with our spirits, and it is this amalgamated unified fusion that makes us brand new creatures that never existed before—that's who we have become in Christ.

"By this we know that we abide in Him, and He in us, because He has given us of His Spirit" (1Jn 4:13). Did you notice that it is not only He who abides in us, but it is also we who abide in Him? When asked where the Holy Spirit is, we point to ourselves and say, "He is within us". Perfectly right! But are we aware that if we were to ask God where our spirits are, He would point to Himself and say, "You are within Me". Mind blowing, isn't it? This is not heresy; it is exactly what 1 John 4:13 says. This revelation opens us to far greater possibilities in the spiritual realm than religion has told us.

Often, religion reduces us in order to magnify God. But God is not glorified by our smallness; He is glorified by what He has made of us. He did not come to earth to reduce us; He came to elevate us to the position of sons and daughters of the living God. Jesus is our older brother and God the Father is our Daddy. We cannot be a different species to the Father who gave us birth. This does not infer that we should not humble ourselves before God. But God is not glorified by our religious self-effacement—it is an insult to the One who went to so much trouble to elevate us from sinners to sons of God—new creatures of the species 'divine royalty'!

We are so much more than mere humans with God's presence within; we are as much in God as He is in us. How else can we be here on planet earth, while at the same time be seated together with Christ Jesus in heavenly places? (Eph 2:6) This is too big for mortal minds to comprehend; too wonderful to imagine! No wonder Paul described us as a new species that never existed before (2 Cor 5:17).

So, being of the god species, on a scale of one to ten, how much of our divine capacity are we actually experiencing in our day to day living? I would venture to guess that we have barely made it to "one" on the scale. In the light of our merger with divinity, we are infinitely more than we may have given ourselves credit for. Though we are thoroughbred race horses, we have confined ourselves to giving kiddies pony rides at the fair.

We are not being humble when we take on a lesser identity. It is ungracious to belittle what He has made of us—He exalted us to royalty at great personal cost. We show Him our gratitude by operating in the princely status that He so lovingly bestowed upon us. If we want to operate at our full potential, it is not something that we can suddenly make happen; our stifling religious thinking gets in the way. But we can step out, little by little into greater supernatural living. It is God honouring to enjoy what He has so lovingly made of us. It is not our attempts at being politically correct that please Him— neither our attempts at being religiously correct. Like a doting parent, He is pleased when we are pleased with the grace He has given us— our pleasure becomes His pleasure.

We, as New Covenant believers, are the chosen generation that Peter referred to in 1Peter 2:9. *"But you are a chosen generation, a royal priesthood, a holy nation, His own special people, that you may proclaim the praises of Him who called you out of darkness into His marvelous light"*. Old Covenant believers were not part of the royal priesthood—royalty was only granted to believers by virtue of what Jesus had achieved on the cross. The installation of the priesthood of ordinary believers put the professional Levitical priesthood out of business—they were decidedly outranked by common people. But then again, Jesus elevated commoners to the rank of princes and princesses, and royalty can hardly be thought of as common.

When speaking of the Holy Spirit, Jesus said, *"The world at large cannot receive Him, because it isn't looking for Him and doesn't recognise Him. But you do, because He lives with you now and later will be in you"* (Joh 14:17 KJV). By using the word *"later"* Jesus made it perfectly clear that the born again experience had not yet taken place; it was promised for a time yet to come. The Holy Spirit was only *"with"* Old Testament saints—He certainly was not yet *"in"* them—they were not temples of the Holy Ghost. In saying this, Jesus made it crystal clear that they were definitely not yet born again. Jesus was talking to His disciples when He made this statement. From what He said, it is clear, that not even His dearest friends and disciples were born again. He was pointing to a *"later"* date when the Holy Spirit would *"be in you"* for the very first time in human history.

If God had required Old Testament believers to be born again this side of the grave, it would have been grossly unfair of Him to have hidden this information from them throughout the ages; only revealing it to one person (Nicodemus) after most of them had already died without this knowledge. Quite obviously, Jesus was prophesying the born again experience to Nicodemus. Except for prophecies that foretold of the coming era of grace, there is no instruction to be born again in any Old Testament writings!

"For the law was given through Moses, but grace and truth came through Jesus Christ" (Joh 1:17). Please notice in this scripture that grace came through Jesus. If Jesus brought grace onto the scene, then we can safely say that it wasn't here in quite the same measure before He brought it. Although God never changes, He has chosen to remove anything that could possibly mar a perfect Father and child relationship. The law, being the knowledge of good and evil, exposes our sin and makes us guilty before God. Guilt would spoil what ought to be a sublime relationship with our heavenly Daddy. Not wanting sin and guilt to spoil a loving relationship, He had to dispose of the thing that ensnared us in guilt, and therefore the law had to be abolished from the religious observances of all believers. He replaced the law's knowledge of good and evil with a direct connection with Himself by way of His indwelling presence in the person of the Holy Spirit, and in doing so, He ushered in the era of grace.

"Extreme grace" does not regard the Old Testament as irrelevant; it cherishes the Old Testament, because among many other good reasons, Christ is concealed in its pages. The Old Testament is not only about the law, it is about faith, love, real life experiences, wisdom, prophecy, prayer, praise, patterns for godly living etc. It is a compilation of various covenants, some of which are still applicable to New Covenant believers. Even the law within its pages has a valid function. No, it cannot make us right. Yes, it demonstrates God's high standard among many other wonderful uses. Of course, we finally come to meet Christ in the pages of the New Testament, and in Him discover what was promised in the Old Testament. The entire Bible revolves around Christ, ultimately culminating in a covenant of grace.

There is no doubt about it, our sins are dealt with very differently under each covenant, and God's presence is now in a different place (omnipresence aside). In the Old Testament, He chose to hide His earthly presence behind a curtain, while in the New Testament He resides within us. We dare not ignore the significance of the tearing of the veil. The barrier has been removed—God has opened the way to fulfil His desire to have intimacy with His family. Now we have privileged access—something that Old Covenant saints never had. We are invited to come *"boldly"* into the throne room of grace without any regard for our sin. For that the promise of *"mercy and grace"* awaits us. Isaiah could not do this—he cowered in his shame—*"Woe is me, for I am undone!"* (Isa 6:5)—there is obviously no boldness in that. John the Revelator, being born again, had a very different experience to Isaiah's in God's presence.

The doctrine of "un-extreme grace" imprisons believers in their shame and undone-ness. While they perceive themselves to be undone, they simply cannot obey God's invitation to express brazen boldness in the throne room of grace. Conversely, "extreme grace" believers have discovered that they are no longer undone, even may I add, while in the very act of carrying out a dreadful sin. Whether believers acknowledge it or not, all humanity of every grace persuasion sins regularly—let's not kid ourselves; none of us have arrived—mankind is simply not capable of anything remotely close to sinlessness.

There is undeserved love and acceptance without the slightest hint of condemnation in the throne room—that's why God calls it the throne room of *"grace"*. God would be a liar if He were to get us to enter a place on the pretext that it is a place of *"grace"*, when in reality it is a place of accusation and judgement.

Hallelujah! Because of Jesus, we are no longer undone. We may enter the throne room of grace with our sin. But beware! The love and acceptance that we receive there, is so overwhelmingly heart altering that sin soon loses its appeal.

God would not have called His throne room *"the throne of grace"* unless he wanted to accommodate sinful humanity exactly as they are in their sinful state. Every single sin that we carry with us into this room has already been nailed to the cross. God turned His face, unable to look at Jesus for the terrible sin, though none of His own, that He carried to the cross. But for us, we bear not a single sin that has not been fully atoned for by Jesus. Ever since, God no longer has to look the other way when we sin. Every molecule of the blood of Jesus vibrates with complete reparation, and it is this that allows God to look past our sins, and to accept us as though we have never put a foot wrong. The *"throne of grace"* is not a place for cowering and shame— it is a place of boldness, love and acceptance, where sin is never an issue.

With such overwhelming love and acceptance, aren't we likely to sin more? It is a valid question. The answer is only known by those who have experienced divine generosity from their most Holy Father. In the face of such overwhelming love and acceptance, sin becomes unthinkable—even the thought of it becomes distasteful. Obviously, that does not mean that sin becomes a thing of the past; Satan is not going to lie down and play dead just because we have been with God; he is likely to up the ante. Temptations do not cease, but thanks be to God, His loving grace gives us all the more reason to not give place to them.

While we were of the world, our sins were counted against us, but at the precise moment of our rebirth, we entered into Christ, and that was enough to change everything forever—in heaven's *"throne of grace"*, none of our sins, whether past, present or future, will ever be counted against us.

Way before the foundation of the earth, in God's mind, His Son had already been slain for our benefit. Knowing this, would you allow me some leeway to tell Jesus' story my way?

Earthly parents desire that their sons find virtuous wives, and it is no different for God the Father. Seeing that His Son would be bringing His bride home to be with His family forever, she would have to fit in with the family's holy ethos—her character would have to be beyond reproach. But His Son did not choose a woman of virtue—His choice of a partner was anything but worthy of the affections of the most eligible Bachelor of all time—her life was a mess and her reputation stained with unthinkable iniquity.

What did His Father have to say about His choice? Well, His Father loved Him so much that He could not deny Him His request. He gave His approval, but warned Him that His choice of a wanton wench would prove to be very costly. She is a hopeless case—a sorry individual—beyond help—incapable of redeeming herself—she would always be letting Him down.

His Son was so love struck and blinded by His desire for her that He declared that no cost would deter Him from going through with His union with her. Then His Father revealed the cost. It would cost Him rejection, pain, agony and the cruelty of the cross. It would be the only way to make His bride acceptable to the family. This was a high price, but His Son was not about to allow anything to come between Him and His dearest love.

He was brave at first, but when push came to shove, He was heard to say, *"O my Father, if it be possible, let this cup pass from me"*, and then at the thought of losing His most cherished desire, He added, *"...nevertheless, not as I will, but as You will"* (Mat 26:39). He looked beyond the pain and saw the prize. In going through with it, He would be able to seal her in perpetual perfection, and that would be enough to satisfy His Dad. *"... preserved blameless at the coming of our Lord Jesus Christ"* (1Th 5:23). We are not preserved blameless because we have ceased to sin or because we are up to date with our repenting; we are preserved blameless because we are *"in Christ"*. Peter goes so far as to say that we are blameless and without spot (2 Pet 3:14).

Obviously, this story is not a perfect metaphor. In reality, the Father loves us every bit as much as does His Son!

I have attended many a funeral of great men and woman of God. Not one of them led blameless lives. Each and every one of these glorious heroes of the faith were buried with the *"spots and wrinkles"* of the imperfections of their humanity. Fortunately, they did not have to qualify to pass from death into eternal life by living perfectly, or for that matter, by repenting timeously; they had passed from death into life by being reborn into Christ. When Christ made His bride perfect, she became eternally perfect, pristinely pure, magnificently glorious, forever faultless, and in His eyes, without a single spot or wrinkle! And if that's what He thinks of us, nothing else matters!

HOLINESS

Is our salvation measured by how
broken and contrite we are?

The rumour goes that people of grace are soft on sin. Is this just another rumour, or could it be true? How could it be? After all, grace is God's one and only solution for our penchant for sin—there is no plan B. In God's estimation, any good living on our part falls into the category of sin—to Him it is *"filthy rags"*.

Grace does not focus on our behaviour; it focuses on our hearts. Love inspired hearts produce a different kind of behaviour without effort. That being the case, what does it take to reach a believer's heart? It takes a revelation of just how completely we are loved, redeemed from the curse, and made to be as righteous as Jesus. Jesus is so desirous of our company, so enamoured with us, that He took the curse of our sin upon Himself, and issued us with His very own spotless righteous standing, not only despite our many flaws, weaknesses and sins, but because of them.

Unless we make an effort to comprehend, seize upon and personalise the length, breadth, height and depth of His love for us, it remains in the realm of nice to know academic information, but does nothing to change our hearts. This leaves us to tame our errant ways with sheer grit and determination. If this is required of us, then how do we differ from unsaved people who also try to live virtuously? No! We are not expected to change ourselves. We have been invited to rest in the finished work of the cross. Our kind of striving is usually fruitless anyway. No matter how much cowering, contriteness and pleading we may apply, we tend to revert back to our less than perfect ways. After all our trying, eventually we either give up, and settle for a life of pious pretence, or wake up to the fact that we are in serious need of help. Without the help of grace, we are hopelessly incapable of eradicating our innate penchant for sin.

Hardened hearts are not contrite hearts. The only influence that has any meaningful impact on stony hearts is agape love—nothing else has the power to crack our innate resistance to submission.

"The sacrifices of God are a broken spirit, A broken and a contrite heart—These, O God, You will not despise" (Psa 51:17). It is clear that brokenness and contriteness are essential stepping stones on the glorious grace walk with our Lord. Nevertheless, it would do us well to bear in mind that our waywardness has no bearing on God's degree of faithfulness and love towards us. When we appeal to Him for forgiveness, He reminds us that He has already suffered the penalty for our clemency—acquittal was decided upon long before we even committed the offence. Even before creation, He had already made up His mind to forgive us, and later went to the cross to validate His decision. With this, He promised not to keep a single record of our sins; in fact, not even to make a mental note of them.

That doesn't mean that we shouldn't ask for forgiveness, but when we do, I can just imagine Him thinking, "Funny, I don't remember that one". When God gives us His word, we can bank it. He will never be able to recall our sins, and that is final! *"Their sins and their lawless deeds I will remember no more"* (Heb 10:17).

Repentance is the part that we play in returning to the righteous pathway when we have strayed from it. The pathway is straight, but try as we may, we don't always walk straight. Repentance helps us to find our way back to the pathway. This pathway avoids the harmful pitfalls in which we can so easily end up battered, bruised and stranded. Just as uprightness has its own consequences, so does wickedness. God, in His grace, has done all He can to help us avoid the pitfalls of sin. We should not blame Him saying, "God gives and God takes away, blessed be the name of the Lord". The harmful consequences of our wayward actions are not of His making.

God does not have to force Himself to keep His side of our relationship right, but for us it is different. For our own good, it is incumbent upon us to keep our side of the relationship genuine. We don't do this to stay saved; we do it to keep our side of the relationship honest.

Where it all goes pear shaped, is when contriteness inverts into condemnation—guilt can so easily sour into shame. That's when we enter into partnership with *"the accuser of the brethren"* who drags us into regret and despair, and does all he can to keep us there. As we buy his lies and adopt his destructive agenda, he takes the opportunity to bring our faith into question—in the process, we forego our peace, joy and wellbeing. Falling into guilt and condemnation is as good as shaking hands with the devil.

Could God really be ungracious? How could He insult our utmost efforts of sincerely doing good works to please Him, referring to them as *"filthy rags"*? Doesn't He have an ounce of appreciation for our sincerity? There must be more to this than meets the eye. God looks beyond our efforts at doing good works, and sees the condition of our hearts. We tend to look at the outward, while God looks at the inward. God is not in the least bit impressed with outward displays of godliness when that godliness is not a true reflection of what's going on in our hearts. If it were remotely possible for us to walk completely blamelessly, we would have achieved absolutely nothing. The Holy Spirit's sanctifying process does not involve self-effort; it involves heart change, and hearts do not change merely because we have decided to behave better; hearts change when they're overwhelmed with love and acceptance, despite their less than perfect condition.

If we must plead for forgiveness, then we must ask how much pleading becomes forgiving enough—can we ever be quite certain that we have taken contriteness to its sin cancelling level? Developing out of this confusion comes all kinds of erroneous penitent extremes—contriteness evolved into superfluous religious penance in Orthodoxy and Catholicism, and a modified version has crept into the misguided self-recriminating devotions of modern day Evangelicals, Pentecostals and Charismatics.

Thank God—Jesus has shown us emphatically in the parable of the prodigal son that pleading is entirely uncalled for—the Father expects nothing more from us other than that we return to Him. The prodigal's speech of repentance was one short sentence. The woman caught in adultery didn't even utter a single word of repentance, yet Jesus said, *"neither do I judge you"*. It is thought that she was the one who later poured the contents of the alabaster box over Jesus in worship. One wonders how Jesus could have been so gracious to someone who may just as easily have walked straight back into the arms of her paying customers. Yet Jesus exalted her story above every other story in the Bible when He said that her story would be retold wherever the gospel is preached (Mar 14:9).

"So you should not be like cowering, fearful slaves. You should behave instead like God's very own children, adopted into his family, calling him, "Father dear father" (Rom 8:15 NLT). Children do not cower before their earthly dads—while their dads are around, they take on an unusual boldness—nothing frightens them. In the face of such unqualified fatherly love from our heavenly Dad, there is no place for cowering.

We do well to repent, but we cannot make ourselves anymore righteous than we already are in God's sight. From His perspective, all our very best attempts at right making, miss the mark.

Grace is decidedly more effective than self-effort—it goes directly to the problem in our hearts. If on the other hand, by sheer white knuckling it, we manage to change our behaviour—we have achieved little. Our changes do not go deep enough to affect the way our hearts operate. We have missed the point—gone about it the wrong way around. Are we really being true to ourselves and others when our behaviour is at odds with our hearts? It is not uncommon for believers to outwardly love and forgive a person, yet secretly rejoice in that person's calamity. Can hypocrisy be any more blatant than that?

Coming to know the extreme love of God is enormously influential upon the way we behave, because it starts by winning our hearts, and it does so without hidden agendas, conditions or strings attached, and asks not for any promises to change. Hearts that have undergone a love transformation, reflect this change in the form of loving actions. When God's unconditional love has conquered a particular sin within our hearts, that sin ceases to manifest outwardly. In surrendering to the One who loves us so unconditionally, we trigger an effortless progression of behavioural adjustments—ultimately, our errant behaviour falls into line with what we believe.

Create *"a clean heart and a steadfast spirit within us."* is the motto of "extreme grace". It is a prayer; not a boast—it is something that God does; not something that we do. In the course of being so overwhelmingly loved, our hearts begin to function differently—next, we find ourselves thinking and processing information differently. Right thinking, almost as if mysteriously, results in right behaving.

We can so easily be so intent on honouring God that we overlook how enormously He honours us. He started this love affair. When we recognise how honoured we are to be adopted into His wonderful family, and how He continues to honour us with His presence, His wisdom, His guidance, His love, His compassion, His understanding, His help, His grace, His mercy and so much more, it becomes obvious that He values us dearly. The way He honours us has a way of awakening honour within us. Instead of demanding honour from others, we are delighted to honour them without expecting the faintest hint of reciprocation!

God's grace allows Him to serve us—to chase us down with His love, even at times when we have carelessly slipped into shame. When we allow ourselves to believe that we are highly prized by God, this awareness translates into self-esteem, which in turn translates into esteeming others more highly. It all starts with right thinking.

"Brood of vipers! How can you, being evil, speak good things? For out of the abundance of the heart the mouth speaks" (Mat 12:34). These were the words of Jesus spoken to the respected religious elite. If we have religious achievements to boast of, it isn't necessarily a commendation. When under pressure, people's words and deeds betray

what is hidden in their hearts. Anybody can give the illusion of godliness—religious pretending is commonplace. Just because people don't smoke or dance does not mean that they are not control freaks, manipulators, offense takers, grudge bearers etc. They may strongly object to the use of bad language, but not think twice of indulging in rumour mongering. Tell me, which is worse? To hear unrefined chit-chat that is peppered with unsavoury language, or to have a knife thrust to its hilt between ones shoulder blades by a trusted fellow believer who thinks nothing of making public what has been shared with him in confidence? This is especially painful when it is perpetrated by someone who has gained our trust and respect.

Jesus gave us broad outlines to work with—He seldom gave us specific instructions, but if He made one point crystal clear it was that we should not judge one another (Mat 7:1). Christians get around this injunction by legitimising their judgementalism, saying that they are not judging the person, but merely judging their fruit. What else can one judge about them? It should be obvious to see hypocrisy in this. No-one has been appointed to the position of fruit inspectors by the heavenly department of agriculture.

So often when believers speak of someone's fruit, they are referring to their perceived holiness. But that is not what Jesus was referring to in John 15. *"By this My Father is glorified, that you bear much fruit"* (verse 8). The question to ask oneself is, "By what kind of fruit is my Father glorified?" The answer is given in the preceding verse. *"If you abide in Me, and My words abide in you, you will ask what you desire, and it shall be done for you"*. In this scripture, Jesus was not referring to our state of holiness; He was referring to the state of our faith as demonstrated in answered prayer—answered prayer is the fruit of our faith, it reveals that we are abiding in Him and His words are abiding in us. The fruit of the Spirit as listed in Galatians is a different issue.

Did you notice that Jesus set out requirements for the outworking of grace in this scripture? *"If you abide in Me, and My words abide in you"* are the requirements for having our prayers answered. Because of our legalistic training, we are apt to jump to the conclusion that *"abiding"* in God is a reference to holiness. But, when read in context, we get a very different meaning. Abiding in Him is not a state of holiness; it is a state of sticking to our confession of faith when the odds are stacked against us. It is about hanging in there in faith even when our prayers seem to go unanswered. Part of the meaning of the original text which was translated *"abide"*, is a Greek word meaning to "stay in expectancy". It takes the tenacity of a bulldog to stay in faith when the evidence does not appear to support our stand.

The second condition that Jesus mentioned is, *"My words abide in you"*. How do His words abide in us? They abide in us when we doggedly hold on to the promises He has given us. None of this has anything to do with our state of holiness. To the contrary, the fruit that Jesus was referring to has everything to do with the state of our faith, and our faith is bolstered by what we know of His grace. In this verse, Jesus made it clear that it is our faith that glorifies Him.

—oOo—

By definition, the church is comprised of believers of all degrees of maturity, ranging from immature new born babes in Christ, to seasoned men and women of godly wisdom. But how often do we find believers who would rather suffer harm than break their word. Thankfully this does not apply to all, but look a little closer and you may notice what is different about people of honour. People who are only too aware that they do not deserve the love and acceptance they get, are able to extend the same love and acceptance to others who don't deserve it either. The love they drink from at the fountain of God's affection, overflows in the form of love towards others—it is not something that they must force themselves to do; they don't even have to strive to do it; it is something that love does all by itself.

According to Jesus, other than that we should believe in Him, everything in our Christian walk hinges on one command and one command only—it is to love God and people (Luk 10:27). When this happens, there is no further need for rules to tell us how to live right. Our love for others starts and ends with the degree of our understanding of the extent of God's love for us—the unfolding of which is without end—it is inexhaustible! Of course, if we insist that God's grace is not extreme, we will not expect more to unfold—how unfortunate!

Jesus did not instruct us to tolerate each other; He instructed us to love each other. As if this isn't difficult enough, He went on to raise the bar even higher by saying that we should love one another as much as we love ourselves—if ever there was a high goal, this is it. But we are not to despair; Jesus tells us how to go about achieving this lofty ideal. Simply put: to the degree that we discover God's love for us; we find ourselves being more accommodating towards others. His love inspiring our love.

"Un-extreme grace" cannot convince its followers that there is more to God's magnificent grace—they have settled for a scaled down version, and deny that it is extreme! The very thing that ignites a passion for God in the hearts of the followers of "extreme grace" is the thing that "un-extreme grace" views with scepticism—they have been conditioned to see it as a new-fangled gospel, when it is actually the old old story unfolding in a first-handed experiential way. Paul did his level best to convince us of this, but religion in its "wisdom" knew better. It has taken us a long time to get back to basics. I am sure Paul must be sighing with relief in heaven, "At long last, they are beginning to get it—my work was not in vain". I hope the angels are keeping him posted.

This magnificent love is something that can only be a reality in the lives of those who have not placed a cap on what they believe God's love and grace includes. If they have decided that God's grace does not stretch far enough to cover all sin, past present and future, they will not be able to live in the luxury of this reality. Religion cannot afford to allow its followers to discover such freedom. If religion were to allow it, religion would immediately lose its reason to exist.

Irrespective of our state of holiness, or for that matter, un-holiness, God's love for us is without end. This discovery can be pretty overwhelming. By the time we wipe grateful tears from our eyes, we are surprised to see that our affections for wrong things have disappeared. Such is the irresistibility of being loved in such a pure way. How can the world even begin to compete with the satisfaction and fulfilment of a divine romance? Oh, the sheer bliss of divine contentment! When Jesus is everything, the lure of worldliness loses its appeal. How can sin's empty promises possibly compete with the pleasures of full blown agape? When it comes to pleasure, sin promises much, but delivers little—there is always a sting in its tail—it's just not worth the trouble.

The boundless freedom experienced by the followers of "extreme grace" can seem frightening to the followers of "un-extreme grace". They do not understand that love without bounds is life changing. In their personal battles with sin, they may pray for help, but when help comes in the form of unconditional agape love, known as grace, they are likely to reject it as error—especially if they have been taught to be suspicious of the freedom that comes with grace.

God's love is very different to ours—it is given without reason and demands nothing in return. Just knowing that we are freely accepted and completely loved, seemingly without reason, is life changing in itself.

No! The re-emergence of the message of grace is not a new revelation; it is discovering what the Bible reveals about the boundlessness of God's love. None of us fully understand it—nobody has even scratched the surface in coming to comprehend the big heartedness of God—there is always so much more of it to be revealed. In the adventure of discovering it, we find our affection for wrong living disappearing, almost as if by accident.

We only find out what a lifetime of "un-extreme grace" has done for believers when their toes have been stepped on. Some of us have had the misfortune of being within range of their rage. Others have been wounded in the malicious crossfire of angry opponents involved in church splits and the like.

Anybody who has been in business for any length of time knows how little religion has done for the ethics of believers. Sad to say, whether Christian or not, when it comes to doing business, one cannot risk doing it on a handshake. In many cases I have found the corporate world to be more reliable than religious folk. This indictment is a sad reflexion on graceless religion. But to dilute grace is to dilute Jesus, and what we get for diluting Jesus is diluted godliness!

What can be said of these religious offenders? Have they fallen out with God? No! As disappointing as religious shallowness is, we all remain His much loved glorious blood bought children—more than that; we are the apples of His eye. I do not raise this point to cast aspersions on believers; rather I raise it to expose the failure of graceless religion. "Un-extreme grace" does not possess the power to deal with deviant attitudes. I love and respect God's children too much to pussyfoot around this issue. For our own good, this information should not be piously swept under the carpet.

In my long career in business, I have often heard the harsh reality of what the world thinks of Christians. Believe me! Those who have been hard done by, by the "sweet and gentle holier than thou's" are not for one moment fooled. How often haven't we heard the words, "And He calls himself a Christian", spoken by those who have become casualties at the hands of the "pious".

"Extreme grace" does not teach the shrugging of shoulders in view of the fact that we are already forgiven. "Extreme grace" stands for something that involves genuine contriteness and a desire for genuine godliness. God's unconditional love overwhelms and melts hearts; making it easier to choose to do the right thing and repent. This cannot be understood by a person who has not found that his or her state of righteousness is purely God's doing; permanently fixed by what Jesus achieved—not exposed to contamination from his or her personal sins and weaknesses. Consider for a moment. If we could be contaminated by sin, and then be required to neutralise these contagions with repentance, we would be unholy for longer periods than holy. If this is how it works, we would not be able to claim to be *"the righteousness of God in Christ"*. At best, we could only claim to be as righteous as our current actions.

To reduce God's glorious righteous making plan of atonement to such a flimsy arrangement, is sin in itself. It diminishes and trivialises the completeness of our redemption—not to mention what it says of the One who went through so much anguish to achieve it for us. Our eternal destination would be determined by the toss of a coin—death could easily occur during a period that has not yet been covered by repentance. No! This would be insanity! It is not in character with a God who is holy!

Either a person is totally and completely righteous or they are totally and completely unrighteous. Our righteous condition does not hang on the fragile thread of our last confession—Jesus' blood sacrifice settled this status for us once and for all—regardless of our current state of holiness, sin or repentance, we are totally and completely righteous in God's eyes—end of story! Such a stable state is not even remotely possible under "un-extreme grace's" temporary righteousness granted between our last repentance and our next sin.

"Un-extreme grace" has this idea that our sin cancels our right standing. It purports that it requires contriteness and repentance to reinstate it. This is not at all good news, yet it is mislabelled the good news of the gospel. The ups and downs of "un-extreme grace" are sanity destroying—peace comes and goes like the waves on a beach. This is not how the God of all grace works. We are invited to enter into our Sabbath rest, and ideally speaking, never leave it.

Of course, it is seldom that simple, because Satan does his level best to convince us that we are not secure in God's rest. He did it to Adam and he is out to do it to us. He doesn't have to get us to sin; he just has to get us to doubt that God's grace could be so extreme? He is a haggler of note—a past master at negotiating our God given privileges away. If he can get us to perform to obtain the righteousness that we already have, it is as good as getting us to deny that we already have it. With this mind-set we forfeit the privileges that accompany right standing and Satan wins the day. It is how he minimises the atonement, our redemption and justification. Let's face it, with him around, we are always going to be involved in a fight of faith—we cannot afford to put our guard down for a moment. We must be ready to pull down every thought that dares to exalt itself above the knowledge of Christ. Beware! Our blood bought liberty poses a threat to our enemy—he will do anything to convince us that grace is less than it is.

"Come to Me, all you who labor and are heavy laden, and I will give you rest" (Mat 11:28). When our right standing with God hinges

on the undependability of our fickle religious actions, we are *"labouring"* for right standing. God's kind of rest cannot be laboured for with any amount of law keeping. Gifts are only gifts if they can be *"received"* without effort.

"And to whom sware he that they should not enter into his rest, but to them that believed not?" (Heb 3:18 KJV). Interestingly, the reason given here for not being able to enter His rest had nothing to do with sin, and everything to do with that they *"believed not"*.

What is the opposite of God's Sabbath rest? It is purely unbelief! Except for two people, none of the Israelites who left Egypt to go to the Promised Land, lived long enough to enter the Promised Land. What was it that these two had that the others lacked? Was it holiness? Certainly not! They were allowed to enter for no other reason than that they believed. The rest of them were refused entrance for one reason and one reason only! That reason was that they *"believed not"*!

How can "un-extreme grace" followers find rest when they insist that we have to add more to something that is already complete? May I suggest that to require us to perform in this way is a distortion that falls into the category of *"believed not"*. There is no possibility of entering into God's rest for those who cannot bring themselves to believe that the work of the cross has left no further requirements to be fulfilled from our side. We get this rest, by accepting that the work of the cross is entirely complete and forever *"finished"*. There is nothing left for us to do except believe, be loved and love others!

Yes the King James Version says that we are to *"labour"* to enter this rest, but that labouring is not in the sense of making ourselves right with law keeping, but rather in the sense of making an uncompromising decision to find rest in grace. There is only one effort required and that is to fight off every thought that would rob us of our sense of rest. The thought that we haven't done enough to deserve rest, is a typical thought that must be pulled down. It takes a disciplined determination to replace these thoughts with Jesus' words, *"I will give you rest"*. He says to those who are heavy laden, *"Come unto me"* (Mat 11:28).

When we have entered His rest, we rest from all efforts to make ourselves right. But for as long as we insist on stopping short of believing in the finality of Jesus' redemption, it stands to reason that we cannot rest in the finality of it.

The question arises; can Jesus be trusted to make us righteous all by Himself? Or does He need a little help from our unrighteous efforts? The answer should be obvious.

The truth of the matter is that we have been purchased. We are the flock that *"he purchased with his own blood"* (Act 20:28). Once purchased forever owned. I take special care of my watch because I paid a lot of money for it. In the same way, God takes special care of those for whom He paid so dearly. He does not mislay His possessions—nor does He need a repurchase scheme to keep buying us back every now and so often. What He has done He has done, and it is enough!

WILL HE CAST US AWAY?

How secure are we in Christ?

"Do not cast me away from Your presence, And do not take Your Holy Spirit from me (Psa 51:11). Does this danger apply to New Testament believers? The writer of Hebrews quotes Jesus' words, *"I will never fail you. I will never abandon you"* (Heb 13:5). We can safely take Jesus at His word; He will never cast us away!

Taking away His Holy Spirit was certainly possible before the cross. But something significant took place at Calvary. Not only were our sins paid for, but the Holy Spirit came to make Himself one with us—a divine merger took place. Our oneness with the Holy Spirit makes all the difference. We did not gradually mutate over time into "new creatures"; it took a millisecond—transformed from one species into another. Our new identity in Christ bears no resemblance to our former identity. We are wall to wall Holy Spirit, fused together with God into something entirely different—we are in the god-class. As children of God, we carry the self-same spiritual genes as the Father who gave us spiritual birth. *"And the glory which You gave Me I have given them, that they may be one just as We are one* (Joh 17:22). Did you get that? We are one with the Father in exactly the same way that Jesus is one with the Father! If we can describe the oneness and unity between Jesus and His Father, we can describe the oneness and unity between us and the Father. According to this verse, it is precisely the same. This is very reassuring—if Jesus is secure, then so are we! Can Jesus be separated from the Father? Well of course not! Then neither can we! If this is difficult to accept, consider that the words of this scripture were spoken by Jesus.

Of course Hebrews 6:6 suggests that separation can take place. But the writer goes on to say, *"We really don't believe that it applies to you. We are confident that you are meant for better things, things that come with salvation"* (NLT). Yes, the possibility does exist, but it would take a complete rejection of grace. Grace cannot be cancelled by sin; it can only be cancelled by law keeping! God specifically conceived grace to make intimacy with sinful humanity possible? Like blotting paper, grace simply absorbs sin—the bigger the stain the bigger the blotting paper.

"Where sin abounded, grace did much more abound" (Rom 5:20). In the original Greek text, this concept is expressed in even stronger terms. Our language has limitations—English has only one word to express various levels of "abounding". Paul used a stronger word for "abounding" grace than he used for "abounding" sin. He said that when sin abounds, grace abounds "exceedingly more". In reality, there can never be more sin than grace!

If we were able to achieve our own holiness, grace would be entirely unnecessary. Seeing that grace was specifically established to overcome wickedness, how could wickedness possibly overcome grace? Which is greater? The devil's wickedness or God's grace? The poison or the antidote?

Grace does not exist for those who have made themselves holy; it exists for those who have difficulty with holy living. But then again, those who have attempted to make themselves holy are equally unholy by God's measure.

Consider the possibility that the writer of Hebrews 6:6 is posing a rhetorical question. Could he be saying that it is impossible to stay saved by any means other than grace? In other words, the writer could be making the point that if grace is rejected, there is no plan B—God has no other means to keep us saved.

What about Ananias and Sapphira who were carried feet first out of the place of meeting? Does this not suggest that sin can separate believers from God? It is interesting to note that Ananias is described as a *"certain man"*, and not as a *"disciple"* as was the usual way of describing believers in the New Testament. From this it seems that Ananias was not a believer; he was in all likelihood an imposter trying to impress the believers with a false display of piety?

What about the unforgivable sin? *"Therefore I say to you, every sin and blasphemy will be forgiven men, but the blasphemy against the Spirit will not be forgiven men"* (Mat 12:31). What is this blasphemy? I have asked many people this question and hardly any of them were able to give me a definitive answer. But when read in context, the answer is plain. This statement was made by Jesus in response to the Pharisees' claim, *"This fellow does not cast out demons except by Beelzebub, the ruler of the demons"* (Mat 12:24).

The point that Jesus was making was that it is unforgivable to claim that the work of grace through the Holy Spirit is actually the work of Satan. In other words, the unforgivable sin is to give the devil credit for God's grace.

Bear in mind that Jesus was speaking to un-regenerated people living under the Old Covenant—it is different for regenerated people living under the New Covenant—all their sins were taken care of at Calvary.

In the early days of the Pentecostal movement, people who were baptised in the Holy Spirit came under severe criticism from other evangelical denominations. They claimed that the baptism and gifts of the Holy Spirit were actually the work of the devil. I believe that although these critics blatantly blasphemed the Holy Ghost, they did not fall foul of Jesus' warning, because as born again believers, they had already been made one with Christ at Calvary.

—oOo—

The potter begins to knead the clay, but it is too stiff to work with. He adds water until he gets a malleable consistency that can be shaped into something useful. Our hearts are often hardened by life's unfortunate twist and turns. To soften them, the divine Potter applies the water of His Spirit together with the graciousness of His love. The more bedraggled we are, the more love He applies—unloved hearts are too hard to be shaped. The more convinced we are of His unconditional love for us, the more pliable we are in His hands—our instinctive resistance melts in the warmth of His affection.

In the environment of love, we find a place that is safe enough to open up and allow the Holy Spirit to deal with unwholesomeness within us. *"Hardened through the deceitfulness of sin",* is a condition more likely to inflict those who have set limits to the extent of God's grace—they feel compelled to resist extremeness and therewith miss their opportunity to be softened by God's loving grace. We can all do with a little more love—it draws the very best out of us. His goodness makes repenting appealing (Rom 2:4).

We don't invite accusers into our hearts, but when our Lover comes knocking—well now, that is an entirely different matter—we throw our hearts' doors wide open and welcome Him home.

BORN INTO RIGHTEOUSNESS

Does our holy living contribute additional
righteousness to our right standing with God?

As with Abraham, our righteousness comes from right believing and not from right behaving. If righteousness came to us through believing despite our sinfulness; it cannot subsequently be lost through our sinfulness. I do not say this to excuse sinfulness—sin will always be deplorable; I say this to be in agreement with what redemption is.

"And whoever lives and believes in Me shall never die. Do you believe this?" (Joh 11:26). This is a very emphatic statement followed by a very direct question from Jesus. When Jesus makes a categorical statement it is not open to religious modification. We must all give answer to His question. He asks you if you accept that living and believing in Him is enough to assure eternity? I trust that you can put aside all reservations and answer Him in the affirmative?

Jesus is not asking whether or not you have done what religion expects of you; He doesn't want to know if you live up to a certain holiness code or if you are up to date with repentance; He only asks one question, "Do you believe that you will never die purely because you live and believe in Him?" Or do you insist that it couldn't possibly be that simple? If you agree with Jesus that living and believing in Him is enough, then He assures you that you will *"never die"*! He is waiting for your answer. He asks, *"Do you believe this?"*

—o0o—

"Pursue peace with all people, and holiness, without which no one will see the Lord" (Heb 12:14). If we were required to reach a certain level of holiness before being allowed to see God, then we would need to know what that level is. It most certainly cannot be perfection—there isn't one single perfect specimen upon the face of the planet. So this verse cannot mean what religion would have us believe. Obviously, it is not about the attainment of holiness; it is about the "pursuit" of it. The only perfection we have any claim to, is the perfection graciously imputed to us. Thankfully, we do not have a holiness score card in heaven. On one issue He was entirely clear— nobody is holy in a practical sense.

Obviously, Hebrews 12:14 cannot cancel Jesus' words, *"Whoever lives and believes in Me shall never die"*. There is a distinct difference between, on the one hand, losing our salvation, and on the other hand, failing to walk in God's gracious provisions. We dare not misuse our grace to be out of step with God. If we want to partner with Him, we need to be of the same mind as Him. Seeing that He is the Prince of Peace and the Lord God of everything, it behoves us to live by His principles. Obviously, we cannot expect God to join us in doing something that is out of character with Him—He simply cannot forsake His holiness for the sake of helping us to succeed at doing something ungodly. If we are in step with ungodliness, we are out of step with God.

To have right standing with God and yet to neglect to express it in our day to day living would be an unfortunate waste of God's kindness. *"Either make the tree good and its fruit good, or else make the tree bad and its fruit bad; for a tree is known by its fruit"* (Mat 12:33). What makes us as trees either good or bad? Is it the righteousness imputed to us by Christ Jesus, or is it our own ineffective attempts at trying to be righteous? In view of humanity's inability to make itself righteous, the answer should be obvious. But if something must change, what is it? It is our thinking (our believing). Actions are governed by thoughts.

"Not me!" I hear you protest. "I am led by the Spirit!" Though you are Spirit led, don't discount the role that your thinking plays. *"Let God transform you into a new person by changing the way you think"* (Rom 12:2 NLT). Unlike spiritual transformation, which is instantaneous; mind transformation is progressive. Paul says that we are transformed to the degree that we allow God to transform our thinking. If we don't do it God's way, our actions become works of the flesh—a poor substitute for fruit of the Spirit. But although the Spirit leads, we don't necessary follow His leading—we are often inclined to give more credence to what our five senses tell us.

Our thinking and thought processes take place in the soulish realm. Either we take our lead from circumstances encountered in the sensory realm (the flesh), or from the indwelling Spirit of God. For example, the doctor may tell us that we have an incurable disease, but the Spirit tells us that *"by His stripes we are healed"*, and therefore we are in good health. Our souls must choose which report to believe. Logic may say that we are done for, while the Spirit says we are not! Again our souls must decide either to go along with our five senses or with the Spirit.

If we desire to behave differently, we need to think differently, and if we want to think differently, our minds need regular renewing. But what sort of mind renewing information would be impactful enough to change the way we behave? The kingdom is a place of love, acceptance and privilege. We need to remind ourselves of our privileged standing with God.

Our Bibles reveal how much we are loved, and this, more than anything else, gives us personal value, which in turn enables us to value others more highly. Let's not kid ourselves; not everybody out there is lovable. How do we bring ourselves to love repugnant and obnoxious individuals? God may have the grace to do it, but we are incapable, unless of course, our love has been ignited by His love. They say that loved people love people. Praise God! There is no effort in that!

—oOo—

Quite obviously, it is not even remotely possible that we initially gained our salvation by repenting from each and every individual sin—nobody could possibly remember all of them. That being the case, how could the rules suddenly change after re-birth, requiring us to repent of each and every sin to assure that we stay saved? If this is what we have come to believe, then it is obvious that we don't understand what we were saved from; it wasn't only from our sins; it was from the whole sin issue. John the Baptist said, *"Behold the Lamb of God, which taketh away the sin of the world"* (Joh 1:29 KJV). Note that the word *"sin"* is used in the singular, meaning that the whole issue of sin has been dealt with.

Repentance, is a change of mind (heart), the consequence of which is a change of conduct—righteous thoughts that manifest in righteous actions. When this happens, there is no further need to engineer holiness. Rather, we are surprised to discover that we are behaving differently. And it all started with thinking differently. In Jesus' words, *"Out of the abundance of the heart the mouth speaks"* (Mat 12:34). Our unguarded words and instinctive conduct is purely an expression of what is in our hearts.

But when Jesus and the apostles used the word *"heart"*, what exactly were they referring to? We know that our hearts are responsible for circulating blood through our bodies, but the word *"heart"* was not used in this sense. There are approximately 150 references to the word *"heart"* in the New Testament. The original Greek word which was translated *"heart"* is not some ethereal term. *"Heart"* is used in the figurative sense to describe thoughts and feelings. For example, when Jesus referred to committing adultery in our hearts, He was referring to committing adultery in our thoughts and emotions (Matt 5:28). Jesus used *"heart"* in the same sense when He said, *"A good man out of the good treasure of his heart brings forth good things, and an evil man out of the evil treasure brings forth evil things"* (Mat 12:35). Our hearts do not operate purely on rationale; they operate at a subconscious level with emotions and passions.

If repentance is a change of perspective, then we can safely say that repentance is not what religion has made it out to be.

A change of perspective may seem easy, but in reality it is not. In a manner of speaking, we do not own our perspectives; they own us— we become the road we have travelled. Perspectives did not come to us easily; it took a lifetime of both positive and negative experiences, and all sorts of other influences, including both good and bad role models to determine the way we process information in our subconscious minds (hearts). Discarding these embedded paradigms can be very difficult—to adopt opposite thinking is nigh impossible. It takes more than a sermon or two to undo a lifetime of wrong thinking. Mind renewal is not a once off occurrence; it's an on-going process of discovering ever greater depths of God's love for us.

Of course, when emotions are added to the mix, a passion arises that makes change so much more effective. God is an emotional God, and love is a very strong emotion. Grace is God's love language and He dispenses His goodness to us with loads of understanding and mercy. Love is a very powerful tool for change, and God has a lot of it to give!

CONFESSION

Are only confessed sins forgiven?
Do we remain guilty of the rest?

"If we confess our sins, He is faithful and just to forgive us our sins and to cleanse us from all unrighteousness" (1Jn 1:9). Confession should not be confused with repentance—the one is a matter of owning up; while the other is a matter of mind reversal.

There is no doubt about it; confession is vitally necessary to keep us out of foolish pride. Besides, it has many other edifying benefits. We are cautioned not to think too highly of ourselves. Having said that, consider the following:

The big Question is: Does this scripture apply to sinners or believers, or maybe to both? To answer this question, we must ask who it was that John was addressing. It is interesting to note that all the epistles commence with a greeting to a person or church except this one. Why so? John was not addressing a group made up exclusively of believers; He was addressing Gnostics—a cult that did not believe in the concept of sin. It was a mixed assemblage of both Gnostics and confused followers of Jesus who had been thrown off course by the heretical philosophy of the Gnostics. They were of the opinion that sin does not exist. John's first task was to convince the Gnostics that sin does exist. Next, he went on to convince these heretics that they needed to confess their sins in order to be saved—hence 1 John 1:9. Only after he had made this point with the Gnostics, did he go on to address the confused believers.

When unbelievers confess their sinful condition, God is faithful and just to forgive them and to cleanse them from all unrighteousness. It is significant that this step invokes a cleansing from *"all"* unrighteousness in one fell swoop; not just the ones mentioned. The emphasis is on the word *"all"*. At rebirth, every form of unrighteousness is immediately and totally forgiven and expunged from the record books of heaven. This does not happen because each and every sin is confessed individually; it happens when our sinful "condition" is confessed. i.e. "I am a sinner".

I have never met a single believer who can claim to have confessed each and every one of his sins. If that was required, then nobody could possibly be saved. Fortunately, it is not! Such a task would be physically impossible—thousands upon thousands of sins in both thought and deed would have to be dragged out of a lifetime of less than perfect living.

It is obvious that this verse deals with receiving salvation for the first time. Although these words were said to Gnostics, they apply equally to any and all unbelievers, no matter what their religious bent may be.

Chapter two takes on a very different tone; it is addressed to John's confused disciples. Here John speaks about forgiveness without making any mention of confession. *"If you sin there is someone to plead for you before the Father. He is Jesus Christ, the one who pleases God completely. He is the sacrifice for sins. He takes away not only our sins but the sins of all the world"* (1John 2:1-2 KJV).

There is another issue. If on-going confessions were required to keep us saved, one would expect the other writers of the epistles also to have mentioned it, but there is no such teaching from them on this subject. Yes, they do mention confession, but certainly not confession of sins. They speak of a very different kind of confession—confession of faith! James calls on us to confess our faults to each other, but makes no mention of confessing our sins to God. Other than 1 John 1:9, every New Testament reference to confession is in regard to a confession of "faith", not of "sin". Not even Jesus used the word "confess" or "confession" in respect of sin—doesn't that tell a story all of its own?

We ought not to dismiss this vital difference offhandedly. It may seem like splitting hairs, but it is certainly not the case. The two concepts of confession are not even remotely similar—in fact they are diametrically opposite. Confession of sin involves introspection, self-examination and humility; while confession of faith involves trust, belief and boldness. It takes the focus off our puniness and places it on our merciful, loving, almighty Father.

Obviously, this does not mean that once we are born again we cease to confess our sins. While our spirit man, and therefore our salvation is secure in what Jesus has done for us, nevertheless, as they say in the classics, "confession is good for the soul".

Of course, everybody benefits from our readiness to confess. Honesty hides nothing—always open and transparent—it is grace in action. Besides, confession is the most appropriate response to God's graciousness. Nothing is hidden from Him. Confession happens in healthy families—it's known as "familial" confession and forgiveness.

In the setting of an earthly family, one would expect a son to ask his father to forgive him when he has done something that is offensive to his dad. It is obvious that his relationship with his father is not held together by his confessions; it is established and sustained by way of the family he was born to—confession or no confession, the family genetics remain unchanged.

Quite obviously, a Christian who offends his Father, yet never asks for forgiveness, can hardly be thought of as being sensitive. Thoughtless, yes; callous, yes; arrogant, yes; sensitive, no! But even in the rockiest of family relationships, family remains family—it is held together by blood!

Unlike the transformation of our spirits at rebirth, our bodies and souls were not transformed—if we had warts before we were born again, the warts are still there after rebirth. It is up to us, in partnership with the Holy Spirit, to cause our bodies and souls to fall into line with what has taken place in our spirits.

The reality of life in the kingdom is that our souls (minds) continue to be tempted by sin until the day we die. There is always a battle raging, and our minds are the battlefields where this warfare takes place. On a daily basis, we are confronted with a myriad of choices, and we don't always choose well. It doesn't have to be big blunders to be sin; the niggly irritations of our day to day relationships with others often get us into a whole heap of trouble. Do we fly off the handle, or do we take the trouble to understand why others behave the way they do?

Under which of these two scenarios are we more likely to succeed in these crucial battles: (a) when we are convinced that we stand accused by God, or (b) when we are convinced that we have been acquitted by Him? Secondly, are we more likely to have victory when (a) we are in fear of losing God's love, or (b) when we are secure in His love? The answers to these questions should be obvious.

Sadly, religion puts the onus upon us to hold our salvation together through confessing each and every sin. In other words, they have taken God's promise to *"never leave nor forsake"* us, to mean that He will leave us and forsake us except if we are able to keep up to date with our confessions and repentances. But when the buck is passed from God's almightiness to our puniness, we are in deep trouble! Surely we all know that humanity is too fickle to go the distance? And that's why salvation can neither be achieved nor sustained except by a Saviour. Much of religion still refuses to concede that salvation is not only established by redemption and atonement, but also sustained by the same redemption and the same atonement. It does not rest on how current and up to date we are with confessions. There just aren't any other scriptures to support religion's ideas on confession.

In this regard, the theological principle of having more than one witness in scripture to confirm the validity of a doctrine is simply ignored. This principle says that we cannot base a doctrine on one isolated scripture. The perceived message of any scripture must be confirmed and supported by other scriptures that concur with its perceived message before it can be accepted as a Christian doctrine. The notion that God only forgives a believer's sin after it has been confessed, cannot be corroborated by other scriptures. That being the case, we must consider the possibility that religion has misunderstood the context of 1 John 1:9 and therefore misconstrued its meaning.

Religion would also have us "plead" for forgiveness. But we are not instructed to do this. John makes it perfectly clear that *"there is someone to plead for* (us) *before the Father"*. That someone is Jesus! But religion has got us convinced that His pleading is not enough. In order for religion to validate its existence, it must put more weight upon our efforts than upon God's. Sadly, this malpractice depreciates the finished work of the cross, and cancels the promises of God. We have an advocate who takes care of all "pleading". To plead for our Heavenly Father's forgiveness would be tantamount to snubbing Jesus who has promised to take care of this requirement for us. If it were not for His commitment, we wouldn't have a snowball's hope in hell.

No! There is not even the slightest hint in 1 John 1:9 that we should plead for forgiveness. In the face of the Blood Covenant, I cannot imagine that we are required to plead for anything from God, but if there is something, it is certainly not forgiveness—that is a done deal. God is more willing to forgive than we are to be forgiven. This is made obvious by the painful lengths that Jesus went to in order to make our forgiveness possible. Never mind pleading for forgiveness, there isn't even the slightest suggestion in 1 John 1:9 that we are required to "ask" for forgiveness. All that John calls on us to do is to confess or agree with God concerning our sin. We are simply to agree with what He said about our sin—namely that it is wrong and that we should desist from continuing with it. But more than that, we acknowledge that it has already been atoned for by Jesus some two thousand years ago.

Paul was pretty angry with the Galatians when he discovered that they were trying to stay saved by some means other than grace. *"Are you so foolish? Having begun in the Spirit, are you now being made perfect by the flesh?"* (Gal 3:3). We continue to see this error being perpetrated in our day and age.

There are not two different kinds of grace—one for getting saved, and another for staying saved. The same grace that saved us, when we had nothing to bring to the party, is the grace that keeps us saved, because we still have nothing to bring to the party. After all, what can we possibly offer? "Filthy rags?" Is that all we have to offer? Nothing that we are capable of bringing can help the blood of Jesus be more effective than it already is. Anything added to the *"finished"* work of the blood of Jesus does not prop it up; it cancels it! In Paul's words, *"Christ is become of no effect unto you"* (Gal 5:4 KJV).

Hebrews 10:10 makes it perfectly clear that we are made holy once, and that this one time is enough to keep us holy for all time and eternity. *"...made holy by the sacrifice of the body of Jesus Christ once for all time"*. In verse 14 the writer goes on to say, *"For by that one offering he perfected forever all those whom he is making holy"* (KJV). It took one single grand act of atonement for us to be *"perfected forever"* and always. Forever is a very long time! And because it is promised to last forever, there can be no interruption to it. If it were possible for our sins to interrupt our perfect standing with God, then the writer of Hebrews lied. If our reluctance or neglect to repent could interrupt it, then what does that say about the writer's integrity? Fortunately, we are not dependant on the writer's integrity; we depend on the integrity of the Spirit of God who moved the writer to promise that we are *"perfected forever"*, and therefore this statement is indisputable.

This verse clearly separates the two life changing occurrences, namely: *"perfection"* and *"making holy"*. The one is our perfect position before God and the other is the practical outworking of this perfect position in our day to day actions. These two concepts are vastly different. The one is established and unchangeable—it is *"forever"* the same; while the other is progressive and ever improving—a process of being *"made holy"*—an on-going process of character moulding. Here again, this is not something that we are required to do; it is something that the Holy Spirit has undertaken to do for us. Of course, for this to take place, He needs our submission and co-operation.

Our positional perfection is immediately and permanently established at rebirth, while our behaviour changes gradually—it changes at the pace that we are prepared to yield and submit to the guidance of the Holy Spirit. Despite knowing and accepting this, believers are nevertheless often duped into believing that sanctification is the part that we must play, but this is far from the truth—this verse makes it perfectly clear that it is *"He"* who *"is making us holy";* certainly not us! But He can only do this when we get out of the way and stop trying to do it for Him. It's not about doing; it's all about surrendering. As humans, we are apt to avoid surrendering to something that is imposed upon us, as is the case with law, but readily crumble into submission when loved. Unconditional love has a way of making the thought of surrendering appealing.

Whosoever Jesus, in his infallibility has made perfect, cannot be made imperfect by mankind's fallibility. If our actions could make us imperfect, we would have to admit that our actions carry more weight than His actions—an assertion that is not at all clever. Just in case we didn't quite get it, the writer takes it a step further in verse 17 by saying, *"I will never again remember their lawless deeds"* (KJV). *"Never again"* denotes eternal blamelessness. How dare we tag any conditions or exceptions to such an emphatic statement? Our right standing with God was not established by anything deserving that we did or did not do; it was established by God. And when He put us in right standing with Himself, He was fully aware that it would not bring our sinning to an end.

Seeing that, by our most excellent actions we were hopelessly incapable of saving ourselves, what in the world would make us think that God would expect us to stay saved by our flawed endeavours? No! In as much as we were incapable of making ourselves righteous to begin with, we are equally incapable of making ourselves righteous ever after. We should not be deluded—no one can attain God's holy standard—it is beyond the capacity of humanity.

Security that hinges on us being up to date with repentance is not at all secure. Nobody is ever entirely up to date; there is always a time lag. For some strange reason, we are prone to delay getting around to it. David murdered his most loyal of loyal allies for no other reason than that he lusted after the man's wife. Does sin come any more deplorable than that? Did he repent immediately? No! It took him two long years to get around to it.

They say that procrastination is the thief of time, and it is so, but it also steals so much more from us when repenting is delayed. It saps our peace, robs us of our joy, affects our health and sucks the vitality and fun out of what should be an abundant life—it is a relationship breaker, and it makes us miserable to be around. We often push repentance to the back of the queue, and have little regard for how self-destructive these delays can be. At any given moment, for the vast majority of believers, there is a backlog of un-repented sin. It is unthinkable to imagine that this would be salvation cancelling. Such a conclusion could only be drawn by those who do not understand that their state of justification and righteousness, received as a free *"gift"* at rebirth, stands unmoved and unaffected by their sin. How can sin possibly trump God's plan to annul sin? We did not get salvation by earning it and therefore cannot be expected to earn the right to keep it.

Sometimes we may even rationalise our sin by saying that it is not gross sin. But sin is not just heinous atrocities like adultery, rape and murder; it is also impatience, prejudice and intolerance. It is harbouring unspoken anger and irritation; it is the slightest disregard of the traffic code; it is spiteful and ungracious thoughts, even the ones we don't carry out; it is doing our religious duty by telling somebody that we love them, while secretly rejoicing in their misfortune, and so on and so on… Our motives are never entirely pure. Nobody ever manages to actually get entirely ahead of sin. And the moment we think we have got it licked, we hear God's words ringing in our ears, *"Filthy Rags"*!

There is nothing more crucial than our eternal destiny. It is unconscionable to imagine that a responsible God would carelessly entrust irresponsible people, who couldn't save themselves if they tried, with the responsibility of staying saved. He is too holy for that! Salvation simply cannot be held together with *"filthy rags"* and because so much of what we do is tinged with faulty motives, we can never be entirely up to date with repentance.

But doesn't God hate sin? He sure does! But He is fully aware that we have an innate propensity and penchant to continue sinning for the rest of our days—for this He has got us covered with mercy and grace. Besides letting us off the hook, His Holy Spirit has committed Himself to guiding us through a process of behavioural realignments. And He is fully aware that that process will not be completed during our sojourn on earth. But we can take heart—even our vilest sins cannot cancel the words of Hebrews 10:17—He will never record nor remember, and therefore never accuse nor judge us of our sins—end of story!

By imagining that Jesus' atonement requires our righteous making actions to keep it propped up, we are inferring that the atonement was incomplete and therefore Jesus cannot take all the glory—we end up stealing the glory for the part that we supposedly play. To deny that our atonement and redemption stand complete on their own, without our assistance, is to trivialise the work of the cross and to reduce the honour due to the one who hung on it. Jesus was dead serious when He declared that the work of our atonement was *"finished"*. Atonement was made and redemption was paid for in full and final settlement. Once redeemed, there is no further need to be slightly more redeemed from time to time.

We must make up our minds—either Jesus paid in full, or He just made a small down payment, relegating us to take care of the outstanding debt in a lifetime of instalment payments. We must decide—either His blood redeemed us totally and completely, or we were not redeemed at all!

Colossians 2:13 states, *"...having forgiven you all trespasses"*— every single one of them. Note that he did not say, "Having forgiven our pre-born again trespasses and the subsequent ones that we have gotten around to repenting of". The truth of the matter is that Jesus died prior to each and every one of our sins, so when He said *"all"*, He really meant *"all"*, from the moment of atonement on the cross, stretching all the way back in history to Adam, and extending all the way forward to the end of time. He included every sin that had not yet been committed, and then made this clemency available to whosoever will receive it. It seems that "un-extreme grace" has decided not to receive it. It is difficult to understand why anyone would settle for a lesser salvation than Jesus provided. He went to a lot of trouble to obtain it, only to have it spurned by the very ones for whom He suffered so much.

In 2 Corinthians 5:19, Paul said that God keeps no account of our sins. They are wiped from His memory—He cannot recall them. That being the case, it is obvious that somebody else is involved in keeping us conscious of our sins—there are no prizes for guessing who he is—he is better known as the *"accuser of the brethren"*.

Paul wrote the biggest chunk of the epistles. If confession was necessary to hold our salvation together, then one would have expected him to at least have made one tiny mention of it. He does not have a single word to say on the subject. Not in Romans; not in 1st and 2nd Corinthians; not in Galatians, Ephesians, Philippians, Colossians, 1st and 2nd Thessalonians, 1st and 2nd Timothy, Titus, Philemon or Hebrews of which he was possibly the writer. If successive confessions were a prerequisite, then we would have to conclude that Paul was in error and the gospel he preached was heresy. Quite obviously, to make such an assertion would be to make a blunder of heretic proportions.

Hebrews 9:28 says, *"He will come again but not to deal with our sins"* (NLT). The writer did not say that He will come again to deal with our sins with the exception of the ones that we have confessed and repented of. We have to seriously twist this verse to fit doctrinal boxes. Verse 26 says, *"He came once for all time, at the end of the age, to remove the power of sin forever"* (NLT). We did nothing to remove *"the power of sin"*, except that we received the finished work as a free gift—it was all Jesus' doing—all the praise belongs to Him alone! Note that He removed *"the power of sin forever"*. No amount of sin has the power to condemn us. For those who are in Christ, sin has been dealt with in full, for all time and eternity.

Would coming into the knowledge of such liberation cause us to want to sin more? If that is the case, it would demonstrate just how little religion has done to change our hearts. Unconditional love is hugely influential—with His kind of love upon us, ethically good choices become second nature to us. But sadly, for many believers, religion has had the last say—believers are not permitted to consider grace as a solution to their sin, and that leaves them to do battle with stuff that Jesus has already conquered on their behalf.

Jesus forgave the paralytic who was lowered through the roof, without so much as first getting a confession out of him. He did the same for the criminal on the cross. Jesus is the same yesterday, today and forever—He never changes. Many years earlier, Joel prophesied that whoever calls on the name of the Lord would be saved. He made this statement without qualification—let us take care not to put words into Joel's mouth by tagging anything onto them that he did not say.

"Extreme grace" does not for one moment suggest that we allow our sin to go by unnoticed. When we sin, rather than take Satan's bait and fall into guilt, condemnation and shame; we remind ourselves of the victory that Jesus has obtained for us to overcome that sin; always cognisant that, come what may, we remain the *"righteousness of God in Christ"*.

We turn to God in godly sorrow. What we have done is not consistent with who we are in Christ. Godly sorrow comes with a desire for change. Desire is not something that can be forced upon a person; it is a deep emotion called passion. God's passion for us arouses our passion for Him. To refuse to be sorry would be awfully ungracious on our part. In the light of such loving grace, how can we not be sorry?

The next question is, "Aren't we repenting when we turn to God?" Of course we are! That is exactly what repenting is. But our future is not secured by something as unreliable as our often shaky commitment to get around to repenting on a particular issue. Jesus took full responsibility for providing a reliable plan of salvation, and He has completed His assignment with aplomb.

Our prayer of repentance could conclude with something like, "Thank You Lord that there is no condemnation to those who are in Christ Jesus, and thank You for keeping our relationship perfectly intact by what you did for me and not by what I did for myself".

The words, *"There is therefore now no condemnation to those who are in Christ Jesus"*, do not only apply when we are up to date with confession, as if such a state were remotely possible; they apply every bit as much when we fail to do right and neglect to be current with repentance. Although our state of *"no condemnation"* commences instantly at rebirth; yet it soon becomes evident that this wonderful happening did not bring about an end to our sinning. Let's face it, there are many sins that never come to an end this side of eternity. Yet despite our fickleness, there is absolutely *"no condemnation"* upon us whatsoever.

If we were to suppose that our state of *"no condemnation"* expires when next we sin, then we must conclude that everybody loses their state of *"no condemnation"* a split second after receiving it. The mere notion of a continuously alternating state, vacillating between "condemnation" and *"no condemnation"* is insanity itself! If that were remotely possible, then every time that we manage to reinstate our position of *"no condemnation"* through repenting, it would soon be lost in the rough and tumble realities of everyday living. How crazy is that? No! The permanent state of *"no condemnation"* can be enjoyed by every believer, because of one thing, and one thing only—every believer is *"in Christ!"*

We say rather jokingly that Jesus gets out of the car when we break the speed limit. We infer that He leaves us when we sin, but this is not even remotely possible, because being *"in Christ"* makes us inseparable from Him. Just as tea cannot be separated from the water in a teapot; so it is for us when we are inseparably combined with Christ at rebirth; we are transformed into a commodity that is different to its former constituents, and this merged composite cannot be unscrambled.

Sin cannot trounce grace (Rom 5:20). In any given situation, there is always infinitely more grace than sin. Unholy people get more grace than supposedly "holy people". I say this rather tongue in cheek, because quite obviously, there are no such creatures as holy people on the face of the planet. We are all deficient in godliness, except of course for the *"gift"* of godliness that was imputed to us by God. God decided on righteousness by imputation, because it simply cannot be attained by any other means—it is either by grace or it remains *"filthy rags"* (Isa 64:6).

I do not speak of righteousness by imputation to excuse sin—they are Paul's words—grace does not merely excuse sin; it cures sin. Paul quotes David's prophetic words that the man is blessed *"to whom God imputes righteousness apart from works"* (Rom 4:6). Once this *"gift"* of *"righteousness apart from works"* has been bestowed on an individual, sin is never again imputed to that person. Two verses on, he reiterates, *"Blessed is the man to whom the Lord shall not impute sin"* (Rom 4:8). Who is the fortunate person referred to in this prophecy? It is every born again believer, from the most saintly to the least saintly. It is *"to him that does not work"* for his salvation (Rom 4:5). Righteousness by imputation is only for people who don't deserve it; they simply *"believe on him who justifies"* (Rom 4:5).

Sad to say, but religion is often responsible for keeping the cycle of sin turning. The reality is, that like fosters like. Preach against sin and reap sin. In 2 Corinthians 3:9, Paul calls the law the ministry of death. Jesus came to give us abundant life; we dare not contaminate that life with a consciousness of sin. In Romans 7:8, he says that *"Without the law sin is dead [the sense of it is inactive and a lifeless thing]"* (Amplified). In this verse it is clear, that not only are we freed from the law and from sin, but also freed from the *"sense"* or consciousness of sin. When righteousness is sought through law keeping, a consciousness of sin is awakened. But we are numb to the laws demands and take no instructions whatsoever from it—we have been disconnected from it so that we can be connected to the Holy Spirit who is infinitely more competent at producing holiness than the law could ever hope to be.

No longer do we allow the law to badger us with fatal alternatives—it can no longer hold a gun to our heads—it cannot force us to obey or be cursed! Jesus used "extreme grace" to bring an abrupt and complete end to it. He wants to have an intimate relationship with us, but instead of badgering us into it with the law of "do or die", He has chosen to coax us into it with love, and has graciously connected us to His Holy Spirit who gently guides us from within. He doesn't accuse or stand in judgement of us; He never scolds, but is always ready to encourage, guide and edify—He is ever with us, and His still small voice is loud enough to lift us out of the doldrums; to warn us of impending danger; to take us on to better things, and to remind us of His undying love for us.

Some would argue that if God the Father rebukes, then we can expect the same treatment from His Holy Spirit. But it is important to distinguish between "loving admonishments" and "judgemental condemnations". *As many as I love, I rebuke and chasten. Therefore be zealous and repent"* (Rev 3:19). God's admonishments emanate out of a deep sense of love for His cherished children—not out of a sense of indignation.

If sin is dead except where there is law, then we ought to distance ourselves from the law so that we do not arouse sin. It is a strange quirk of human nature to want to do the very things that are forbidden. As a child, I found the adventure of stealing fruit from our neighbour's trees to be more adventurous than eating fruit from our own trees. Why? Because it was forbidden, and that made the intrigue of it immensely exhilarating!

The law does not curb sin; it fosters sin! Take prohibition in the United States for example. In 1920 laws were enacted with the best of intensions. While trying to protect society from the disastrous effects of alcohol abuse, all it managed to do was to turn law-abiding citizens into criminals, making a mockery of the justice system and causing prohibited drinking to seem glamorous and fun. It made celebrities of thugs and brought the justice system to its knees. It became acceptable, no, even cool to dispense with social values and to engage in debauchery. Liquor consumption, and with it liquor abuse, sky rocketed, especially amongst the youth and women. Previously alcoholism was almost unheard of amongst women. Prohibition spelt the end of the conservative culture of America. Deep seated Christian values, that were the social norm of that time, gave way to the appeal of being risqué. The intrigue and excitement of breaking the law became more than socially acceptable; it became appealing!

Instead of improving society, it turned good honest law abiding citizens into dishonest law breakers. It put a shine on what was previously regarded as wrong. The police were no longer allies; they had become the enemy, and dodging the enemy became a national pastime. Scheming and cheating the system added a thrill to socializing. It turned "innocent" neighbourhood gangs into national crime syndicates, and with it, corrupted government officials.

With prohibition laws, the scourge of alcohol abuse did not wane; it flourished. It was Protestant Christians—the moralists of that era who campaigned for the introduction of this law. In their attempts to moralise society, they succeeded only in corrupting it.

The bottom line is that moral laws do not reduce sin; they incite sin. Legalism is out to get you—don't fall for its fraudulent offer of "holiness"—it is not even vaguely holy—it's a religious sham! Now grace is quite a different matter. God's love, expressed in mercy and grace, is infinitely more influential upon how we behave, than any law could ever hope to be!

NO CONDEMNATION

Can believers be condemned?

To indulge in self-condemnation is to defy Paul's statement that *"There is therefore now no condemnation to those who are in Christ Jesus"*. Although God bears no thoughts of condemnation towards us, we are not always as easy on ourselves—often turning on ourselves in self-accusation.

"I am never good enough," we disparage ourselves.

The original Greek, meaning of *"no condemnation to those who are in Christ"* is that for anybody who is *"in Christ"*, there is absolutely no possibility; not now, nor at any time in the future of being condemned by God. This scripture doesn't say that there is no condemnation to those who are up to date with repentance. It is aimed at all people who are *"in Christ"*—no matter whether pious or sinful; repentant or unrepentant. The truth is that even while in the very act of committing sin, there is still zero condemnation on those who are in Christ Jesus—a hard pill for pharisaic Christians to swallow.

The fact of the matter is that every individual upon the face of the earth is either *"in Christ"* or *"in sin"*. There is no getting around it—it is one or the other. A woman cannot be slightly pregnant. She is either pregnant or she is not. Similarly, there are no degrees to being *"in Christ"*. We can't be slightly *"in Christ"* and therefore can't be slightly in sin. For those who are *"in Christ"*, not even the sin they continue committing can reduce their "in Christ-ness". *"In Christ"* is a position and status that we were reborn into. It was established by the blood of Jesus; not by the level of our good intensions and sincere resolve to stay out of trouble. In as much as our best behaviour could not gain right standing with God; our worst behaviour cannot undo the right standing we have in Him.

At any given moment, every believer on the face of the planet is either doing something good or something bad. Or to put it another way: right now every believer, including you and me, are either doing *"sin"* or *"filthy rags"*. Each as bad as the other!

This is a catch 22 situation. The bottom line is that there is absolutely no possibility of holding our salvation together through sinlessness, law keeping or the current-ness of our repenting—it doesn't work that way. The status of being *"in Christ"*, having *"no condemnation"* and being the *"righteousness of God in Christ"* are continuous states of being, established by rebirth, and continuing into eternity, unhindered by the less than perfect choices that all believers make. We are either entirely *"in Christ"*, or we are entirely in sin. We are either eternally in *"no condemnation"*, or we are eternally condemned. We are either permanently the *"righteousness of God in Christ"*, or we are striving to be righteous yet never achieving it—God calls it *"filthy rags"*. Romans 3:12 is clear on this point: *"there is none who does good, no, not one"*. That being the case, we have only one hope, and that one and only hope is for us to be *"in Christ"*; a stable position that cannot be manufactured; it can only be imputed once in a lifetime. But once is enough, because it is permanently sustained for all time and eternity, not by personal effort or good behaviour, but by Christ Himself.

Believers may say with conviction that they are not into law keeping. But their self-condemnation belies their words—providing sufficient evidence of law keeping. Whether we live by Old Covenant law or by modern day legalism, a sense of guilt and condemnation is inevitable.

Although entirely contrary to redemption, yet we feel obliged to wallow in shame—we consider it our "religious duty". But feigned humility is false humility. Sadly, in belittling ourselves, we are belittling God's redeemed. How sad to reduce Christ's redemption to fit our small view of His goodness.

The Bible is clear, it says that no righteousness can come through keeping the law; all that it can produce is a consciousness of sin. But there is an answer for those who are determined to find true righteousness. We find that answer in Romans 3:21, *"now a righteousness apart from the law has been given to those who believe"* (KJV). Righteousness in God's sight does not come through living right; the one and only way to obtain it is through believing right. But then again, right believing produces right living without effort.

The glory of God is grace's closest ally. But in the absence of grace, there can be no glory. If we don't have the splendour of grace, what do we have? Nothing but a set of laws that consign us to guilt, and make us as intolerant as we believe God to be! Both Christians and non-Christians have to put up with our pious intolerances. Legalistic holiness makes us miserable to be around.

No self-respecting believer would turn to religion for belittlement—it is quite natural to expect edification from it. Yet, when religion doesn't live up to its promises, believers are often persuaded to try harder. There is always this sneaky suspicion at the back of our minds that we have not done enough. We press on and keep trying regardless—hoping against hope that our religious endeavours will eventually pay off. Sadly, religion is big on promises, but small on delivery—hopes are often dashed with unfulfilled promises.

How unfortunate—we could just as easily be luxuriating in grace. But for as long as we remain sceptical of the extremities of grace, we will have difficulty indulging in, and resting in, the peaceful serenity of the finished work of the cross. Dear Lord, how do I bring the importance of this point home? The cross is not just a vital doctrine of Christianity; it is Christianity! And the cross is as extreme as grace gets!

How unfortunate it is to miss out on God's best! Sadly grace and condemnation do not mix—it is like oil and water. We simply cannot have God's glory operating in our lives without embracing the glory of His grace—the glory of God is packaged in grace, and grace comes without the slightest hint of condemnation.

To the extent that we manage to rid ourselves of a consciousness of guilt; to that extent we experience the supernatural glory of God. There are signs and wonders; miracles and healings; greater works than Jesus performed locked up and held imprisoned in our personal sense of guilt and shame. Without grace, the glory simply cannot come out.

How far does God's grace go? Is there a sin bigger than grace? To the same extreme extent that we feel condemned; the opposite extreme is actually true of us. No amount of unrighteousness in our lives can outweigh our perpetual state of the *"righteousness of God in Christ"*, period!

Whole mega ministries have been built on the shaky foundation of "Christian" performance. It's all about how much we have fasted; how much we have prayed; how much we have repented; how much we have pleaded; how much we have sacrificed. It is all about me, me and more of me! We regularly see these ministries tumble. They end up shipwrecked, in church splits, nervous breakdowns, divorce amongst leadership and all kinds of other spiritual tragedies. It is such a common catastrophic charismatic phenomena that it doesn't surprise us anymore—it is almost expected.

The moment that performance outweighs grace on the scales of religious expectations, the scales tilt in favour of the flesh. It becomes an exchange of God's ability for our inability—God's limitless almightiness for our feebleness. When we are not plugged into grace, we are not plugged into God's provisions; we are plugged into our own limited capacity to provide for ourselves. Unless we are walking in the glory of grace, we are walking in the frailty of the flesh.

Whether it be Mosaic law, denominational law, the high expectations of church leaders, or even unspoken religious pressure, it is all the same. The problem is that by giving more prominence to our pious accomplishments, we give less prominence to God's gracious accomplishments. We revel in the glory of our achievements, when we ought to be revelling in the glory of His achievements. Conversely, with grace, God gets all the glory, because it is all His doing and none of ours. Fulfilling law is self-honouring, while living by grace is God-honouring.

One of our previous senior pastors was extremely passionate about holiness. He took repentance to another level; insisting that it be done publicly in front of the congregation. One of His holiness endeavours was to get our youth to promise before God and the congregation to remain sexually pure until married—a commendable ideal. Then he went on to spoil it all by sealing their promises—proclaiming dire consequences for failing to keep their pledges—declaring an Old Testament curse upon any who would dare to break their covenant.

Sadly, this had the immediate effect of bringing these innocent young believers into all kinds of self-condemnation. Instead of purifying their relationships, he succeeded only in encouraging the proliferation of sexual desires for each other. The effect that this had on their relationships with God was devastating to say the least. His associate pastors were left to deal with the aftermath of the radioactive fallout, as one after another, the youth succumbed to the radioactive sickness of guilt and condemnation. This pastor made no bones about it; he was fiercely opposed to "extreme grace".

Then came the devastating news. At the very height of his strong demands for holiness, he disappeared, leaving the elders with a lot of explaining to do. Sheepishly, they disclosed the details of the tragic "soap opera" like events to the congregation. This "virtuous" senior pastor was having an affair with one of his lady pastors. With his marriage in tatters, this nationally admired church leader vanished with his lover, bringing his highly acclaimed public ministry to a shameful end, and destroying the lady pastor's ministry to boot.

One of America's sternest moralistic televangelists made it his business to crack down on immorality in the church. He took every opportunity to expose sin in Christianity. He was responsible for exposing the sexual impropriety of one of America's biggest TV Channel founders, and in the process shut the channel down permanently. He also uncovered other indiscretions that ensured the incarceration of this man on a lengthy prison sentence. The televangelist wielded the avenger's sword of holiness, smiting unholy compromise wherever he came across it. In his words, he described the channel's founder as, "A cancer on the body of Christ." In the name of holiness, he went on to destroy other ministries, and in his religious indignation, campaigned for the banning of the sale of pornography in convenience stores—a commendable crusade.

Then tragedy of tragedies! This very same "paragon of virtue" and self-appointed moral policemen was himself caught in a compromising position with a prostitute. As though this was not embarrassing enough, he was found to be in possession of pornography. As it turned out, he was a regular customer of the prostitute. What a shock to the Pentecostal community!

He was repentant, but the public were left to wonder whether his remorse was genuine, or merely a ploy to save his multi-million dollar evangelical empire. With tears streaming down a tortured face, he apologised on television, begging his family and followers to forgive him. His outward display of remorse, contriteness and repentance was very touching. I found it difficult to hold back my tears as my heart went out to the man. Sadly, it wasn't long after this that he was found in a similar compromise with prostitution once again. Clearly, his repentance did not stick.

This man was a prominent "holiness" preacher. Quite obviously, his heart had not been touched nor changed by grace. His ministry had often been marked with public outcries of "holy" indignation. Although he often sang about grace, his pharisaic denunciations told a very different story—his "holy" accusations belying his songs of grace. Not even if he had had a flashing neon sign above his pulpit spelling out, "I stand for un-extreme grace", could he have made his un-graciousness any clearer—his proclamations of "holy" outrage said it all!

From the hard line that he took against those who preached "extreme grace", it was obvious that he did not see grace as a solution to his own sin. Grace had the power to conquer his iniquitous ways, but was of little value to him while he so fervently campaigned against "extreme grace". God loved him just as deeply in his most dreadful sin as He loved him when he was at his godliest best. But without grace his efforts to shake his penchant for secret lewdness remained weak and ineffective.

God's unfaltering love is the power behind "extreme grace". There is infinite life changing love and acceptance available to us, but we are unlikely to access help from a concept that we have been cautioned to avoid. With such strong opposition to anything that doesn't fit neatly into religious moulds, it is not at all surprising to encounter grace scepticism whenever the subject of grace is broached.

To be so completely loved when we don't deserve it, is heart altering stuff! Who knows how this man's battle with pornography and prostitution may have turned out if he had understood the life changing implications of God's gracious embrace? God's kind of love is extremely honouring—nothing is more edifying, and edified people make better choices in life. One thing is certain; the gospel of performance that he so zealously championed, failed to change his own heart and his heart let him down when it really counted.

The doctrine of holiness by performance is flawed! Our hearts do not change simply because we manage to master our behaviour. Hearts are moved by unconditional love, and when this happens, behavioural changes follow without effort. No matter how "holy" we may appear, unloved hearts are troubled hearts, and troubled hearts produce troubled behaviour.

When push came to shove, the message this man so zealously proclaimed was put to the test and found wanting. It is clear that the brand of holiness and repentance he so passionately preached is not workable! He was powerless to deal with outward iniquities, while his heart remained entangled in them.

The very same "sloppy agape" and "greasy grace" that he had so vehemently slated, could well have been his closest ally.

After betraying the trust of his family and millions of loyal followers, one can only imagine how low he must have sunk into self-blame and shame. But guilt, remorse and self-condemnation do not free us from sin—these self-destructive emotions hold us hostage to sin. Self-condemnation is one of our most terrifying foes—self-loathing is fertile ground for the cultivation of sin—only God's kind of agape love can lift us out of it.

Rob Rufus says we are to, *"Condemn condemnation; accuse accusation; grab guilt by the throat; get out the religious boat and float wearing our Father's glory coat!"*

THE PERFECT CHRISTIAN

Believers have wonderful ideals; more kindness, more tolerance of the faults of others, more generosity, more of the works of Jesus etc. As commendable as these are, there is a trap worth bearing in mind. It's the trap of self-retribution. When we fail to meet the commendable standards that we set for ourselves, we tend to turn on ourselves, at times beating ourselves half to death with self-condemnation.

Satan, that snake in the grass and *"accuser of the brethren"*, does not have to accuse us when we are doing his work for him. We defeat ourselves with our own misguided self-accusations. If he can keep us focused on our inadequacies, our attention will be diverted from God's grace and His glory within us. No glory, no miracles—a form of godliness that denies the power thereof—job done! Without Satan having to lift a finger, we have disenfranchised ourselves. And it all started with something as innocent as raising our "Christian" bar. If we fail often enough, we may even come to accept failure as our lot in life.

Don't get me wrong, idealism can be used to encourage and uplift. But when it is used to shame rather than inspire, it has the opposite effect. Religion endeavours to edify and uplift, but often places more weight on believers' shortcomings than on their right standing. There is no fun in being put down. We don't need religion to convince us of our deficiencies—every person on the face of the planet is deficient in one way or another—at least before grace is factored in!

Healthy idealism is not the problem, but when idealism is used to show us how poorly we measure up, it engenders a sense of unworthiness, which can so easily lead to self-blame. Often religion does not afford its followers the privilege of a relaxed life of peace and contentment—it cannot accept us as we are—it must always force change upon sincere seekers. But we do not truly change simply because we have been pressured into doing so. It takes love to effect real change at heart level.

Religion has a lot to say on the subject of peace and contentment, but the required level of performance to obtain these prised ideals, is the very thing that distances us from them. How can we be content when we are punishing ourselves for failing to accomplish what is expected of us? The reality of the matter is that we will fail to meet the standards that religion requires of us—it is not optional; it comes with the territory—all people are afflicted with the frailty of their humanity.

Jesus was more impressed with the calm relaxed attitude of Mary than with the driven-ness of Martha. Martha wasn't doing anything wrong; she was doing good, unselfishly serving others with kindness. But as selfless as her ideals were, her obsession with them caused her to fall into the trap of judgementalism. She criticized Mary for not meeting her high expectations. It wouldn't surprise me if she was just as hard and condemnatory on herself. But Jesus was not impressed. He said *"But one thing is needed, and Mary has chosen that good part, which will not be taken away from her"* (Luk 10:42). What was this one thing that Jesus found so commendable in Mary? Was it her service to Jesus or was it her appreciation of His service to her?

Have we fallen prey to the demands of religion and become performance junkies, or have we entered into the place of rest where Jesus is doing the serving?

"Jesus serving me? Surely not?" Yes Jesus serves you, and it gives Him enormous pleasure to do so! Jesus said, *"The Son of Man did not come to be served, but to serve"* (Mar 10:45).

"In that case, does it follow that we cease to serve Him?" Certainly not! The question is, "Are we serving to be rewarded, or responding to His love with our love? Are we under the impression that our performance initiates His performance?" In reality, it is not our performance that initiates His performance; His performance is initiated by His love for us—all He requires of us is to believe, trust, love, and relax in His loving embrace. After all, wasn't it He who started this glorious romance? Dashing about to do this and that religious duty can so easily breed a sense of "spiritual" smugness.

Why did God go to the trouble of creating us? He created all things for His pleasure and that includes you and me. Knowing the pleasure He gets out of having us around is sufficient reason for us to take pleasure in being with Him. We respond to His pleasure with, *"Thou art worthy, O Lord, to receive glory and honour and power: for thou hast created all things, and for thy pleasure they are and were created"* (Rev 4:11 KJV).

Restfulness and trust go hand in hand—faith is incubated in the tranquil serenity of knowing the depths of God's love for us—He demonstrates His love in acts of graciousness!

Imagine how empty your wife's love would be if she only gave it to get something out of you. When she gives that special gift to you, instead of feeling loved, it would cause you to be suspicious of her, wondering what she was surreptitiously trying to inveigle out of you. In other words, her service would be nothing other than a sneaky form of manipulation—putting the squeeze on you—trying to obligate you to her whims. This is better known as the spirit of Jezebel—another Bible word for it is witchcraft.

It sounds so devilish doesn't it? Yet believers often indulge in it when they need something badly enough from God. They do stuff to obligate Him to bless them. When things are not going well for us, we may resort to turning up our level of "Christian" performance in the hope that He will appreciate it and reward us. This distorted notion manifests when we get the covenants mixed up. Sadly, wherever there is a blend of Old and New Covenants, there is a bad blend; it's how we forfeit grace and bring Christ to nought in our lives (Gal 5:4).

In reality, we do not need to put God under any kind of obligation to do anything for us; He has already placed Himself under obligation in terms of an unbreakable covenant; it is a one sided covenant to bless and favour us. He is not looking for any other inducements from us to force His hand. He has committed Himself to serving us; He doesn't expect us to give Him any other reason to do so. His love for us is reason enough.

How do we participate in His generosity? It takes nothing more than childlike faith—it's a matter of believing Him to be true to His word. When He says that He loves us unconditionally, we can indulge ourselves in that knowledge.

Yes, He has given us spiritual laws such as declaring blessings and sowing seeds towards an expected end, but we should not confuse these wonderful kingdom principles with the thought that our performance earns favours.

Could we have gotten this whole servant thing back to front? The truth is that Jesus does not relate to us as servants, but as friends. *"No longer do I call you servants ... but I have called you friends"* (Joh 15:15). Sure we serve the Lord, but let's not kid ourselves; we are only serving in response to His service to us. We didn't go to the cross for Him; He went there for us.

Who is serving who? It was not the disciples who washed Jesus' feet; it was Jesus who washed the disciples' feet.

God is not glorified by what we can boastfully say that we have done for Him; He is glorified by what we allow him to do for us. If we want to glorify Him, then we need to allow Him to serve us. *"Human hands can't serve his needs—for he has no needs. He himself gives life and breath to everything, and he satisfies every need there is"* (Act 17:25 NLT). It is not we who satisfy every need there is; it is He who satisfies every need there is. Let us glorify Him more by allowing Him to serve us more.

God said, *"If I were hungry, I would not mention it to you, for all the world is mine and everything in it. Trust me in your times of trouble, and I will rescue you, and you will give me glory."* (Ps 50:

12&15 NLT). How do we give Him glory? This verse is clear—we give Him glory when we trust Him to rescue us. Again it is He who offers to serve us.

Even at the second coming, He will still be serving us. *"He himself will seat them, put on an apron, and serve them as they sit and eat"* (Luk 12:37 NLT).

"You have got to be kidding Jesus—aren't you the King of Glory—don't You have myriads of servants at Your beck and call—are You seriously going to serve us in heaven?" For the religious mind this is pushing the envelope a bit too far. Religion has had us on the hop, but then again, religion is not God's idea.

"For since the world began, no ear has heard and no eye has seen a God like you, who works for those that wait for him! You welcome those who cheerfully do good, who follow Godly ways." (Isa 64:4-5 NLT). My goodness! The creator of the entire universe works for the likes of you and me!

How fortunate it is to be under *"no condemnation"* from God. Yet, we often find ourselves unwittingly undoing this wonderful privilege—it happens when we allow ourselves to slip into self-condemnation. The truth is that people do not live in reality; people live in what they perceive reality to be. If in reality, we are not condemned, yet perceive ourselves to be condemned, we will not be able to indulge in what it means to be free of condemnation. We end up moping about in doom and gloom instead of blissfully resting in God's divine love and acceptance. There is nothing restful about condemnation; nether is there any joy in it!

Mankind is the pinnacle of God's creation—an incredibly wondrous work in itself. Yes, mankind fell into sin, but that condition was rectified; not by the creature, but by the Creator—we have naught to boast of! Those who have received God's atonement for sin are just as blameless as their Creator in His sight. To Him, it is as though they have never put a foot wrong. What a disservice we offer our Creator when we belittle His marvellous creation with self-condemnation. And then we take belittlement to an even darker level as we wallow in our shame. Our self-despisement does not only reflect poorly on us, it also reflects poorly on our Redeemer.

Sadly, religion must accept responsibility for leading many of its followers into the self-destructive gloom of self-condemnation. Religion has created an idol. What is the name of that idol? "The perfect Christian" is its name. When we are led to believe that we don't measure up to what's expected of us, we find more reason to despise ourselves and end up living under a cloud.

It's like women's magazines that portray the western ideal of a perfect female form. In their glossy pages, flawed complexions are airbrushed out with all kinds of digital wizardry to make them appear flawless. All the same, many women measure themselves against these illusions, and in doing so, find reason to despise their bodies. In reality no one can measure up. The illusions on the pages may appear to be perfect, but they are far from real. Is there any wonder that there is so much self-loathing going on?

According to Psychologist Carl Rogers, "The personality is composed of both the "Real Self" and the "Ideal Self". Our Real Self is who we actually are, while our Ideal Self is the person we would prefer to be. The Ideal Self is an idealized version of ourselves, created out of what we have gleaned from our personal experiences, the demands of society, and what we admire in our role models".

"Ideal Self" means different things to different people. For as long as their ideals remain unfulfilled, they have reason for discontent. Christians are inclined to form these ideals from the picture of perfection often painted from pulpits. When our "Real Self" does not measure up to our idealized image, we are inclined to be dissatisfied with our lives and consider ourselves to have missed the mark and to have failed God.

When religion gets caught up in fostering holiness at the expense of grace, it unwittingly aids and abets *the accuser of the brethren* in creating holy standards that are humanly speaking unattainable. Although we are not naturally equipped to attain them; God has provided the wherewithal—He calls it grace!

When idealisms come without grace, rather than edify, they disparage. Being less than our idealised image can foster low self-esteem and inferiority complexes that easily regress into antisocial behaviour. When we stoop to self-loathing, loathing others soon follows. In modern day vernacular, grace "cuts slack"—it gives leeway and understanding. When we cannot cut ourselves any slack, we cannot cut anyone else any slack. When we can't let ourselves off the hook, we don't let others off the hook either. We become pedantic, unforgiving, unbending—expecting them to hold to our opinions; have difficulty accommodating their differences; show more respect for our opinions than for people. Our intolerances, though concealed in niceties, ultimately show through, often in embarrassing ways.

Rather than lifting us, our "Ideal Self" pulls us down, and this brings about another behavioural dysfunction. We resort to punishing ourselves; thinking that feeling bad about ourselves would somehow make up for our deficiencies. But what we get for our trouble is an ever worsening self-image that manifests in cynicism, crustiness and criticism. It can even devolve into outright hostility. Our attitudes become harsh and overbearing; we become unreasonable and demanding; we get a sense of being out of control; our discontent makes us unhappy, and we end up taking others down with us.

The danger is that we may come to accept the curve balls that come our way as though they are our just deserts, and welcome the bum hand life deals us, as though we deserve nothing better. Next, we cease to expect the best from life, and fail to stand in faith. In the process, our intimate social relationships take a knock, and at times suffer irreversible damage. Could this be a contributing factor to the high divorce rate in the church?

Sadly many believers do not consider grace to be a force for change—they cannot accept that grace is sin defeating. Instead, religion uses guilt to manipulate and coerce followers into "holiness". This mal-practice, borrowed from the Old Covenant, has no place in Christianity.

Christian perfectionism is a bondage akin to legalism. When we can't live up to the "Christian standard", we turn on ourselves, punishing ourselves with derogatory self-talk.

We often hear believers talk about being "hard on themselves" as though they are proud of inflicting guilt upon themselves. They find it difficult to allow themselves the luxury of believing that God continues to love His children when they miss the mark. Their self-denigration makes them miserable to be around. They cannot bring themselves to accept, that as much as God hates sin, He is unfazed by their penchant for it.

The religious practise of inflicting guilt and condemnation, only succeeds in producing the precise opposite of what it aims to achieve. Under an ominous cloud of self-loathing, how can we possibly keep Jesus' commandment to love ourselves; let alone others.

Our lack of esteem for ourselves robs us of peace and contentment, and wrings the last drop of confidence out of our faith. When we believe that we don't measure up to God's expectations, we find it difficult to expect anything good from Him. Low self-esteem immobilises faith.

A friend of mine fell into the trap of self-condemnation. It took him to the lowest ebb of his life, but the church had no answers for his sorry condition—in fact, all that the church could offer him was more self-loathing. He turned to psychology, but he was so down on himself that the psychologist could do nothing for him. In sheer exasperation, the psychologist eventually gave up and referred him to a Jewish Rabi, psychologist.

The Rabi asked him to tell his story. He began to berate himself—a non-stop barrage of self-condemnation flowed from his lips. At first the Rabi let him ramble on with his self-denigration. And then he did something quite unexpected. While my friend was still midsentence, in full flight of slating himself, the Rabi embraced him. My friend doggedly did his best to finish his self-condemnatory story, but was so touched by the Rabi's extravagant display of unconditional love that he broke down and wept—his crying seemed to come from deep within—he fell to the floor in a heap, and sobbed his heart out. This cathartic experience of unconditional acceptance and love was a giant stride towards healing his guilt warped soul.

If the feeble attempt of a Rabi to give unconditional love achieved this much good for a self-despising individual, how much more good would the perfect unconditional love of our most Holy Father achieve?

This might be an extreme example of damage wrought by religious perfectionism, but I feel sure that we have all experienced it to some degree. It is so prevalent in religion that it is not reckoned to be evil. In fact, condemnatory "holiness" preaching is often held in high regard. But this kind of preaching cannot touch us nor change us; only God's unconditional love can do that. When believers live under a cloud of guilt and shame, you can be quite certain that they have not come to understand that there is absolutely *"no condemnation"* hanging over their heads.

My friend's story is not too different to the story Jesus told of the prodigal son. His father was not looking for perfection in him—his son's sin and blatant disregard of the family's high principles did not faze him in the least bit. He continued to love him in the same fatherly way as though he had never put a foot wrong. To us, his waywardness was inexcusable, but to his father, nothing, not even his son's darkest sins could change the intensity of his love for him. Ultimately, it was his father's unconditional love that won the day. So much more is achieved by love—nothing in the world can change a life in the wonderful way that love of the unconditional kind can.

Life in the Spirit is delightful! That being the case, why do believers seek comfort elsewhere? Not purely in the iniquity of downright sin, but in wallowing in sin's aftermath of guilt and shame. We all know that there is no fun in indulging in guilt and condemnation—it leads to stress, anxiety, fear, worry, panic attacks, despair and desperation.

Believers can't be blamed for being down on themselves. It is difficult to be upbeat after been religiously bullied. When they are led to believe that the Holy Spirit is responsible for accusing them, what chance is there that they will want to entrust themselves to His care. Sadly, with this paradigm, the *"accuser of the brethren's"* accusations are often mistakenly attributed to the Holy Spirit.

One cannot know what is hidden behind the smiling faces of the congregation. Then, when they are not smiling and looking the part of happy Christians, preachers have been known to ask, "If you are happy in the Lord, why don't you tell your faces?" In reality, the expressions on their faces are a perfect reflection of their religion. If they really had the abundance that Jesus promised, the joy of it would show up on their faces without coaxing.

While we are feeling bad about ourselves, there is little chance of moving in the glory. When we feel that it is our duty to God to despise ourselves for our shortcomings—we cannot bring ourselves to enjoy the abundant life that Jesus promised. We feel that we must be hard on ourselves for eating too much, praying too little, giving too little, procrastinating etc. Each believer holding to his or her own reasons for loathing himself or herself.

How does Satan attack God? He cannot touch His impeccable self-esteem, so he attacks the self-esteem of His children. Satan does not have to do very much to convince believers that they have missed the mark. When we are low on self-esteem, self-retribution kicks in and Satan's work is done. The less we like ourselves, the shorter our fuses. The more we dislike ourselves, the weaker our resistance to Satan's diabolical plan to bring us to ruin.

Satan is powerless against Christ, so he targets His body, and that's you and me. But he is powerless except to influence those who lack the knowledge of their changeless state of righteousness in Christ. He cannot afford for saints to discover that they are without blemish. It would shut the door on his accusations. And without accusations, he cannot intimidate.

Grace and religion are poles apart. Grace does not use idealism to shame us into holiness; it uses love, and love is edifying enough to inspire us to come up higher, to a place of acceptance and rest, where God's desires for us are accomplished without effort!

MORAL POLICEMEN

Who do I answer to?

Wherever you find legalism you find self-appointed moral policemen. When they step into this role, they step out of grace. Grace has nothing to contribute to the dubious practice of legalism—ungraciousness is out of character with God. The spirit of the Pharisee is just as much alive and well in religion today as it was in Jesus' time! And in the same way that the Pharisees of old could not see error in legalism; so it is in our day and age.

These spiritual sheriffs adopt personal responsibility for keeping their flocks pure, so when sin befalls their congregants, they take personal blame and construct all kinds of moral fences in the form of more moral rules—calling for more accountability—anything to hold the moral fibre of their congregations together. They resist the message of grace, thinking that it would dismantle their moral fences. These policemen have a lot to say about who should or should not be listened to or read etc—they must prevent their flocks from discovering freedom in grace, lest the "grace heretics" cause them to slip from "holiness" into licence.

With all the accountability structured into religious institutions, one would think that it would be enough to contain the proliferation of sin. But restrictiveness has proved to be thoroughly ineffective—sin continues—often secretly. Grace cannot be blamed for this sad state of affairs—sin was in the church long before the re-emergence of the kind of grace that Paul so passionately championed.

The grace message does not promote sin; to the contrary, it is God's way of dealing a deathly blow to sin. Long before the liberating message of grace was restored to the church, church leaders' marriages were falling apart, and sin was at work in their congregations. The message of grace cannot be blamed for what religion failed to do. If change doesn't happen at heart level, it doesn't happen at all! Unless our hearts are captured by God's love, we have no more than a good moral code—just another world religion. How sad to live by a gospel stripped of glory. Many have settled for ineffectiveness. Clearly, a gospel lacking grace, is no gospel at all!

Grace does not put heavies on believers; it lifts burdens from their shoulders—unlike the heavy handed words often used by religion to frighten people into "godliness". Grace has the answer, but it cannot carry out its life altering assignment when it is being drowned out by voices of guilt and condemnation.

It is impossible to police believers and to love them at the same time. Apostolic religious shepherding structures have failed to contain sin. Nobody has been called to the dubious business of meddling in other peoples' affairs, and nobody is expected to allow themselves to be manipulated by religiously exalted father figures.

We are called to be witnesses. In a court of law, a witness is not permitted to offer an opinion, an instruction, an accusation or a judgement; he may only relate the details of what he personally witnessed. If he dares to tell more, the prosecutor or Counsel for the defence will object and the judge will sustain the objection. We ought to be making ourselves the bearers of the message that we have personally received, and keep our hands from meddling. It is God's business to change hearts; not ours.

How does condemnation affect us?

- We feel that we are not doing enough.
- We feel insecure.
- We lack confidence in prayer and before men.
- The heavens appear to be as brass.
- We tend to avoid God.
- We feel estranged from Him.
- We turn to escapism to avoid facing up to our failures.
- We get a distorted impression of the loving character of God.
- It leads to a defeated and depressed state of mind in which sin is easily incubated.
- We take our frustrations out on others.
- Our shame causes us to want to shame others.
- Our lack of self-esteem causes us to esteem others less.

Condemnation is a bad paymaster. God is not responsible for it—all the blame lies with *"the accuser of the brethren"*—it is his job description. Most of his fiery darts are attacks on our integrity. When we fall into guilt and condemnation, we are conceding defeat and handing Satan victory on a silver platter. We are supposed to block his darts with the shield of faith and go on the offensive with the sword of the Spirit; declaring that we are the *"righteousness of God in Christ"*. *"And they overcame him by the blood of the Lamb and by the word of their testimony"* (Rev 12:11). We defeat Satan's accusations against us by declaring our testimony that our sins are covered by *"the blood of the Lamb"*. This is what the believer's confession is!

Satan would have us believe that we have overstepped the mark and therefore must plead for more atonement. He doesn't mind us doing this—it is further proof that we don't understand our blood bought privileges. He enjoys it when we look for security in our actions rather than in our redemption. Satan is out to keep us ignorant of our perpetual right standing—he cannot afford to risk us discovering that our past, present and future sins are entirely covered by *"the blood of the lamb"*.

Of course, we ought to repent whenever our conduct falls short of our righteous standing—repentance is better than remorse. But it is not our conduct that holds our salvation together—salvation, by its very nature, cannot be attained nor sustained by anybody other than a Saviour—that's why it is called salvation!

When the woman caught in adultery was brought before Jesus, rather than condemn her, He exposed sin in the hearts of her pharisaic accusers. The religious Pharisees of our day and age are up to the same inexcusable judgemental nonsense. But it is not the way of Jesus to accuse.

Religion ties us up in the knots of do's and don'ts. It misuses Old Covenant requirements in its mistaken quest to invoke New Covenant promises. The outcome of this bad mix brings about a very opposite outcome to what is desired. Failure is inevitable; it cannot be avoided—without the help of grace, we are not equipped to live up to religion's impossible standards. Like the Pharisees of old, each religious stream tacks on their own list of additional requirements. They do this despite Paul's many warnings—to add to grace is to cancel grace! Grace plus anything else, equals nothing at all! Grace plus nothing at all, equals everything!

Legalistic blends of the gospel are proclaimed with the best of intentions, and before we know it, we have become enslaved to a regime of religious performance. The unfortunate outcomes of bowing to these religious requirements, must be hidden from us. We needlessly bear the burdens that Jesus would bear for us. We do this and that, hoping that God would appreciate our religiosity. Sadly sincerity is not necessarily godliness!

Bible teachers who dilute the veracity of the gospel with legalism are not out to get us—they have our best interests at heart—they are God's chosen vessels. It is easy for them to get caught up in something religious, especially if it was passed down to them by trusted mentors.

In Philippians 3:2, Paul warns us to beware of evil doers—he calls them *"dogs"*. *"Dogs"* sounds like a good name for sinners, doesn't it? But He wasn't referring to sinners; he was referring to religious leaders who impose legalism on believers. Calling people dogs, is very strong derogatory language from the saintly Paul, but that's how strongly he felt about the diabolical nonsense that they were up to. He urges us to be on the alert for grace destroying *"dogs"*.

If you are anything like me, you will have difficulty using such strong language against well-meaning religious guardians. He must have felt very strongly about the matter to berate them so harshly. I prefer to regard them as innocently misled—dogs is too harsh a word for my liking—but then again, who am I to argue with Paul?

Could Paul have taken his lead from Jesus? This is what Jesus had to say to the legalists of His time, *"What sorrow awaits you teachers of religious law"; "Blind guides!"; "Blind fools!"; "Hypocrites! ... whitewashed tombs"; "Snakes! Sons of vipers!"* (Mat 23 NLT). "Wow! Are you serious Jesus?" And to think that these ungracious words were uttered by our gracious Lord. He never had a single ungracious word for the worst of the worst of offenders, yet had not a single word of grace for legalists. He could not have made His loathing of the ungodly practice of legalism any clearer! Jesus hates legalism with a passion!

It is time for the grace revolution to arise! The religious prison gates need to be torn down for God's wonderful people to be liberated from guilt motivated religious performance. It is time for ordinary believers to perform signs and wonders as a matter of routine, but they can't do it while under a cloud of religious condemnation.

Nothing could convince the woman caught in adultery to forsake her sinful way of life. A whole plethora of "righteously" justified insults from respected religious leaders had failed to influence her to change her sinful ways. But her obstinacy was about to meet its match. A showdown awaited her that would take her sinful defiance out at the knees. It wasn't a double barrelled shotgun blast of "righteous" indignation that floored her; it was just a few gentle words of grace, *"Neither do I condemn you; go and sin no more"* (John 8:11). By releasing her from condemnation, Jesus wasn't giving her more reason to sin; to the contrary, it was this gracious gesture that empowered her to overcome her sin—that's what unconditional love achieves in sinful humanity.

Jesus knows that little forgiveness invokes little love, and that much forgiveness invokes much love. He put it this way, *"To whom little is forgiven, the same loves little"* (Luk 7:47). The depth of our love for Him is in direct proportion to our understanding of the depth of His love for us. And nothing reveals His love more clearly than grace.

When Jesus desperately needed Peter's support, Peter deserted Him, repeatedly denying that he even knew his best Friend. Surely this is enough reason for Jesus to haul him over the coals, but that is not the way of Jesus. He handled it very differently. Jesus dealt with Peter's denial with love and understanding; restoring him—setting him free from condemnation. This non-judgemental act of grace elevated Peter from a yellow bellied, lily livered coward, into a mighty leader with a backbone of steel. It was not the law's accusations that propelled Peter into His world shaking ministry; it was grace. In partnership with the Holy Ghost, even Peter's shadow was enough to bring healing and deliverance to hurting humanity. Isn't His grace amazing? Sorry, there has got to be a better word than amazing! I am at a loss for superlatives to describe how amazing His grace is!

Can you imagine how differently things could have turned out for Peter if Jesus had chosen to dress him down for his shameful behaviour? He may well have turned into a guilt driven religious performance zombie, instead of the spiritual giant he became.

PERFORMING FOR FAVOUR

What must I do to benefit from the promises?

Consider this scenario: Your brother died and left you a small fortune in his will. What must you do to obtain your inheritance? Do a good deed to show the executor that you deserve it, or give him your banking details? Well this is exactly what has happened to you. Your older brother died and left you a fortune. Your older brother's name is Jesus.

New Testament promises are bequests, not rewards, yet religion would have us qualify for them with all kinds of religious gymnastics. Who is responsible for misleading believers? It all started in the Garden of Eden. Adam was tricked into believing that he could become like God if he performed for it. He did not have to eat from *"the tree of the knowledge of good and evil"* to become like God—He was already like Him—within the confines of his humanity of course. He was made in God's image, and had the living breath of God's Spirit within him.

Do you recognise what *"the tree of the knowledge of good and evil"* symbolises? There is another religious symbol that also reveals knowledge of good and evil. It is the law! Both of these symbols make us conscious of our sins. Fortunately, we are no longer subjected to nor controlled by the knowledge of good and evil, neither from the forbidden tree, nor from the now forbidden law. Christ redeemed us from the law's power to curse and condemn. The purpose of the law is not to bring us holiness—it can only find fault (Rom 3:20).

If we are under the impression that the law was given to teach people how to conduct themselves, then how do we explain what took place under its jurisdiction? Sin abounded all the more! Paul gave a very different explanation of the law's purpose. He said, *"The law entered that the offence might abound"* (Rom 5:20).

"Why, then, was the law given? It was given ... to show people their sins" (Gal 3:19 NLT). But thankfully, God does not use the law to influence New Covenant believers to live right. In the same verse Paul went on to explain, *"But the law was designed to last only until the coming of the child"*, and we all know that the child has come (Gal 3:19 NLT).

Furthermore, the Covenant of law was faulty. *"If the first covenant had been faultless, there would have been no need for a second covenant to replace it"* (Heb 8:7 NLT). God Himself found fault with the Covenant of Law. *"For the law always brings punishment on those who try to obey it (The only way to avoid breaking the law is to have no law to break!)"* (Rom 4:15 NLT). Did you notice that the law punishes us for merely trying to obey it? Scary, isn't it? I cannot make it any plainer.

It is interesting to note that the Covenant of Law has never been applicable to gentiles—it was given to a small group of people called the Israelites. At no time did it apply to the greater population of the world—not to Romans, Greeks, Egyptians or Philistines. Nor did it suddenly become applicable to them when they eventually received Jesus as Saviour. By the time we as gentiles came onto the scene, the previous Covenant had already been annulled by the cross, and therefore never applied to us—and no theological synod nor doctrinal pronouncement can change that. *"When God speaks of a "new" covenant, it means He has made the first one obsolete"* (Heb 8:13).

People of grace have the Holy Spirit to lead them. *"But when you are directed by the Spirit, you are not under obligation to the law of Moses"* (Gal 5:18 NLT). It is plain that New Covenant believers' conduct is to be shaped, not by the law, but by the Spirit.

Did you notice that both the followers of grace and the followers of legalism are clearly defined in this short verse? The one group is *"directed by the Spirit"*, while the other continues to look to the *"law of Moses"* for moral direction.

The bottom line is: we are not favoured because we have managed to keep the law. When the Israelites left Egypt, they were not under law—it had not yet been instituted. Although far from holy, they were exceptionally favoured without any help from law keeping—God parted the Red Sea for them and drowned their enemies in it— probably the most remarkable miracle of all time. But once the law had been installed at Mount Sinai, it was a very different matter—they had to earn favour through obedience to its dictates. How did they fare under its guardianship? Not at all well! Did the law succeed in bringing about moral change? Not in the least bit!

Now that Jesus has put the law aside, we are once again favoured without the slightest regard for our ability to keep law—we are favoured purely at Christ's expense!

Before the time of the law, there was much sin yet no transgression. There can only be transgression when there is something that can be transgressed. Strange as it may seem, the law did not result in less sin; it resulted in more sin (Rom 5:20).

The law directs sinners to a Saviour, but once saved, religion in its quest for holiness, misguidedly redirects them straight back to the law so that the law can frame their actions and way of life. It sounds so religiously prudent, doesn't it? But in this way, sincere followers, who were saved from these accusations, are sent back to be accused all over again. *"The accuser of the brethren"* stands by with open arms, ready and waiting to welcome us into his territory. Although misguided, religion does this with the best of intentions. Regretfully, forbidden practices do not suddenly become divinely acceptable simply because they are well intended.

Sadly, the law requires us to make decisions based upon our knowledge of what is right and wrong. But, as New Covenant believers, we have acquired a better way; we are instructed to be led by the Spirit. *"The knowledge of good and evil"* embedded in the law of Moses failed in its quest to influence good living. But New Covenant believers do not rely on good and evil knowledge; they rely on Holy Spirit perceptions. And while the Spirit of God is directing them, He produces His fruit through their actions.

If we are looking to the law for moral direction, we are effectively blocking the Holy Spirit from playing His assigned role in our decision making. In so doing, we like Adam are eating from the forbidden *"tree of the knowledge of good and evil"* when we should be eating from the *"tree of life"* who is Christ Jesus Himself.

Jeremiah spoke of the coming New Covenant saying, *"I will put My law in their minds, and write it on their hearts; and I will be their God, and they shall be My people"* (Jer 31:33). Paul confirmed this in 2 Corinthians 3:3. Whilst we are being led by the Holy Spirit, there is no need for Old Testament commandments to help us distinguish right from wrong. After all, His assessment of right and wrong is infinitely more reliable than our resolve to keep the law. This is what it means to have God's laws written in our hearts.

Before eating from the *"tree of the knowledge of good and evil"*, Adam had no *"good and evil"* knowledge at his disposal. But his ignorance on this issue did not cause him to fall into sin. No, he fell into righteous living, as the Holy Spirit effortlessly guided his decision making. His choices were entirely directed by inner perceptions and promptings, rather than academic knowledge of right and wrong.

For Jesus it was the same while He walked the earth—He often said that He "perceived" rather than "knew". When the women touched the hem of His garment, He "perceived" her faith.

The gift of the word of knowledge is not head knowledge; it is perceptions dropped into our hearts by the Holy Spirit. Wisdom is imparted to us in much the same way. Perception is something other than head knowledge—it is intuitive knowledge. But when we are taking our lead from the *"knowledge of good and evil"* as revealed in the law, we are not taking our lead from the Holy Spirit. If we want to be led by Him, we must be prepared to abandon any thought of being led by the law. It is infinitely more beneficial to develop a sensitivity to His promptings.

Despots demand loyalty from their subjects, but that is certainly not God's way—He does not relate well to puppets. He allowed Adam to choose—he could live by what would become a flawed sense of right and wrong, or he could be led by the Spirit of God. It had to be one or the other. Sadly, he made a poor choice and we have been left to live with the unfortunate consequences of his poor judgement.

Although Adam was entirely holy, his freewill had to be tested to prove that his perfect relationship with God had not been imposed upon him. He was quite at liberty to choose badly. The test was set. Would he be content to continue to be guided by the Holy Spirit's intuitive promptings, or would he turn to the *"knowledge of good and evil"* for moral guidance. Clearly, with this knowledge, He would be left to walk in His flawed wisdom rather than in the Holy Spirit's flawless wisdom.

The choice was clear. Either eat from the inspiration of the *"tree of life"* or from the forbidden tree of *"the knowledge of good and evil"*. Today, like Adam, you and I stand before the same two trees. We can go to the law engraved in stone to obtain the *"knowledge of good and evil"*, or we can go to the Spirit of God to draw from the very life of God—He is *"the tree of life"*. The choice is set. Will it be the law, or the Holy Spirit? Choose the law, and like Adam suffer God's displeasure. Or choose to have the Holy Spirit prompt us from within, and with it, find true life in the Spirit. Bear in mind that to choose the Spirit will require us to make a complete break with the law—no longer allowing it to have the slightest influence over our choices—the Holy Spirit's guidance is infinitely superior. This does not make us mindless; it makes us Christ minded—in fact, there is no other way to be Christ minded.

Prior to obtaining *"good and evil knowledge"*, Adam and Eve lived in a sublime state of holy bliss without the slightest consciousness of sin. They didn't need a consciousness of *"good and evil"* to keep them from sinning—the Holy Spirit was enough!

To break the word "conscience" down into its constituent parts; "con" means "together with" and "science" means "knowledge". Our con/sciences function on the sum total of the knowledge we have accumulated—it is this that establishes our convictions as to what is right and what is wrong—it becomes our measure of good and evil, similar to the knowledge imparted by the forbidden tree. I am not suggesting that we abandon our human judgement. No! Let's not kid ourselves, we live in an imperfect world, and as such, are not always sensitive to the guidance of the Holy Spirit. Our basic knowledge of good and evil becomes our second line of defence. But seeing that we have the privilege of being guided by a divine moral compass, why on earth would we want to turn to the feebleness of a human moral compass? Ideally speaking, while we are led by the Spirit, there should be no need for this, but then again, we do not live in an "ideal" world.

Jesus said, *"My sheep hear My voice... and they follow Me"* (Joh 10:27). His voice is infinitely more reliable than our acquired *"knowledge of good and evil"*.

We have Adam to "thank" for this dastardly knowledge imposed upon mankind—it brought shame and disgrace. This "enlightenment" caused him to be afraid of hearing from God. And the same goes for those of us who seek righteousness through legalistic expectations and religious laws. They make us aware of our wretchedness, which in turn causes us to fear the voice of God.

Some would say that they appreciate the law's accusations because it causes them to turn to grace. But praise God! Grace is not only a refuge from the accusations of the law of sin and death; the law of life in Christ Jesus provides us with a permanent dwelling place of perpetual rest and contentment, far from any accusations levelled against us by the law—the guidance of the Holy Spirit is enough! (Heb 4:10).

Whilst we are being led by the Spirit, the lusts of the flesh lose their allurement. Paul said, *"Walk in the Spirit, and ye shall not fulfil the lust of the flesh"* (Gal 5:16). Problem solved—at least it would be in an ideal world—but in reality we tend to go about our days leaning upon our flawed and skewed understanding of good and evil rather than upon the infallible wisdom of the Holy Spirit within us. In doing so, we are often left to deal with the toxic fallout of our poor judgements. For the most part, this is not purposely done—decisions are usually made on the spur of the moment—our poor judgement serving as a backstop.

"But isn't the Spirit always in agreement with our assessment of good and evil?"

"Not necessarily."

"Now come on Deon! You are taking this a bit too far! God would never ask us to do anything contrary to our consciences."

"Really! May I ask you; would your conscience allow you to kill your son?"

"Absolutely not!" you protest in holy indignation. "Even the thought of it is preposterous!"

"Well then, what if God were to tell you to kill him?"

"He would never do any such thing!"

"Really! Then how do you explain His instruction to Abraham to kill his son?"

In the Garden of Eden, Adam and Eve *"were both naked ... and were not ashamed"* (Gen 2:25). After eating the fruit of *"the knowledge of good and evil"*, they suddenly became ashamed of their nakedness and hid from God. What changed? Their nakedness hadn't changed; it was their perceptions that had changed. This tree, as a symbol of the law, had imposed a relationship damaging concept called shame upon mankind. This is what the law is still doing in this day and age to those who prefer legalistic frameworks. The law perpetuates shame in the lives of believers, and as with Adam and Eve, this shame is wrecking what should be a sublime relationship with our heavenly Father.

For as long as Adam and Eve fed from the tree of life, they felt no shame. We have the same choice in our day and age—we can feed from the shame that the law offers, or we can feed from the life offered by the Spirit of grace. It is not sufficient to say that we feed mostly from the grace of Jesus and only occasionally from the law. As it was for Adam and Eve, only one tiny bite of the law is enough to bring us into shame. And shame is all it takes to damage the perfect relationship we have with our heavenly Father. Although His grace towards us never changes, our perceptions of it do. When we misperceive that we have damaged our good standing with Him, our confidence in His generosity takes a knock.

We are to pull down every thought and imagination that dares to exalt itself above the knowledge of Jesus. The knowledge of Jesus concerning you and me is that we are *"the righteousness of God in Christ"* and that there is now *"no condemnation"* upon us for all time and eternity.

What was Adam's sin? Did he go on a rampage of evil? No! All he did was attempt to become what God had already made him to be. For believers the same applies—we don't have to do something evil to disappoint God; just using law keeping and good deeds to find justification is disappointing enough—He has already accomplished our righteousness for us. Yes, good deeds, confession and repentance are commendable, but we do not use them to prop up our right standing with God.

We do not curry favour with God by doing good works; we do good works because we are already favoured by Him. The bottom line is, that we as believers are already *"the righteousness of God in Christ"*; trying to obtain righteousness through law keeping is nothing other than eating from the forbidden tree. This is how deceptive religion is. In our innocent attempts at making ourselves right, we are in danger of subtracting from, rather than adding to our right standing.

Repentance is not only good, but vitally necessary. If while rowing downstream, we become aware that we are approaching a waterfall, we need to make a quick U-turn and beat a hasty retreat before the raging torrent draws us over its precipice. If we do not live a life of ready repentance, we become unnecessarily bruised and disfigured believers. We dare not risk taking on the Christian journey without committing to a routine of regular repentance.

Satan tried to pull the same stunt on the second Adam that he had so cunningly pulled off on the first. He challenged Jesus, the second Adam, when he said, *"If You are the Son of God, command that these stones become bread"*. Jesus was already the son of God; He did not have to perform anything to become the son of God. Today, you and I do not have to perform a single thing to make us the *"righteousness of*

God in Christ"—it is the *"gift"* that we received at rebirth—the work of righteous making is all God's doing. Although it is a finished work, its process of working its way into our actions is continuous.

According to James, the proof is in the pudding! When we accept that we are *"the righteousness of God in Christ"*, our works will provide all the proof necessary to demonstrate that this is so. Religious thinkers have twisted James's words to mean that we have to work to stay saved. What a travesty to destroy something as precious to believers as their blood bought liberation from such onerous obligations. We have been freed from the deathly grip of guilt itself—a privilege that was paid for with the precious blood of our Saviour. Sadly, sincere believers soon become victims of this kind of religious abuse, and nobody seems to care.

WOE IS ME!

Am I undone?

When Isaiah saw the Lord *"high and lifted up"* in His holiness and heard the seraphim calling out, *"Holy, holy, holy is the Lord of hosts; The whole earth is full of His glory"*, he became profoundly aware of his sinful state and cried out, *"Woe is me for I am undone!"* The seraph took a coal from off the altar and with it touched his lips to purge his iniquity from him (Isa.6:1-5).

Interestingly, he did not confess his individual sins; he confessed his condition, and it is no different for us. As New Covenant saints however, our condition is no longer *"undone"*. The question to ask New Covenant believers is not whether or not we are undone, but rather, whether or not Jesus is undone. If He is not, then neither are we; after all we are *"the righteousness of God in Christ"*. And *"... as He is, so are we in this world"* (1Jn 4:17). John made this statement after Jesus had already returned to heaven. Regardless of whether we reckon ourselves to be "holy" or not, we are nevertheless like Him in His present glorious state in heaven.

Isaiah had his sins purged by a coal from off the altar, but we have had our sins purged by the blood of the Lamb of God. Consequently, our sins have no bearing on our righteous standing with God. In as much as Jesus is in right standing with His Father, so are we (Php 3:9). In as much as He is loved by His Father, so are we. Jesus said to His Father, *"You love them as much as you love me"* (Joh 17:23 NLT). In as much as He is glorious, so are we. *"I have given them the glory you gave me"* (Joh 17:22 NLT). In as much as He is one with the Father, so are we. *"I in them and you in me, all being perfected into one"* (Joh 17:23 NLT). In as much as He is the Son of God, we are sons and daughters of God. Jesus is our older brother.

To suggest that New Covenant believers need coals from off the altar to cleanse us a little more, is to suggest that Jesus didn't do a proper job of atoning for our sins. It is as good as saying that the task was beyond Him—His blood was not enough! Such a suggestion would trivialise the cross. It is tantamount to inferring that coals carry more weight than the blood of the Son of God. But of course, the blood of Jesus does not need any help from coals. His blood outranks coals a gazillion to one! No, that is not descriptive enough! There isn't a number big enough to express just how vastly superior Jesus' blood is!

Jesus didn't make us almost whole; He made us completely whole, thus totally remedying our undone-ness. We are either dead or we are alive—we can't be slightly dead. By the same token we are either dead *"in sin"* or we are alive *"in Christ"*. We can't be slightly alive *"in Christ",* neither can we be slightly redeemed nor slightly undone. New Covenant believers are certainly not undone, for we are *"complete in Him"* (Col 2:10). But, for as long as we see ourselves as undone, we will live as though this is so, and consequently have to live within the limitations of our perceived undone-ness. In doing so, we reduce redemption to something less than it is.

But there is a better way—a way that honours God for His wonderful plan of redemption. It is to accept that our salvation was in every respect fully accomplished on Calvary. We should be living in the privileged significance that comes from being entirely as righteous as Jesus in God's sight.

There is nothing humble about claiming to be undone. It is yet another form of contrived religious piety. To call ourselves undone is to take issue with Jesus about the completeness of His atonement and redemption. We are not left in undone-ness—we are made entirely whole. Wholeness speaks of nothing lacking, nothing broken. Jesus did a magnificent job—He transformed New Covenant believers into a brand new species of being—we are the glorious *"chosen generation"*—something that Old Testament saints could only dream of.

We are invited to be bold in His presence—something we cannot do while convinced of our undone-ness. Not even honoured Old Covenant prophets could be bold in God's presence. But there are New Covenant believers who choose to approach God as though they are undone. Sadly, what they have chosen disqualifies them from obtaining mercy and grace in time of need (Heb 4:16). This is what God has reserved for those who dare to be bold.

Satan cannot afford to allow us to accept this truth, so he has made it his business to keep us imprisoned in a state of religious "undone-ness". If He can get us to accept undone-ness as though it were piety, he can keep us away from participating in the finished work of Calvary. When we, albeit in complete sincerity, piously adopt undone-ness as a way to demonstrate humility, Satan takes the gap. He welcomes religiousness—it gives him opportunity to ply his devilish talent for skulduggery.

Shortly after I was saved, I was immensely impressed with the prayer of a respected brother, who in his humility referred to himself as a worm. Being young and impressionable, I admired such humility. Little did I know that his feigned piety was not in the least bit God honouring. These were the destructive words of a believer who was discrediting the work of the cross—unwittingly denying that it had elevated him to royalty.

For New Covenant believers, drawing near to God is decidedly different to what it was for Old Covenant believers. *"Let us therefore come boldly to the throne of grace, that we may obtain mercy and find grace to help in time of need"* (Heb 4:16). In verse 14, the reason given for this privileged invitation and promised immunity from the consequences of sin is not holiness and repentance, but rather that we have a *"great high priest"*. As with Old Testament high priests, Jesus, our New Covenant high priest, presents the sacrifice in heaven for our sin. The difference is that there is only one sacrifice required and that is Jesus himself. The sacrifice has already taken place and all sin, from the beginning of time to the end of time, has been atoned for in one grand gesture of grace.

His presence is not a place where New Covenant believers have any reason to feel uncomfortable; to the contrary, His presence is the most comfortable place for any believer, no matter how far he or she may have progressed or failed to progress on the road towards spiritual maturity. When we enter a place of mercy and grace, our practical holiness ceases to be an issue before God!

If holiness were a prerequisite for entry, and none of us are perfect, because we *"all fall short of the glory of God"*, then how could it be possible for anybody to accept God's kind invitation to enter His throne room with boldness?

Certainly, on our own credentials, none of us could possibly feel comfortable in His presence. But then again, we do not enter on our credentials. The doorkeeper of the throne room of grace does not require us to produce a personal résumé of merits and achievements in practical holiness; he only asks to see our *"righteousness of God in Christ"* royal invitations. Each and every New Covenant believer has been invited in writing. The invite is headed "Hebrews 4:16". This room is a place of extreme mercy and grace.

As New Covenant believers, we do not have to reach a certain level of perfection before daring to enter His presence; rather upon entering, we discover that we are already every bit as perfect as Jesus. Even if we can't see it ourselves; it is how He sees us.

Isn't it just so wonderful to listen to the accounts of people who have returned from death experiences? None of them come back with any hint of Isaiah's experience in the presence of the Lord. They come back with tales of incredible beauty, love and acceptance. Many of these visitors to heaven are not what one would call fine specimens of virtue and godliness. Obviously, Jesus achieved enough on the cross to make up for what they lack in practical holiness.

We stand a good chance of being accused anywhere except in one place, and that place is in God's presence. *"Who dares accuse us whom God has chosen for his own? Will God? No! He is the one who has given us right standing with himself. Who then will condemn us? Will Christ Jesus? No, for he is the one who died for us and was raised to life for us and is sitting at the place of highest honour, pleading for us"* (Rom 8:33-34 NLT).

In God's throne room of grace we are entirely safe from accusations—if God has named it the throne room of grace, then we can rest assured that in that place, grace reigns supreme—accusations and judgements of any kind are not permitted there. After all, accusations are entirely opposite to mercy and grace, and we are invited to enter in to *"receive mercy and grace"*.

Interestingly, mercy and grace are only offered to people who deserve neither mercy nor grace. Or to put it another way, we only qualify to receive this promise if we have failed to make ourselves right. After all, mercy and grace would serve no purpose if it were not to accommodate our shortcomings. But then again, those who have found this kind of love and acceptance in God's presence, have also found something far more valuable than anything offered by sin. How can sin possibly compete for our affections? God's extreme love and grace outshines anything and everything the world has to offer!

If God expects us to feel undone and uncomfortable in His presence, we would not be able to obey His invitation to be *"bold"* and confident in that gracious place. If He were to accuse us in a place of mercy and grace, we could say that He had gotten us there under false pretences, and that would immediately make Him unholy. If He were to lose His state of holiness, His position as supreme Lord of the universe would immediately become vulnerable, making it possible for Him to be overthrown and ousted. Of one thing we can be quite certain; God is holy, and He will never do anything underhanded—His holiness assures us of this. And this knowledge gives us sufficient assurance to be unflinchingly *"bold"* when we are with Him. And we are with Him all the time without interruption, in fact, at this very moment, we are seated together with Him in heavenly places!

GROWING IN GRACE

How do we grow in grace?

Certainly not by good behaviour and repentance. We know that plants gain nutrition from the nutrients in the soil. When Peter instructed us to grow in grace, he was instructing us to draw nutrients from God's grace. We grow in grace as our roots sink deep into the love of God. Love, in the form of mercy and grace provide nutrients and nourishment—empowerment for victorious Christian living.

Think of a tree in the desert. It doesn't grow unless its roots tap into a source of nourishment deep beneath the burning sands. Ephesians 3:17-21 says, *"May your roots go down deep into the soil of God's marvellous love"*. As our roots penetrate deep into the soil of His love, divine nutrients nourish, edify and inspire. We discover *"... how wide, how long, how high and how deep his love really is"* (verse 18). Paul is not suggesting that we gain this love purely from the pages of our Bibles. It is so much more than that. We grow in grace by discovering God's love in a personal experiential way that unfolds, develops and grows without end.

Our Bibles are not just pages of divine information; they are love letters enticing us into a love affair—whispered words of love, drawing us into intimacy. He is not looking for an acquaintance; He is looking for a real live lover—He desires an all-consuming romance.

His word reveals His love to us, but the romance is not a single episode; it's a series. In enthralling instalments, an intense love story unfolds, not purely in Bible pages, but in personal experiences. And as the romance blossoms, we grow in grace. The more we draw from His grace, the more we grow in grace.

When we *"experience the love of Christ, though it is so great we will never fully understand it"*, we grow in grace (verse 19). The fact that nobody has ever, nor will ever *"fully understand it"*, is enough proof that God's love is a lifelong journey of discovery that involves so much more than mere head knowledge gained from the pages of our Bibles—romance simply cannot be scripted.

When religion redefines grace by setting limits to it, it makes itself culpable. We should not be reducing grace to fit our denomination's small thinking about God—His love is infinite and therefore immeasurable. At the point where we draw the line on grace, we draw the line on God. He has no other means of winning our affections. When we reduce His grace, we reduce our glorious divine romance into an arm's length arrangement, and consign our love affair to shallowness.

Our religious scepticism only serves to block His affections from reaching our hearts. Quite obviously, we can only be romanced to the degree that we allow our Lover to romance us. He dearly wants us to know how deep His feelings for us run, but we can't *"experience"* something that we have been persuaded to avoid. Sadly, wherever grace is religiously reduced, the depths of His love cannot be known.

How do we grow in grace? By growing more holy? Certainly not! It is in the love affair—the journey of discovering ever deeper aspects of His love for us—this is the process of growing in grace! What is the promise for those who *"grow in grace"*? The next verse says, *"Then you will be filled with the fullness of life and power that comes from God"* (verse 19). Moving in this power and fullness of life is made possible by our personal *"experience"* of *"growing in grace"*. This power is a life force that takes care of shaping our behaviour in divine ways.

The moment that we think we know the limit of how extreme God's love is, is the moment that we stop growing in grace. In other words we stop short of believing that it could be extremely greater than our capacity to imagine—God's loving grace is too extreme to be put into doctrinal boxes. It is unfathomable—the quest of discovering it is endless. When something is infinite, it is inexhaustible!

There is more to growing in grace than simply just a matter of living in unconditional favour. Love is the oxygen of grace. The thought of being so generously loved, when we are only too aware of our undeserved-ness, can be pretty overwhelming—enough to soften our hearts and melt our innate resistance to submission. Nothing can boost confidence in the way that grace does. When it comes to faith, grace gives us good reason to trust. It's a shot in the arm—a confidence booster. It is an exchange of human fallibilities for divine infallibility—our insufficiencies for His all-sufficiency.

Even in heaven, we will not stop growing in both our knowledge and *"experience"* of God's love. We will spend eternity worshipping God; not because we must, but because we will be in perpetual awe of the endless unfolding of unimaginable revelations of His gracious goodness—the extremities of which we will never fully grasp— eternity is not long enough.

Worship is not something that can be genuine if it "must" be done out of a sense of duty—worship can so easily regress into nothing more than empty chants. Worse still, it can degenerate into flattery for favours, and nothing could be shallower than that.

In our exploration of grace, we come to discover what real love is—we see it in the extreme measures He took to gain our affections. On our journey of discovery, we get an ever clearer picture of the pleasure He gets out of connecting with us.

Worship is not something that must be coerced out of us—it is an effortless enthralment—forever overawed by His magnificent beauty. Our worship is continuous—way beyond church hours and daily devotions. We find ourselves expressing our pleasure in Him in the most unlikely, and often unchurchified of places. We cannot help it—we are enthralled with His kindness!

Like an attentive lover, He takes pleasure in dropping little reminders of His love here and there throughout our busy days—often breathtakingly thoughtful! We come across caring tokens of kindness when least expected—He knows exactly what it takes to bring a thrill to each of His loved ones. To one it may be a dramatic sunset, to another the laughter of a child. To me it's the power and punch of a swing band in full flight, or the mellow tones of a flugelhorn overlaying the breathy tones of a tenor saxophone, doing a laidback jazz number to the exotic rhythms of the bossa nova.

Then there are those spontaneous spurts of joy that we experience when a favourite athlete publically devotes his moment of glory to his God and mine. Grace enthralled believers don't have to try to respond in worship—gratitude seems to jump out of their chests when least expected.

Lovers enjoy surprising each other with thoughtful gestures, and our divine Lover is no different. There is no effort in worshipping a god who is as caring as our God! What a joy to discover that we are His pride and joy—the focus of His affection!

Who could have said it better than Louis Armstrong?

> *The colours of the rainbow... so pretty in the sky*
> *Are also on the faces... of people going by*
> *I see friends shaking hands... saying how do you do*
> *They're really saying... I love you!*

It's the small things in life that remind us that our God is mindful of us. The convenient parking; the kind word of a friend; a loving family to come home to; an encouraging word when we are about to give up; the unexpected Skype phone call from a daughter living far away!

Every now and then, something big comes our way. Closing a major deal; getting a refund from the Revenue Service when we thought we would be required to make another payment; the birth of a child or grandchild! Oh what a thoughtful Lover He is! It is obvious to me that He is smitten with His bride!

His grace and mercy gives us a window into His deep love for us—it also gives us some idea of His need to be loved—He looks to His dearest ones to fulfil that need. By allowing mere sinful mortals to put His son through the pain, shame and torture of the cross, He demonstrated the lengths that He is prepared to go to in order to win our hearts, and with it our affections. It is obvious that He wants our company and will stop at nothing to get it.

As the King of the universe, one can only imagine that He has everything His heart could possibly desire. But He lacks one thing. He lacks that dimension of our affection that we withhold from Him. We may do this on the pious pretext of distancing ourselves from any form of grace that we believe to be too extreme. If we will not allow ourselves the luxury of receiving the extremities of His grace, we will never know how deeply we are loved. It is a fact of life—we cannot return more love to Him than we have allowed ourselves to receive from Him. Lovers thrive on each other's affection—a lack of reciprocation can be pretty painful! But it is a joy to reciprocate, if only a small token of the love we receive from Him.

I have heard it said that it is not He that benefits from our worship; it is we who benefit from it. There is no question that we benefit greatly, but I think one day we will be surprised to discover just how pleasurable our loving gestures of worship have been to Him.

How would our worship holdup if there wasn't a worship band or church organ to rouse us to worship? Would our worship be any different if we couldn't meet with fellow Christians in worship? Are we externally stimulated or internally stimulated—is our desire to worship aroused by a slick worship team, or by our love affair with the God who dwells within us?

It has been said that when a glowing coal is removed from the midst of other glowing coals, it soon loses its heat. In saying this, it is inferred that we are externally motivated. Whilst getting together to encourage and edify is certainly a biblical injunction, the analogy of the coals misses the point—there is no need to seek spiritual stimulation from external sources when we have the greater One dwelling within us.

Is our worship love inspired or merely a good religious routine that must be dispensed with before the sermon can be delivered? When worship has to be cranked out of congregants, it can so easily degenerate into mindless boredom—empty chants that lack worship's fundamental elements of heartfelt love and adoration. *"... They honor me with their lips, but their hearts are far away. And their worship of me amounts to nothing more than human laws learned by rote" (Isa 29:13).* In order for worship to truly be worshipful, it must come from our hearts. But our hearts have little to offer, unless we have been overwhelmed with the extravagant love that God expresses to us in the form of grace.

When our bridegroom's love has awakened love within us, genuine heartfelt worship flows naturally in torrents of gratitude and joy! All of this is triggered by our discovery that our heavenly Father enjoys having His children around, no matter whether they are naughty or nice.

When we come to acknowledge that we are purely the beneficiaries of such extravagant love, we become aware that worship is welling up from deep within. When we sense the depth of God's adoration of us, adoration of Him erupts in spontaneous outbursts of emotion! We are almost surprised to discover that our eyes are wet with joy.

Programmed worship or not—we don't need to be cranked up— we don't have to create special worshipful atmospheres with the right kind of mystical background music—we find ourselves enthralled with Jesus because He is enthralled with us.

With His generous love upon us, there is nothing arduous about adoring Him. Our interaction with Him ceases to focus on our holy contribution or lack thereof—it's not about what we have managed to do or not do; it's all about who He is and what He means to us. After all, grace has no regard for our puny righteous making efforts; it's all about God, who in His unconditional love has favoured us beyond measure. He loves us much, and He loves us for His own good reasons.

Charles H. Gabriel penned:

How wonderful! How marvellous!
And my song shall ever be:
How Marvellous! How wonderful!
Is my Saviours love for me!

Eternity will be filled with this amazement:

When, with the ransomed in glory,
His face I at last shall see,
'Twill be my joy thro' the ages
to sing of His love for me.

Paul makes it clear that grace is not withheld where there is sin, because *"where sin abounded, grace abounded much more"* (Rom 5:20). He goes on to ask a rhetorical question, *"What shall we say then? Shall we continue in sin that grace may abound?"* (Rom 6:1). And then answers *"Certainly not!"* The point is that we can make more grace abound; not by sinning less, but by sinning more! But in this verse we are cautioned not to do so, because *"How shall we who died to sin live any longer in it?"* (Rom 6:2). In other words: Yes we can sin because there is enough grace to cover it, but why on earth would we want to indulge in the very thing that grace empowers us to defeat?

There are some who caution their followers to, stay away from extreme grace on the grounds that it teaches that sinning is okay. Really? I mean, really? Where ever did they get that idea from? The Bible is clear, *"For the grace of God that brings salvation has appeared to all men, teaching us that, denying ungodliness and worldly lusts, we should live soberly, righteously, and godly in the present age"* (Tit 2:11,12). This scripture is clear. Grace does not teach that sinning is okay. To the contrary, grace teaches that sinning is decidedly not okay! In fact, grace does not teach us to embrace ungodliness and lusts; it teaches the *"denying of ungodliness and lusts"*, and then empowers us to deny them. The very reason for granting grace in the first place was to empower godly living; not ungodly living! Knowing this, it is difficult to understand why religious people insist that grace people teach that sinning is okay. Obviously, grace presents a threat to the very core of their beliefs. To let go of legalism is to lose control of congregants—a scary thought! In their estimation, grace is simply not religious enough to be godly.

Grace provides an extreme solution to sinning. Anybody who has been in religious circles for any length of time has encountered the shallowness of religious "holiness". Yes, believers do develop a polite form of charm and kindness that on the surface appears to be genuine enough, but the moment the pawpaw hits the fan, and relationships come under strain in conflicts such as church splits, interpersonal feuds and doctrinal disagreements, one soon discovers that this kind of holiness is not real—rather it is a very fragile veneer that is easily scuffed and chipped away to reveal the ugliness of hidden ungraciousness. Religion's idea of "holiness" can so easily amount to nothing more than a contrived level of behaviour that gives one acceptance in one's religious clique. To claim that it amounts to godliness would be tantamount to claiming that God has lowered His standard.

Can grace be set aside? It would seem so. Paul said, *"I do not set aside the grace of God; for if righteousness comes through the law, then Christ died in vain"* (Gal 2:21). From this verse, it is clear that grace is not set aside by sin; it is set aside by the practice of trying to obtain righteousness through law keeping.

"Christ is become of no effect unto you, whosoever of you are justified by the law; ye are fallen from grace" (Gal 5:4 KJV). We do not fall from grace when we sin; to the contrary, when we sin we fall into grace. This scripture is clear—we fall from grace when we try to find justification for ourselves through any means other than grace.

Being *"strong in the grace that is in Christ Jesus"* is exactly what "extreme grace" is all about. Whatever we add to grace, no matter how well intended and noble, effectively dilutes grace. If we work for grace, we cancel grace. Good works simply cannot earn a *"gift"*. However, good works can flow in a natural way from those who walk in grace. Working for grace does not increase grace; it reduces grace!

Our only contribution is to put our trust in the accomplishments of Christ's finished work. To be strong in grace, is to rest in the knowledge that grace alone is enough—in fact it is everything!

There is a level of boldness at the throne of grace that can only be known by those who are convinced of their unshakable righteousness. *"Therefore, brethren, having boldness to enter the Holiest by the blood of Jesus, by a new and living way which He consecrated for us, through the veil, that is, His flesh"* (Heb 10:19,20). This is not the cowering way of Isaiah; it is a *"new and living way"*! *"For the law ... can never with these same sacrifices, which they offer continually year by year, make those who approach perfect"* (Heb 10:1). In God's eyes, we are as perfect as Him. Isaiah's annual sacrifices were not enough—he lacked the perfection of Christ—no wonder he cringed in God's presence.

What does it mean to *"fall short of the glory of God"*? Grace is not only a matter of God being gracious to us; it is also a matter of us being gracious to those around us. What is to blame for *"any root of bitterness"* springing up within us? Bitterness is plain and simply a symptom of gracelessness! If we, as conduits of grace become clogged up with offence taking, we block the free flow of grace to a hurting world around us. Whether we give offence or take offence the same applies—in both instances we simply refuse to grant grace to those, who in our estimation, are offensive. Like an oil well, grace should be a gusher, not a trickle. But with offence taking, our grace splutters to a dribble (Heb 12:15).

The Amplified Bible says, *"falls back from and fails to secure God's grace"*. We fail to secure God's grace when we don't believe that it is extreme enough to allow God to love us when we don't deserve love. And we fail to secure grace when we turn to law keeping for our justification.

"God resists the proud, but gives grace to the humble" (Jas 4:6). Those who through ardent law keeping and repentance have achieved something to boast of, are at risk of falling into pride. But those who depend solely on God's grace have nothing to bring to the party—they depend entirely on His mercy and grace. Seeing that it is all His work, what can they possibly take any credit for? The glory is entirely God's!

At the end of the day, God is not impressed with what we can boastfully say that we have managed to achieve—He calls it *"filthy rags"*.

"Work out your own salvation with fear and trembling" (Php 2:12). If this verse is misunderstood, as is often the case, we may try to work to stay saved. But that is not what is implied here. We are not to work for our salvation; we are to work our salvation out! In other words, the measure of grace we have received is the measure we should grant to others. This verse is all about grace in action—doing as much good to others in word and deed as God has done to us. It's all about loving the ones God loves—and that's everybody. He loves the ungodly *"world"* so much that He gave His only begotten Son to save them! Wow! The *"world"* is pretty all inclusive, isn't it? It includes the most disagreeable and nastiest of characters—including mass murderers such as Osama Bin Laden, Stalin and Hitler. In the same way that we get His favour despite our obvious undeserved-ness, we are to favour others despite their obvious undeserved-ness.

We are to *"Pursue peace with all people, and holiness, without which no one will see the Lord"* (Heb 12:14). It is often assumed that "extreme grace" does not pursue holiness—it is thought that it simply shrugs its shoulders and says sin is okay. It is hard to understand how "un-extreme grace" could have come to such an unfortunate conclusion. But when one understands Satan's diabolical plan, one recognises his devious agenda. He must do all he can to malign God's sin defeating plan. He must convince good honest religious people to be suspicious of grace. If he can convince them that God's one and only plan to defeat sin, is actually a plan to support sin, he can hi-jack God's glory and grace, and offer a religious substitute—legalistic bondage in exchange for divine freedom.

Satan plays dirty—in the guise of an *"angel of light"* he goes about trying to bluff us into believing that grace is too easy to be godly. If he can convince sincere religious folk that grace supports sin rather than defeats it, he can distort their concept of grace to suit his own devious ends. But in reality, "extreme grace" sees sin as sin, and no matter how we look at it, it is abominable! And it cannot be fixed with anything less than grace of the most extreme kind. God uses an opposite methodology to that of religion to achieve holiness. Where religion sternly accuses; Jesus says, *"Neither do I condemn you"* (Joh 8:11).

It is not unusual to discover that the kingdom's way of doing things is precisely opposite to the religious way. Religion requires holiness to be attained by behaving right; while grace goes to the root of the matter and concerns itself with the real issue. The real problem is seated in the hearts of believers. Religion may agree that it is a matter of fixing the heart, but disagree on the method of repair. Hearts cannot be fixed with the best of intentions. Self-effort, fear, instructions or rules cannot do it; hearts can only be fixed with the kind of love that demands nothing in return. Ultimately, hearts that are loved in this way stand a better chance of falling in with God's will.

The truth is that if a heart cannot be fixed with love, it cannot be fixed at all! Criminals leave prisons unchanged by years of incarceration. What was in their hearts when they were imprisoned, is still there upon their release. Often they leave prison even more bitter and twisted with the world. It takes love to build self-esteem, and God has plenty to give!

In reality, there is no holiness in the holiest of actions, unless that holiness is the fruit of the Spirit. It is only when we are backed into a corner that we discover how genuine our holiness actually is. It is not uncommon to see, what is thought to be holiness, crumble under pressure. No matter how sincere, holy making efforts remain works of the flesh, and as such, remain vulnerable—apt to crack under pressure. But fruit of the Spirit is decidedly different!

Minds operate on reason, but hearts are different; they operate on emotion. Fear, hatred, revenge, jealousy, anger, pride and many other destructive emotions—these negative passions motivate less than healthy behaviour, better known as sin. Then there are positive emotions—joy, peace, happiness, pleasure and many other beautiful passions, but there is one that stands head and shoulders above all others—it lifts and motivates us to purity—that emotion is love! (1Cor 13:13).

God loves His children generously. When we allow ourselves the luxury of indulging in His generosity, knowing full well that we are undeserving, it has a profound influence upon the way we do life. Once the roots within our hearts have been revitalised and nourished with the nutrients of God's love, healthy actions follow—they simply fall into line with the loving character that our Lover has instilled within us. After all, actions, whether good or bad, are purely the outworking of what's going on in our hearts.

Love is captivating—especially when it is obvious that we don't deserve it. Because grace starts with our hearts, it has a head start on religion. In fact, how can we ever pursue holiness other than through grace? Holiness by any other means is *"filthy rags"*.

When we walk by faith, we are walking by the Spirit. And He is the Spirit of grace. And when the Spirit is producing His fruit through our actions; it is all His doing and therefore not *"filthy rags"*. Walking in "extreme grace" is purely a walk of faith, and *"... whatsoever is not of faith is sin"* (Rom 14:23 KJV).

Obviously, God's fruit is infinitely more holy than our efforts. There is a direct correlation between grace input and grace output. Grace infuses holiness into us. To reduce grace, is to reduce holiness! Grace by its very nature is an expression of holiness of the most extreme kind!

You are not likely to see "extreme grace" believers complying with the outward requirements of legalism. If they were to do so, it would rob them of their grace privileges. *"For if those who are of the law are heirs, faith is made void and the promise made of no effect"* (Rom 4:14). To fall in with the demands of legalism would be as good as throwing in the towel—there is no point to standing in faith when our faith has been *"made void"*—compromised by our ineffective efforts to earn favour.

Legalists often misinterpret the freedom they see in people of grace as proof of their rebellion. But is it really rebellious to refuse to bow to the religious idols of legalism? One is reminded of the three Hebrew boys who were labelled rebels for refusing to bow to another religious regime. They stood their ground beyond the threat of death, and God honoured them for it.

Legalism cannot produce holiness; it can only make pretenders of us. But *"The law no longer holds you in its power, because you died to its power when you died with Christ on the cross"* (Rom 7:4 NLT). Where religion misses the point, is that it does not teach its followers that when they died with Christ, they died to the jurisdiction and dominion of the law. Consequently, they open themselves to the possibility of pharisaic badgering. Sadly, the rewards of following the law are harmful—fateful curses await those who insist on seeking righteousness through it.

Bobby Salkinder was my childhood hero. He was a showman of note; riding many horses simultaneously. He would hold the reins of a whole herd of galloping broncos, while standing on the backs of two of them. He was in big trouble if they did not gallop in perfect unison. The Old and the New Covenants do not run in unison. The one operates with works that are either rewarded or punished, while the other operates with the guidance of the Holy Spirit. He dispenses grace, love and mercy at Christ's expense.

While the one covenant shows us how sinful we are, thankfully, the other shows us how righteous we are. The one metes out condemnation while the other metes out reconciliation. The one ministers death while the other ministers life. If we insist on having one foot on each covenant, we are heading for big trouble; they will tear us apart as they move in opposite directions. While we insist on practising both covenants, we cannot benefit from either.

No self-respecting saint would like evil desires to be aroused within him or her. But the law is responsible for provoking and arousing these foul desires, for *"... the law aroused these evil desires that produced these sinful deeds"* (Rom 7:5). If we don't want to arouse these evil desires, then we must distance ourselves from trying to obtain righteousness through law keeping. If we dare to dabble with law keeping, we will have to contend with evil desires—they come with the territory. We cannot afford the evil enticements of sin that come with seeking justification through any kind of law keeping. Far better to be Spirit led.

In Romans 4:14 Paul says, *"So if you claim that God's promise is for those who obey God's law and think they are good enough in God's sight, then you are saying that faith is useless. And in that case, the promise is also meaningless. But the law brings punishment on those who try to obey it. (The only way to avoid breaking the law is to have no law to break!)"*. I have never met a Christian who does not aspire to increase in faith, yet I have met many who insist on keeping the law—a faith debilitating pursuit!

Legalism is what Jesus put an end to on the cross. 2 Corinthians 3:3 says that His laws are *"... written not with ink, but with the Spirit of the living God; not in tables of stone, but in fleshy tables of the heart"*. No longer do we follow the letter of the law; we follow the promptings of the Holy Spirit. In verse 6, he goes on to say of the law that *"the letter killeth"*. Thankfully he adds, *"but the spirit giveth life"* (KJV). The law offers nothing but death to those who would try to live up to its impossible demands.

"Now we have been released from the law, for we died with Christ and are no longer captive to its power" (Rom 7:6). In order for religion to retain its unsanctioned governance of believers, it must keep this information hidden from its followers. Although we are released from the guardianship of the law, religion still teaches otherwise. It does this despite the deathly outcomes of these forbidden practises. In the face of so many scriptural warnings, we are left to wonder why so many doggedly pursue them in the mistaken cause of holiness. God has specifically directed us to a new and better way. And that way is the way of grace, because with grace we are Spirit led. It's not a bit of each covenant—if it is not entirely the covenant of grace, it is entirely nothing at all!

Only when we have managed to shake ourselves free from the blight of legalism can we really serve God. *"Now we can really serve God, not in the old way by obeying the letter of the law, but in the new way by the Spirit"* (Rom 7:4). The implication of this verse is that no matter how sincere our service may be, we are simply not serving God when we are *"obeying the letter of the law"*.

There is no sword of Damocles dangling over the heads of the redeemed of the Lord. *"So if the son sets you free, you will indeed be free"* (Joh 8:36). We cannot indulge in this freedom unless we acknowledge that we have it. Sadly, by our sincere endeavours to gain holiness through law keeping, we are effectively denying that it is already ours!

IN CHRIST

What must I do to avoid condemnation?

"There is therefore now no condemnation to those who are in Christ Jesus". The second part of Romans 8:1, *"...who do not walk according to the flesh, but according to the Spirit"* has long been misconstrued by religious thinkers to be a condition for achieving a state of *"no condemnation"*. But these words are certainly not a condition; rather they are a description of a person who lives under the grace of no condemnation. The same verse sets out the one and only condition for the honoured status of *"no condemnation"*, and that is that a person must be *"in Christ"*.

What is walking by the Spirit? According to Hebrews 10:8, the New Covenant is characterised by being led from within rather than being governed by a set of laws, as was characteristic of the former covenant. Consequently, a New Covenant believer can be described as one who walks by the Spirit. To walk according to the law's stringent requirements is to walk by the flesh. This is certainly not the way of grace!

But there is a further problem with the second part of Romans 8:1—these descriptive words do not appear in earlier manuscripts. In the days before the invention of the printing press, scribes would meticulously hand copy from one manuscript to the next. Obviously, in view of the possibility of errors creeping in, and these errors being further magnified by subsequent copying, it is preferable for modern day translators to work from original manuscripts. But in the absence of originals, the best they can do is to translate from the earliest copies available.

So when it came to copying this verse from one manuscript to the next, the early scribes must have felt obliged to add an explanation. A promise to never condemn believers for their sins was far too generous a concept for religious thinkers to accept without qualification. One can only speculate that such overt generosity was too implausible for the scribes to grasp. In later editions of the manuscripts, in their sincere efforts to make this liberating statement more religiously palatable, they ended up appending a description of what they felt a believer *"in Christ"* is, and this description has ever since been misunderstood by religious thinkers to be a condition that must be fulfilled before a state of *"no condemnation"* can be attained.

Instead of helping believers to come to a better understanding, this misleading statement has caused many to wonder whether or not they have done enough to claim to be walking according to the Spirit. But it is not what we do or don't do that determines our state of *"no condemnation"*; it is the person we became at rebirth that qualifies us. Being *"in Christ"* is the sole determining factor! It is simply not possible for a person who is *"in Christ"* to also be in condemnation, unless of course that person mistakenly insists that *"no condemnation"* is only for those who have managed to attain a certain spiritual standard of morality. But scripture is clear—all blood bought believers without exception, are in Christ and therefore fully qualified for the status of *"no condemnation"*.

Sadly, these well-intended yet unauthorised addendums to the manuscripts have caused sincere believers to doubt their good standing with God. Scripture tampering has misled believers to think that grace is conditional. In their zeal, the scribes have confused sincere believers, and in this confusion, many forego their grace privileges—deferring them to the future, when hopefully they will be holy enough to qualify for them. But for as long as they believe God's unconditional favour to be conditional, they cancel grace and forfeit the *"gift"*. Bear in mind that gifts by definition cannot be conditional—not now, not ever—end of story!

Grace is so simple and unreligious, that believers throughout the ages have had difficulty coming to terms with it. They fear that such enormous freedom would lead to licentious living. They do not understand, that in modifying God's grace to fit their denominational boxes, they have cancelled grace. Sadly, the original purpose of grace has been modified into a more religiously plausible doctrine. Much of the church has strayed from the extreme form of grace that Paul and others so passionately proclaimed—the vibrancy of a grace relationship with God has been turned inside out—swallowed up by religiousness.

Religion is culpable—it must take the blame for dividing the body of Christ along doctrinal lines—dogmatic disagreements separating brothers. In many cases, denominationalism is a mere hop and a skip away from cultism. One can only wonder where the fine line between religion and cultism is actually drawn—which side of the line does the average church in the suburbs stand? A church has slipped into cultism when excessive power over congregants has devolved into the hands of a strong cleric who misuses legalism to enforce his ideas. Sadly, his empowerment is obtained at the expense of the blood bought freedom of ordinary believers.

If a strong leader can convince followers that there is virtue in passively accepting everything that is said from the pulpit, then his followers are likely to take everything he says at face value. This is what gives cults their strength. They may say, "Don't take my word for it; check it out for yourselves". But if you do, you had better interpret it in line with denominational thinking. Anything else is regarded as heresy. What can be said about such overt misuse of religious power? Dare I say it? It is nothing other than self-exalted "holy" dictatorship! Scary stuff!

When awkward questions are not welcomed, but met with rebuff and reproof, then it is time to be scared! But is it really rebellious to seek the kingdom for oneself? After all, didn't Jesus Himself instruct us to do so? Pastors are not God's mediators—that's Jesus' role. They have the divine honour of shepherding—ordained to lead in the spirit of servant-hood (Mat 23:8-12).

The coming of Jesus spelt an end to the Levitical order of the priesthood. From the moment of the birth of the church, Jesus alone would take up the position of high priest, and each and every believer would be fully ordained priests in their own right.

At first, the early church stuck faithfully to the biblical model, but it didn't take too long for grace to unravel and regress to the point where a separate priesthood, not too dissimilar to the Levitical order, was instituted. For the first time the clergy was put on church payrolls and exalted above the status of ordinary believers. Make no mistake, workers are worthy of their wages. It is not their wages that are at issue. But an issue arises when the clergy are deputised to liaise with God on behalf of believers.

In the dark ages, the priesthood took the opportunity to empower themselves; insisting on subservience from followers. They passed themselves off as the ones with a direct line to "the man upstairs". Sadly, when God became "the man upstairs" He ceased to be the Spirit within us.

With the inauguration of the clergy as a separate class of believer, more and more of the function of the priesthood of the believer fell to the responsibility of priestly professionals, thus robbing ordinary believers of their priestly standing. The blood bought privilege of ordinary believers' to live in intimacy with their heavenly Father had been turned over to a group of professionals who would do it for them. But in order for them to fulfil this role, Jesus, our High Priest would have to vacate his seat to make way for self-appointed priestly substitutes. Of course, such a notion is absurd!

Even more absurd is the concept that controlling apostles provide a covering for subordinate believers. *"Therefore, holy brethren, partakers of the heavenly calling, consider the Apostle and High Priest of our confession, Christ Jesus"* (Heb 3:1). Jesus is not only our High

Priest, He is also our Apostle. Covering is not the function of control freaks. There is no mention of this in the scriptures. The function of the apostle is to spearhead the spreading of the gospel and to establish and connect new believers to their divine Apostle and High Priest, Jesus. They are commissioned to commission others. But the concept of covering has become so ensconced in Christendom that believers readily bow to religious hierarchies as though they are doing God a service. As an extreme example, the Pope is enthroned and revered. His followers bow before him and kiss his ring. Kowtowing is not restricted to traditional churches; Charismatics have their own version of apostolic worship—priestly superstars abound.

"But Deon, we need apostolic covering to keep us from falling into error". Are you sure that it will keep us out of error? In view of the fact that there are thousands of apostles, each with their own version of the doctrines of the Bible, it is obvious that with their covering we get their errors. After all, if they are in disagreement with each other, then it follows that they can't all be right. It stands to reason that covering does not protect us from error; it aligns us to somebody else's errors. Everybody on the face of the planet is in one form of error or another. While this may appal us, it does not faze God. He knows that we all see through a glass darkly, yet He loves us regardless.

In South Africa, there is an apostle with more than five million followers. He proclaims himself to be the Holy Spirit. This might be an extreme example of cultish apostolic error compared to most, but error is error, even if it differs in finer detail. As long as we get the fundamentals of the gospel right, our disagreements on side issues are neither here nor there in God's estimation. Never forget that the central Person of the gospel is Jesus, and the central theme of His gospel is grace. Grace is the fundamental of fundamentals—the very crux of the gospel of Jesus!

The Holy Spirit is our teacher. The moment we chose to be Spirit led, we cease to be intimidated by legalistic overlords. We simply cannot serve two masters at the same time. Better to suffer their indignation than to acquiesce to their fleshly demands for legalism's fraudulent version of "holiness". To be in step with legalistic expectations, is to be out of step with the Spirit. When the choice is between moral policemen and the Spirit of God, it is a no brainer! Unless we have the freedom to forsake the law, how can we be Spirit led?

Religion often establishes the principal of "passive acceptance" as a highly prized virtue. Followers must feel guilty for holding to contrary doctrines. Once submission to this primary "virtue" is established, the leader's word becomes sacrosanct; followers are expected to allow themselves to be controlled in the name of "holy" submission to God's appointed man. Certainly, God appoints leaders, and as such they should be honoured. Their divine appointment is not in question. But when their divine authority flips over into dictatorship, alarm bells ought to be sounded!

Many modern-day evangelical churches live with "conditional grace" as though it is God's way, not realising that by making grace out to be conditional, they cancel grace. Christianity is built on the firm foundation of God's grace as expressed in the cross. To tamper with grace is to tamper with all that is Christian—without grace the whole plethora of Christian doctrines fall over—they do not even exist without grace. Unless they can be securely bolted with robust corrosion free tungsten bolts onto the fundamental foundation of grace, there is no place for them in Christianity.

Although grace is unconditional, it is not automatically received. Only those who asked Jesus for healing actually got healed. God tells us how to position ourselves to tap into what He holds out to us without conditions.

Having said that, there are nevertheless grace blockers. *"God resists the proud, but gives grace to the humble"* (1Pe 5:5). Proud people cannot walk in God's grace. The choice is simple, it has to be one or the other—either pride or grace, but never a mixture of the two.

More often than not, those who have achieved a religiously acceptable level of "holiness" through adherence to legalism, become puffed up and spiritually proud of their religious standing in the community. This leads to feelings of superiority. Before long they are looking down their noses with disapproval upon believers who have not yet mastered what they have managed to master. These bastions of "holiness" ignore Peter's words that *"God resists the proud, but gives grace to the humble"* and in doing so, they fail to participate in grace.

"Boldness" is a grace door opener (Heb 4:16). Timidity brought about by a sense of guilt, condemnation and undone-ness will fail to obtain mercy and grace in the throne room of grace.

It takes "faith" to make withdrawals from grace. *"... we have access by faith into this grace"* (Rom 5:2). We need to stick our necks out in faith if we want to benefit from the unconditional favour that is available to us through grace. Without faith, grace cannot be appropriated. Another definition of faith is "confidence in the generosity of our gracious Lord".

Unforgiveness is a grace blocker. It should be obvious that unforgiveness is diametrically opposite to grace—after all, if it were not for mercy and grace, we would have to answer for our sins. Jesus' advice to us was that we should treat others with the same consideration that we would want for ourselves.

Honouring others is a grace door opener. So we honour honourable people, do we? Big deal! They are already worthy of honour—even unbelievers honour them. As followers of Jesus, we are empowered with His grace to be gracious to people who are not necessarily worthy of honour. Honour is not something we say; it's something we do. Jesus gave us the example of the Good Samaritan who honoured a man who despised him and his ethnicity. He did not do it with words; he did it with substance. This is true honour, and it opens the door to receive God's grace.

Disobedience is a grace blocker. There is a danger for believers to take the gap, because they mistakenly believe that being under grace gives them a right to be disobedient. But we should be under no illusion; we cannot enjoy the benefits of grace, unless we follow Jesus' instructions to receive His grace. Sadly, there will always be some who will misuse grace to excuse their disobedience. What a travesty! Others insist that grace is synonymous with disobedience! But, nothing could be further from the truth! The Covenant of grace is one of walking in obedience to the voice of the Spirit within us, as opposed to being governed by a list of ordinances cast in stone (Jer 31:33).

In the game of rugby, the full back always appears to be in the right place at the right time to retrieve the ball when punted by the opposing team. It is the same with grace. We can miss it altogether if we are not ready, expectant and in the right place at the right time. Grace does not invite disobedience; it inspires a higher level of obedience! Obedience places us in perfect position for the favour that God has lined up for us. You could say, "No obedience equals no participation in grace". Let's face it—obedience is the key to grace's privileges. But then again, obedience is not onerous to people of grace; it is appealing—their hearts are captivated by love!

Jesus said, *"If you keep My commandments, you will abide in My love, just as I have kept My Father's commandments and abide in His love"* (Joh 15:10). If the requirement of keeping God's commandments is exactly the same for us as it is for Jesus, then we need to be obedient in the same way that He was obedient. If this is how He tapped into His Father's favour, then it is no different for us.

Bear in mind that it is not the commandments of Moses, but the commandments of Jesus that we are to keep. Keeping the law of sin and death will get us nowhere—it breathes death on the most vibrant of divine relationships. But the law of life in Christ Jesus is different— it opens doors to extravagant living! We can also deduce from this verse that God's love is as consistent towards us as it is towards Jesus. We cannot blame Him if we have a lack of favour in our lives; it is up to us to make withdrawals from His gracious provisions.

This verse has often gotten believers thinking that God loves us to the degree that we obey Him. No, it is not His love for us that changes; it's our resolve to tap into His love that changes. We are instructed to abide in His unfailing love for us. In the Bible, the love of God and the grace of God are often interchangeably used to describe the same thing.

Wouldn't it be wonderful if we could have absolutely anything we desire? In John 15:7, Jesus says that we can, and then gives us the instructions to make it happen. He said, *"If you abide in Me, and My words abide in you, you will ask what you desire, and it shall be done for you"*. Wow! Our desires! How about that? It is not just our needs but our desires that will be met.

Sounds pretty wonderful, doesn't it? These scriptures are taken from Jesus' teaching on the vine and the branches. Jesus is the vine and we are the branches—He is the divine source of grace. It stands to reason that a branch cannot be fruitful unless it is connected to the source of life flowing through the vine. If we want to be fruitful, we need to be connected to the source of grace. How do we ensure that we stay connected? Simply by obeying His life giving commandments which are to stay in faith, and to love God and others as much as we love ourselves.

We have a choice. Life or death? What will it be? The Holy Spirit stands by, ready to lead us into a blessed life—grace manifests by way of answered prayer.

Did you notice that Hebrews 9:13-14 says that the blood of Christ purges our consciences from dead works to serve the living God? We are apt to think of dead works as being transgressions and iniquities, when in reality, dead works are nothing other than our attempts to obtain what Jesus has already obtained for us.

Although God has purged our consciences, we have a tendency of re-contaminating them by replaying our guilt and condemnation video tapes over and over in our heads. The more we rehearse and meditate on our failures, the lower we drag ourselves into remorse and regret. Instead of giving in to remorse and regrets that foster doubt and despair, we should be rejoicing in the midst of our failures, counting them as valuable training that we would not exchange for anything in the world. Money can buy almost anything, but nothing can buy the wisdom we gain through experience. Treasure it and use it to reach greater heights! A positive mind-set has the effect of lifting our spirits and reinforcing our faith in a God that can be counted on when the chips are down.

It's all about knowing that God is always on our side and in complete control. We wouldn't have gained the wisdom we have today if we had skipped any of the good, the bad and the ugly lessons learned from the "University of Hard Knocks". If we can bring ourselves to see God's graciousness in all of life's challenges, then praising Him in the midst of our darkest moments will not be difficult. When we are convinced that God is graciously working all things together for our good, we have every reason to be in a continuous state of gratefulness (Rom 8:28). A thankful disposition is calming and restful.

God's Sabbath rest does not come up once a week; it is a permanent 24/7 state of rest where there is nothing more to be earned from God. It's a place of luxuriating in His divine providence! No matter how bleak our circumstances may appear to be, we find rest from our wearisome striving when we rest in His grace.

Hallelujah! God has given us enough reason to enjoy the peace that comes with grace. With grace there is no place for the self-destructive indulgences of shame.

Religion would have us attempt to do the very work that Jesus has already finished doing for us. Whilst we insist on doing it ourselves, we don't come to the point of receiving what Jesus achieved for us, and consequently wonder why the "reward" is always beyond our grasp. But for as long as we mistake His favour to be a "reward", we cannot receive it as a free *"gift"*. Our most sincere efforts to obtain justification for ourselves, serve only to block grace from doing it for us.

We will not stand condemned before the Great White Throne on Judgement day; we will stand before the Bema Seat of Christ. The Bema Seat of Christ is not a place where saints will be condemned for poor performance; it is a place where our works will be acknowledged. This is not a place of retribution; it is a place where we will be brought to account for what we have done with the grace that has been entrusted to us. The motives behind our actions will either validate or invalidate our works. This is where "Extreme grace" has a head start. Grace appeals directly to our hearts, and it is in our hearts where both good and bad motives are nurtured.

The question is; will we stand before God with the *"filthy rags"* that we have managed to accumulate through years of striving for holiness, or will we stand before Him with nothing to offer except the luscious fruit that the Holy Spirit has produced through us? Obviously, His fruit is infinitely more glorious than ours. Grace has nothing to do with "our" accomplishments and everything to do with "Christ's". Grace is entirely about being led by the Spirit, and when that happens, the Holy Spirit produces His brand of delicious fruit through us all by Himself.

Religion calls for holiness, and then uses checks and balances to reward and rebuke. By its very nature, religion cannot allow freedom. Wherever legalism is imposed, freedom is forfeited. These two concepts cannot coexist. When religion uses the curses and blessings of the law as carrot and stick to enforce obedience, there is no room for freedom.

Reading our Bibles, spending time in prayer, and regularly breaking bread are wonderful grace disciplines. Of course, the moment we do these disciplines to make ourselves deserving of grace, is the moment that we miss grace altogether. This is where religion infiltrates grace. But instead of fortifying grace; it cancels grace!

But if in the process of these disciplines, our faith is strengthened, then we will have greater access to the grace that is so freely available to us. No amount of godly service can unlock grace. For that it takes faith, forgiveness and the humility of a saint who knows that his or her actions, though in the process of being sanctified, are nevertheless far from perfect. Yet he or she is entirely convinced of God's love.

Faith works by love; not our love for God; it is precisely opposite; faith works by our awareness of God's love for us. When we are convinced that we are loved without reason, we know that our faith is not misplaced!

GUILT AND
CONDEMNATION

Do our feelings of guilt and condemnation
make our case any stronger with God?

Whether of the "extreme grace" persuasion or not, believers aspire to live in holiness. But "extreme grace" differs in its motivation. Instead of demanding holiness; believers are drawn into holiness with unconditional love and acceptance.

There are two issues. The first is freedom from "the condition known as sin" and the second is freedom from "the act of sinning". We are not expected to pursue the first one. That is a matter that Jesus has already dealt with and settled for all time and eternity. Chasing after the second issue is just as senseless, because whilst we are side tracked into trying to free ourselves from sinning, we will not see the solution staring us in the face.

Let's not kid ourselves—in reality our most determined efforts to forsake our irksome ways usually fail. The way to have victory over sinning is not by disciplining our bodies; it is by disciplining our minds to yield to the Spirit. But there is often resistance to this idea, because we don't welcome the thought of foregoing our independence. The thought of someone else, albeit God, telling us how we should run our lives, can seem intimidating. But once love has drawn us into a relationship, surrender follows without a fight. When we feel loved, we feel safe—trust follows without persuasion. Lives and lifestyles cannot escape the compelling influence of unconditional love! Before we know it, we have been drawn into godliness.

Is it okay to live in the sublime bliss of grace without ever punishing ourselves with guilt and condemnation when we sin and disappoint God? Jesus took all our guilt and condemnation upon Himself. Guilt and condemnation is certainly not the way of the "redeemed of the Lord". Guilt and condemnation are self-destructive emotions that play directly into the hands of our enemy. As *"accuser of the brethren"*, it is his business to get us to loath ourselves for the things we have done.

By indulging in self-condemnation, we inadvertently bring our right standing with God into question and make light of the cross. In pouring scorn upon ourselves, we pour scorn upon the gospel.

We are in perpetual right standing with God—He has elevated us to royalty as sons and daughters of the most-high God. How sad to allow self-condemnation to rob us of our royal standing. To belittle ourselves, is to belittle the royal priesthood of believers, of which we are all members.

I know a man who proudly tells from the pulpit of the many tears he sheds for his sins. This is adequate evidence of his lack of understanding of the grace he stands in. When we make more of an issue of our sin than of our right standing, it is obvious that we are not participating in the glorious *"gift"* of grace.

Yes, we have done wrong. Yes, we feel the guilt of it, but unless we nip guilt and condemnation in the bud with speedy repentance, they can so easily evolve into all kinds of self-destructive emotions such as doom, gloom, despair and self-loathing. And it doesn't stop there; these negative emotions give way to a multitude of antisocial behaviours.

To drink from the cup of guilt and condemnation is to poison oneself with the noxious dregs of sin. As though sin in itself is not damaging enough, we linger over its toxic dregs and allow condemnation to complete the destruction that sin began. The more we drink of sin's noxious brew of guilt and condemnation, the more likely we are to fall for temptation when it comes knocking.

If sin doesn't destroy us, guilt will! Our consciousness of sin is the dreaded killer, and the law is its accomplice—it is the ministry of death! *"Without the law sin is dead [the sense of it* (sin) *is inactive and a lifeless thing]"* (Rom 7:8 Amp). We so willingly stoke our passions for sin and guilt by keeping the law. But according to Paul, once we have cleared the law from our minds, *"sin is dead"*.

Sin in itself is usually not quite as damaging to us as the aftermath of sin. The aftermath is the destruction that we bring upon ourselves in self-denigration. It is *"The accuser of the brethren's"* devious tactic to accuse and lay blame. The question is; do we take his bait and fall into self-blame and shame, or do we block his fiery darts with the shield of faith? If he can get us to accuse ourselves, he can rattle our confidence and disable our faith; it's how he defeats his enemies. To accuse ourselves is to carry out his diabolical work for him.

The awful truth is that sin thrives in the darkness of guilt and condemnation. Sin breeds sin. The less we come to value ourselves, the more likely we are to fall for temptation. Yes, we have a problem that must be dealt with. Yes, we must make right with whoever we have wronged. Yes, we repent quickly. No, we dare not permit ourselves to slide down the slippery slope of guilt and condemnation. We need never go there! These self-destructive emotions take us down to pit dwelling mentality—ideal breeding ground for antisocial behaviour. This is where we are most vulnerable to our enemy's tricks—we become prickly—our actions become horrid kneejerk reactions as we seek to take everybody else down to our level. The nasty ungraciousness of the tall poppy syndrome follows as we cut everybody else down to our size.

Contrary to popular belief, guilt and condemnation are not sin defeating emotions; they exalt sin. These emotions take us down to our enemy's level—it is how we give him the right to wreak havoc in our lives. What then is the solution? Coming into agreement with God is the solution. If He says that I am *"the righteousness of God in Christ"*, then although I have disappointed myself by slipping into sin yet again, I remain what He has made me to be; entirely without condemnation, because *"there is no condemnation to them that are in Christ Jesus"*. Yes! I have not behaved as though this is so. No! That has not changed my right standing with God.

We should not lose sight of the basic truth that we remain *"in Christ"*, not because we have repented on time, but because our *"in Christ"* status was established at Calvary and personalised at rebirth. And if we are *"in Christ"*, we are *"The righteousness of God in Christ"*. This status cannot be diminished by sin; after all, Calvary was the place where sin finally met its match. That doesn't mean that we don't repent. Repentance is noble; it helps us walk uprightly before God and men, among many other honourable virtues.

Repentance is a change of mind that results in a change of conduct. This is the crux of the message of grace—when change takes place "within", it soon manifests outwardly (Mat 23:26).

Must we now live in grace without feeling any guilt or condemnation? It is a given—we all go through these destructive emotions, but unless we turn them into joyous repentance victories, they serve no purpose except to take us down. For the believer, condemnation happens when something as beautiful as being sorry corrupts into something as awful as self-condemnation. Like milk left in the sun, self-condemnation is the joy of life turned sour. Sorrow that leads to repentance is empowering, while self-condemnation and shame are disempowering. No self-respecting believer should ever give way to these destructive emotions—they refute our blood bought status of *"no condemnation"*.

The next verse gives the reason for no condemnation and the reason is certainly not our pious endeavours to live holy. *"For the law of the Spirit of life in Christ Jesus hath made me free from the law of sin and death"* (Rom 8:2). Although Jesus did not free us from sinning; He did free us from the law's awful consequences. *"The law of sin and death"* has lost its power to curse and condemn. When we accept God's way, He gets all the glory. After all, we rightly deserve condemnation and did nothing to free ourselves from it—He did it all!

A problem arises when we acknowledge that we are free from *"the law of sin and death"*, yet fail to fully embrace the grace that God provided for us by way of *"the law of the Spirit of life in Christ Jesus"*. When we do this, we float in a state of limbo; neither under law nor grace—or so we think. The truth is that without the covering provided by grace we stand accused. If it is not all grace with zero Old Covenant law, it will be all law with zero grace, and with the law comes guilt and condemnation.

What does Jesus have to say about condemnation? In His own words, *"He that heareth my word, and believeth on him that sent me, hath everlasting life, and shall not come into condemnation; but is passed from death unto life"* (Joh 5:24). Jesus' words, *"shall not come into condemnation"*, are very emphatic. To allow ourselves to slip into the self-destructive grip of self-condemnation is to challenge the validity of what He said. The truth is that Jesus *"condemned sin in the flesh"* once and for all time and eternity on our behalf (Rom 8:3). As a result, as far as believers are concerned, condemnation has finally met its match. But for unbelievers it is different.

The self-destructive emotions of guilt and condemnation have precisely the opposite outcome to that of the empowering knowledge of our good standing with God. The one destroys self-worth, while the other edifies and bolsters self-worth. Overcoming sin simply cannot be achieved from a position of self-blame and defeat, but is a synch for a mind that is fixed on the victory that Jesus established at Calvary.

It is in the nature of mankind to regret thoughtless words and deeds—our flawed choices often get us into a whole heap of trouble. If we allow these disappointments to drag us into guilt, condemnation and shame, it becomes a simple matter for our *"accuser"* to divert us from marching in *"Christ's triumphal procession"*. He only needs our sense of guilt and condemnation to work with—shame is his stock in trade! Sadly, religion often unknowingly carries out Satan's destructive agenda. He is determined to convince believers that they are less than what Christ has made of them. Sadly, there are sincere churchmen who are convinced that the deeper the guilt and self-blame, the deeper the repentance. Is it any wonder that their flocks flounder in defeat? Once disempowered in this way, their faith is rendered ineffective.

FALL FROM GRACE

Do we *"Pursue peace with all people, and holiness, without which no one will see the Lord"*? (Heb 12:14)

The world out there is hurting; they are crying out for help and the church has the answers. But religion, lacking the fullness of grace, has little of value to offer.

Our actions are not holy unless our hearts are in it. The hidden attitudes of our hearts either nullify or validate our attempts at living holy. Grace is called for—it goes straight to the heart of the matter, to the very place where attitudes are formed. An extreme form of love is required—nothing less has the power to draw a person into holiness.

Love is enormously influential, and so is guilt and condemnation. Godly attitudes incubate and flourish in healthy self-worth, but wither in the shame of self-condemnation. Like mushrooms, sin flourishes in the darkness of self-condemnation, but wilts in the bright sunshine of healthy God edified self-esteem.

Small love inspires small love, while great love inspires great love, and when love is inspired, it can do no harm. Religion, in its quest for "holiness", dispenses a scaled down version of grace to its followers—it feels that it must shield its charge from licence. But scaled down grace is scaled down redemption. Sadly, in this way, we don't come to know how much we are loved, and consequently, have little love to give away. Instead of passing on unbridled grace with love and acceptance, our fellow man must put up with our holier than thou-ness, crustiness and "pious" intolerances—the product of watered down grace.

As much as we desire to fulfil the divine injunction to *"Pursue peace with all people, and holiness"*, religion has reduced grace to the point where it is powerless to do so. We cannot be at peace with all people while we are judging them. And we cannot attain holiness through sheer grit and determination. God's directive can only be fulfilled with godly attitudes. Sadly, watered down grace is watered down power. We need the power of grace to confront our sin, beginning with our attitudes. It takes the extremeness of grace to establish the extremeness of holiness.

Godly character is often desired, but not always attained. We need to stay on track—the love that comes with grace gives us all the motivation necessary to stay the course (Luk 7:47).

"Looking carefully lest anyone fall short of the grace of God..." (Heb 12:15). Some Bible versions say it slightly differently—they say, *"turning away from the grace of God"*. How do we turn away from the grace of God? Certainly not by sinning; that's how we turn to it. We turn away from it when we turn to any means other than grace to find justification for ourselves. But, in reality, grace on its own is enough—our puny efforts cannot improve on something that is already perfect.

Paul related his personal battle with condemnation—it was an affliction that came upon him when he tried to keep the law. He said that he could not live for God unless he completely forsook the law. He put it this way, *"For when I tried to keep the law, it condemned me. So I died to the law—I stopped trying to meet all its requirements—so that I might live for God"* (Gal 2:19 NLT). If he could not live for God unless he completely ditched the law, then the same applies to us.

Religion cautions its followers to stay away from "extreme grace". It may even substantiate its stand by quoting scriptures that it believes will be transgressed. "Stay away from extreme grace, "...*lest any root of bitterness springing up cause trouble, and by this many become defiled""* (Heb 12:15). But the root of bitterness does not exist in actions; it exists in hearts—the very place where grace plays its life changing role. Godliness has no stronger ally than grace—nothing but unconditional love is able to crack our resistance to submitting to the Holy Spirit's counsel. Only love can influence us to walk in a godliness that is transparent and genuine. The personal value that we get from being valued, makes it unnecessary to seek value elsewhere, least of all in the self-destructive pursuit of sin.

I have also heard it said, "Stay away from "extreme grace", *"lest there be any fornicator or profane person like Esau, who for one morsel of food sold his birthright. For you know that afterward, when he wanted to inherit the blessing, he was rejected, for he found no place for repentance, though he sought it diligently with tears.* (Heb 12:16, 17).

We obtained an enormous inheritance upon the death of Jesus— this is our birthright. As with all inheritances, it comes to us free, gratis and for nothing—grace at its best! But like Esau, we can forfeit it, and that is the greatest tragedy that can befall a believer. It is not intentionally done. It happens when we innocently turn to the law for our right standing. But we soon find out that our best law keeping efforts are incapable of giving us what the Spirit of grace gives. But for those who have found fulfilment in grace, they have no need to seek fulfilment in fornication or profanity. Unconditional love and acceptance within their divine romance is fulfilling enough.

To believe that we sell our birthright when we sin, is to believe that we are saved by our conduct. But the only reason we turned to a Saviour in the first place, was because we could not find salvation through good conduct.

Nothing that the world offers can compete with the pleasures of a divine romance with the King of kings. It appeals to the very best in us. When a heart loses its appetite for ungodly behaviour, there is no need to strive for holiness—it comes naturally!

It takes a lot of love to draw us into a divine romance—one where we feel safe to entrust our all to our Lover. Whilst it is not possible to be perfect, we can at least progress towards godliness. Yielded-ness will take us in that direction, and love gives us good reason to yield. When we are submitted to the Spirit, we soon find out that everything He inspires us to do is entirely holy and good for us.

As a fit teenager, like most young men discovering their manliness, I was ready to test my horns on anybody who dared to challenge me. I remember being ordered by a church elder to move to a seat closer to the front of the church. His stern rebuke for choosing to sit near the back gave me enough reason to dig my heels in and remain where I was. This angered him all the more, and the harsh words that followed from him gave me even more reason to resist his demands.

Later, when the visiting speaker got up to speak, he graciously honoured us before respectfully asking that we move a little closer. I quickly obliged as my obstinacy melted in the warmth of his courtesy and respect—it is difficult to resist graciousness! There is no question about it; grace is more powerful than the harshest demands of legalism.

But Jesus wasn't gracious to everybody—he angrily chased the traders out of the Temple with a whip! Consider for a moment—how many did he win over on that day? Probably none! These men didn't suddenly give up their evil practices to become meek and mild disciples of Jesus. It is more likely that they hardened their attitudes and hated him all the more. But Jesus wasn't trying to win them over on that day, He was cleansing the Temple.

God has been in the business of influencing people a lot longer than you and me. Although He could crush us into submission with one flick of His finger, He knows that crushing us will not change our hearts. As much as He desires change, He is fully aware that we respond more readily to love than to bullying. Is it any wonder that He wraps His instructions in grace?

"Therefore, since a promise remains of entering His rest, let us fear lest any of you seem to have come short of it" (Heb 4:1). Interestingly, they *"could not enter because of unbelief"*, not because of sin (of course, we know that unbelief is sin) (Heb 3:19). Grace is purely a Holy Spirit inspired walk of faith, and it is faith alone that gives entry into God's rest.

The question to ask oneself is, "what is it that we rest from doing?" The answer is, "We rest from making ourselves acceptable to

God". That is something that the Holy Spirit has undertaken to do for us. Permission to enter this rest is restricted—not every believer enters. Those who have tried to obtain entry on the basis of their holy living or good works cannot rest; there is always more to be done. Verse 3 of chapter 4 uses the word *"only"* and therefore excludes any way except faith to enter His place of rest. *"For only we who believe can enter into His place of rest"* We rest from religious striving—we cannot afford to rely on any of our right making efforts—we rely purely on what Jesus has done, and what the Holy Spirit continues to carry out in us, period!

"For if you live according to the flesh you will die; but if by the Spirit you put to death the deeds of the body, you will live" (Rom 8:13). Without question, we are expected to put to death the deeds of the flesh, but not without help, for it is *"by the Spirit"* that we *"put to death the deeds of the body"*. Thankfully, this is the way of grace. Grace is the process of being led by the Spirit—the only effective way to put to death the deeds of the flesh.

Grace is immensely endearing and enormously edifying—good reason to keep coming back for more—bringing the very best out of us. Intimacy makes submission appealing!

It took one supreme sacrifice to break sin's stranglehold over our lives. That does not mean that we cease to act sinfully, but thankfully, grace gives us good reason and empowerment to overcome sin.

Of course all our actions, whether holy or not, have consequences. Take care not to blame God for the natural consequences of our careless actions—they are not divine penalties. Although God has forgiven us, we are left to suffer the unfortunate outcomes of our reckless actions. Although God forgives me for making my best friend's wife pregnant, nevertheless she remains pregnant, and I am left to live with the devastating consequences of my shameful actions.

As hard as it may be to admit, our day to day sinning will continue until the day we die. We will spend a lifetime repenting, because quite frankly, we will spend a lifetime sinning, not because we want to, but because it is what we do. God is well aware of this, and has done all He can to empower us to overcome sin. "Extreme grace" is not sin's ally; it is sin's deadliest foe!

CONTRITE SPIRIT

Is there contriteness in grace?

"Extreme grace" is often construed by religious thinkers to be a new revelation. But neither "extreme grace" nor the ungracious practice of slating "extreme grace" is new. "Extreme grace" had its place in the early church long before it unravelled into a less extreme form, also known as religion. The emergence of religious controls spelt an end to the original form of grace that Paul so passionately championed. Freedom presented a very real threat to the dubious practice of clerical control. Anybody daring to question the religious status quo, was quickly labelled a heretic. The price for suggesting that grace was God's idea was high—the threat of death ever present. Religion had become a monster intent on eating itself up.

The past two thousand years have been peppered with the re-emergence of "extreme grace", only to be squashed by Pharisaic oversight. Each of history's great reformers steered the church back to a measure of grace, but instead of growing in this enlightenment, the church very quickly slid back into the bleakness of religiousness. The liberties of grace were viewed with suspicion. Church government assumed a controlling role, and grace was reckoned to be rebellion. Among thousands of Christians martyred by sword and fire were great reformers such as John Huss (1414); Jerome Savonarola (1498); Ulrich Zwingli (1528); Thomas Cranmer (1556); William Tyndale (1536); Patrick Hamilton (1528) and William Hunter (1555). Grace had become a hot potato to the religious establishment—it had to be quelled lest it multiply!

Paul was probably the foremost proponent of "extreme grace". He devoted the greater part of his prolific writings to convincing believers to abandon the practise of making themselves right through law keeping; repeatedly warning that it would void their faith and cut them off from Christ (Gal 5:4, Rom 4:14).

Agape love is a sanctifying force. As it goes about its life transforming work, the allure of sin soon fades. Sadly, for as long as believers are persuaded to stay away from "extreme grace", they cannot enjoy God's benevolence. No matter how doggedly they may pursue holiness, it cannot be achieved without the help of grace. Unless grace has conquered sin in our inner control centre, we are powerless to conquer it in our actions.

Once we have given the Holy Spirit the reins of our lives, there is no further need to strive for change—He can be trusted to steer our thinking in the right direction. When this happens, our actions soon fall into line with our sanctification. Grace has no trouble surviving the turbulent waters of sin, but drowns in our pious attempts at making ourselves right.

With regard to contriteness and humility, James says, *"Let there be tears for the wrong things you have done. Let there be sorrow and deep grief"* (5:9 NLT). He calls for extreme humility. This is where "extreme grace" has the edge. The depth of our relationship with our loving Father, determines the depth of our sorrow when we disappoint Him—it all comes down to intimacy. The love of God packaged in grace, reveals an affection of the most intimate kind!

I grew up at a time when caning was the preferred method of disciplining boys at schools. We lived in fear of that stick. The rod did not endear us to the principal. The sorrow we felt was usually shallow—we weren't sorry for our mischief; we were sorry for being found out.

I had a strict Sunday school teacher who did not appreciate my smart aleck questions—he regarded them as a challenge to his authority. With stern words he would expel me from his class almost every Sunday. Did his harsh treatment soften my heart towards him? Certainly not!

Now my Grandmother was very different. The love that she showed me made it very difficult to do anything that would give her reason to be disappointed with me. So whenever I slipped up and gave her reason, it would wound me deeply—genuine sorrow followed. Her love for me was enough reason to keep my heart soft towards her.

In an environment of grace, where God's love is the central theme, His love gives us good reason to be sorry whenever we become aware that we have done something hurtful to our relationship—it is only natural to be sorry.

Love is a doing word, but also a deep emotion. When we live emotionally connected to God's deep love for us, it stands to reason that we will be sensitive to His hurts. It should be obvious that love would motivate deeper contriteness and sorrow than the most stringent of religious requirements.

Believers who are accustomed to having their lives regulated by the rigid framework of the law, are often offended by the freedom they see in the followers of "extreme grace". Viewed from the security of religious structures, liberty can seem pretty frightening. But then again, it is perfectly understandable for people of grace to be misunderstood. It is a reaction that Paul often encountered—he made an all-out effort to allay religious reservations and fears. True grace is always at risk of religious criticism—especially by those who do not understand that it is the Bible way. Many conclude that if it has no restraints, it must be error. They often see danger where there is no danger. Obviously, when God is in it, there can be no danger.

Somehow grace gets confused with permission to sin, and to be disobedient. And to top it all, they suppose that sorrow for wrongdoing is not experienced. Nothing could be further from the truth!

"Extreme grace" does not open the door to disobedience; it opens the door to obedience at a level that can only be understood by a person who has been loved into obedience. "Extreme grace" does not promote sinning with impunity; it inspires a Spirit led life. "Extreme grace" does not lead to a hardening of the heart; it leads to a heart made soft by love. "Extreme grace" is God's expression of love, and His big heartedness is enough to melt the stoniest of hearts. "Extreme grace" does not shy away from repentance; it draws us into repentance.

For as long as religion shuns "extreme grace", it forfeits the undergirding support and empowerment of grace, and without this empowerment, lofty Christian ideals cannot be attained. Sheer grit and determination, together with any other religious requirements, have failed to bring about real change at heart level. I speak from personal experience, having been an ardent devotee of legalism's watered down version of grace for most of my life. Holiness was expected of me—it was labelled the gospel of grace; yet I saw little grace in the harsh attitudes of holiness people, including me.

One of our most respected leaders had little patience for the faults of others. Members were careful to tread softly in his presence lest they arouse his wrath. Grace was not big on his agenda. Religion holds no answers for the evil in believers' hearts—it is time for us to be honest about it, and to admit what many believers have suspected all along.

Surely there must be another way? Praise God! The Bible has had the answer all along—it is grace, and God's grace is of the most extreme kind!

HOLY MOTIVATION

How holy must we be to escape God's wrath?

Your love is better than life itself (Psa 63:3). It is Your kindness and favour Lord that leads us to repentance (Rom 2:4).

Fearful consequences are sometimes used to persuade believers to repent, but is this really God's way? He motivates repentance with His goodness. David's intimate relationship with God gave him insight into His generosity, love and kindness. He wrote, *"Oh, taste and see that the Lord is good"* (Psa 34:8).

God does not lead from behind with a stick—He leads from the front with encouragement and loving inducements. As human beings, we respond poorly to beatings. It is difficult to respond lovingly to the one beating us. But when we are loved into obedience, it is different! Our capacity for obedience is enlarged by His love.

"Or do you despise the riches of His goodness, forbearance, and longsuffering, not knowing that the goodness of God leads you to repentance?" (Rom 2:4). What are our motives for repenting? Are we doing it out of fear, or out of sensitivity to the One who loves us so

dearly? Are we driven or drawn? Do we have a master and servant relationship, or an intimate friendship with Jesus?

When we sing, "Jesus, Lover of my soul", it can sound so airy-fairy that its profoundness can escape our notice. Somehow, we miss the point—it is not just the vagueness of what our soul may be that He loves so dearly; it is we, personally with whom He is so deeply in love.

When we attempt to modify our actions, change is superficial. Unbelievers see through pious pretending, and are quick to label Christians as hypocrites. Regretfully, they cannot be blamed for coming to these unfortunate conclusions.

We often hear the hypocritical words, "I can't stand so and so, but as a Christian I must love him". And it is not unusual to hear two believers who cannot stomach one another, telling each other that they love each other "in the Lord". It doesn't take a rocket scientist to see hypocrisy in this. This two-faced insincerity is the result of contrived good behaviour from a person whose heart has not been changed by God's love.

Paul urged us to be genuine in our loving. He said, *"Don't just pretend that you love others. Really love them"* (Rom 12:9 NLT). I once heard a church leader say that if you cannot find any love in your heart for a person, then by faith, tell that person that you love them. But this is so opposite to what real love is! People are not easily fooled—they know flakiness when they see it! Is there any wonder that there is so much shallowness going around?

We simply cannot extend more love than what we have discovered of God's love for us. God's graciousness is something that must be received before it can be given away. Unless it originates in God, it is merely charm. And grace should not be confused with the shallowness of charm. We are not inherently equipped to extend mercy to obnoxious individuals—it runs contrary to human nature. But when we realise how merciful God is to us, then giving mercy to others becomes second nature. God's love inspires our love, making it possible to love the least deserving of individuals.

When good behaviour is contrived, underlying attitudes remain concealed. Force of will is not necessarily force of love. To simply resolve to treat others better, is not the same as desiring to treat them better. Unless our hearts are in it, our changes are no more than skin deep—attitudes die hard. Love is needed, and grace has plenty to give! Those who have discovered that they are loved despite themselves, have no difficulty loving others without regard for their deservedness.

What is the answer to shallowness? Quite obviously, it is depth! Unless change takes place at heart level, it is not deep enough to be genuine. Although we are dearly loved, we can miss the significance of it—His love must be embraced in all its extremeness before it can have an effect on our lifestyles. Once our hearts have been captured by His love, our resistance to repentance crumbles—we willingly open up and allow Him into our secret places. When this happens, His compassion becomes our compassion, and loving others changes from "have to" to "want to".

There is a turning away from the truth—it is what happens when we turn to the law. Paul warned about it when he said, *"Christ is become of no effect unto you, whosoever of you are justified by the law; ye are fallen from grace"* (Gal 5:4 KJV).

We must steer clear of fables. It is a fable to believe that we can be made right, or be sustained in right standing with God by any means other than grace. We dare not stray from Paul's original message of pure undiluted grace—we dare not taint it with laws, rules, legalism, restraints, religious routines or strivings, no matter how noble they may seem.

What about people who flaunt sin under the supposed license of grace? We should be under no illusion—what they are into is not grace at all! They have missed the essence of grace by a country mile! Such people have failed to grasp the inherent purpose of grace. Grace was not given for the purpose of promoting sin; it was given for the purpose of defeating sin.

Those who pick and choose bits and pieces of grace to excuse their ungodly lifestyles are deluded. They have no right to claim to be people of grace (Jude 4). They are kidding themselves—their lives have not been revolutionized by grace.

—oOo—

"For if you live according to the flesh you will die; but if by the Spirit you put to death the deeds of the body, you will live" (Rom 8:13). Grace fulfils this scripture perfectly. Notice that we are not expected to strive to put the deeds of the body to death; we do it *"by the Spirit"*. It is by grace that we are led by the Spirit. To describe the covenant of grace, is to describe a lifestyle directed by the Spirit. God only has one solution to sin—it is grace—there is no plan B.

Religion has proved beyond any shadow of doubt that it has not succeeded in putting to death the deeds of the body. It has done a fine job of dealing with surface matters such as smoking, drinking, dancing and adopting a saintly demeanour—inconsequential issues that side track believers from facing up to the real issues. For these it has no answers. The bottom line is that sin cannot be fixed with anything short of grace. The root of evil is not found in behaviour; it is found in the unsanctified thinking of believers.

How did religion come to decide upon what is sinful and what is not? At one time it was no makeup, no slacks for women, no bioscope etc. Over time the code underwent modification, yet remained fundamentally flawed. The list of do's and don'ts is just as ineffective now as it has always been—powerless to change hearts—just weird enough to make weirdoes of us all—a turnoff for those looking in.

Religion lost its way in legalism. Legalism is Satan's counterfeit gospel. Legalism's do's and don'ts are the fables that Paul warned Timothy to avoid. Whilst we are doing our level best to rectify surface issues, inward issues continue to fester.

When religion requires this, that and the other of us, it makes the gospel out to be a moral code, instead of a divine romance. When personal holiness is elevated above grace, change becomes the responsibility of the flesh instead of the Spirit. When that happens, all we are left with is a feeble gospel—one that honours the shallowness of legalism as if it were holiness—breeding a sense of superiority that looks down with disdain upon those it considers to be weaker vessels.

If we don't put the teabag into the tea cup, we end up with nothing more than sticky sweet warm water. When we leave grace out of the gospel, we are left with a sticky sweet religion that is powerless to confront sin in our hearts. Try as we may, we get nowhere fast; it's like trying to chop a tree down with an axe handle.

When religion is obsessed with surface matters, the real issues in the depths of our beings are left to proliferate unchecked.

The truth about believers is that we are not in the process of becoming *"the righteousness of God in Christ"*. We are already *"the righteousness of God in Christ"*. Although we have this wonderful *"gift"*, we all know that our behaviour is never entirely righteous. That's where the Holy Spirit comes in; He is always pointing us towards something better. When we are led towards something better, something worse gets left behind.

Religion often beats us over the head with a list of do's and don'ts—sins that we are expected to deal with. But Paul tackled the problem of sin from an entirely different angle. Instead of instructing us to stop sinning, he instructed us to walk by the Spirit. He was convinced that when we do it this way, we would not fulfil the lusts of the flesh. Problem solved! (Gal 5:16)

What was it that made him so sure that this would be more effective than law keeping? He was well aware, that as good as the law is, it does not possess the power to prevent sin. Sincere believers continue to be plagued by the self-same hang-ups, long after regularly repenting of them. In some cases, people never have victory over certain sins—they just don't seem to get their repentances to stick. Sometimes repeated repenting has only provided brief interludes to sinning. In reality, it is nigh impossible to shake ourselves free from our ingrained hang-ups. Paul went on to say, *"You do not do the things that you wish"* (Gal 5:17).

This comes as no surprise to God who is well aware of our human frailties and limitations, and that's why He has given us an effective solution that really works. How do we live by grace in practical terms? It's all about surrender—it's a yielded walk to the Holy Spirit.

As with New Year's resolutions, no matter how commendable repentance may be, it does not possess the power to bring about lasting change. It might be easy to repent, but it's the follow through that is difficult—old habits die hard—especially when God's grace is not factored in.

Strange as it may seem, preaching against sin does help us to sin less; it draws us into more sin. But thankfully, being reminded of our righteousness has the opposite effect. *"... the sharing of your faith may become effective by the acknowledgment of every good thing which is in you in Christ Jesus"* (Phm 1:6). The sharing of our faith is not made effective by acknowledging every bad thing in us; it is made effective by acknowledging every good thing in us. And being in Christ means that there is plenty of good in us. If you are thinking, "I can't think of anything good about me", think again—you are as righteous as God!

"No, you don't understand, Deon. You don't know what I have done."

"No, you don't understand. Because you are in Christ and He in you, you are filled with all kinds of goodness. But it is of little consequence unless you come to acknowledge it."

Unless we acknowledge that we are perpetually righteous, we cannot translate this truth into righteous actions. Unless we acknowledge that we are filled with light, we cannot light the way for those in darkness. Unless we acknowledge that we are filled with God's love, we cannot love unconditionally. Unless we acknowledge that we contain God's health and provisions, we cannot live in His health and provisions.

A little dabbling in both covenants will not do it—either it is all grace with zero law or it is nothing at all! If we choose to ignore this counsel, and insist on striving for holiness, we end up with something that only resembles holiness in the eyes of fellow legalists. Unbelievers are not for one moment fooled by contrived shows of religious snobbery—they see straight through our charades. I have a vivid picture in my mind of a dear Christian friend bent over with her finger down her throat as she showed her revulsion for a recent encounter with the shallowness of Christian snobbery. We cannot blame unbelievers for not rushing in to participate in something that they have seen through—holier than thou charades are seriously off-putting. Excuse my French—it is vomitable!

There is a more appropriate name for the holiness movement that I was party to—in a nut shell, it is a Gestapo Concentration Camp—to put it plainer, it is all about a kill joy god! He is served hand and foot with all kinds of demands and compulsory legalistic nonsense, even though, thankfully, such a demanding god does not exist. Legalistic demands entrenched in the holiness movement equals "no fun", period! From our freakish idea of holiness, fun bordered on worldliness.

In his youth, my father was not allowed to play cricket or any other school sport because it was regarded as "worldly". Legalism has got Christianity horribly wrong. God has got to be the most enjoyable Person to be around. God doesn't just enjoy His life; He is joy; He is peace; He is love—everything about Him is superlatively pleasurable and gloriously wonderful!

We can only comply with legalism's demand for holiness by gritting our teeth and manufacturing it, but manufactured holiness is not holiness at all. Even if we have given up a whole lot of awful sinning and committed ourselves to a whole lot of godly deeds, our lives do not remotely resemble holiness. Our best efforts fall into the category of human effort, and according to Jesus, *the flesh profits nothing"* (John 6:63). True holiness is not about acting perfectly; it's about the Spirit of God producing perfect fruit through us. When grace plus the Spirit of God plus our faith are working in concert, a symphony of holiness is produced.

"He who believes in Me, as the Scripture has said, out of his heart will flow rivers of living water" (Joh 7:38). This living water is the very life of the Spirit, which includes both the gifts of the Spirit and the fruit of the Spirit. When we experience this natural overflow of the Spirit, there is no need to manufacture holiness; it manifests all by itself without any help from us. Our contribution is faith, trust and yielded-ness.

Grace is a whole different way of thinking—it is Spirit thinking. If we can turn a deaf ear to religion's demands for holiness, and open our hearts to God's love talk, surrender follows, and surrendered hearts open the way for the Spirit of God to produce His fruit. And there can be nothing holier than that! To describe the fruit of the Spirit is to describe holiness—it's the best definition we have!

Sadly, the kind of preaching that demands holiness, is the very thing that keeps sincere believers in self-effort and therefore out of holiness. For as long as we are intent on manufacturing our version of holiness, the Holy Spirit is prevented from producing His version.

Religion demands holiness; whereas grace inspires and empowers us to walk in holiness. The one is characterised by burdensome requirements, while the other, by generosity, love, joy, peace and fulfilment—a reason to celebrate!

Worldly pleasure is nothing other than Satan's counterfeit to God's pleasure. Satan wouldn't bother offering his version if he wasn't trying to distract us from God's version. Counterfeits are designed to appear real, but have very different outcomes. Satan's counterfeits have stings in their tails. The problem with legalistic holiness is that in its efforts to stamp out worldliness, it ends up outlawing God's good things. Merriment is seen to be too worldly to be godly. How sad!

God is not a party pooper; partying is His idea. He instructed His people to buy whatever they wished to consume at the annual party in Jerusalem. *"And thou shalt bestow that money for whatsoever thy soul lusteth after, for oxen, or for sheep, or for wine, or for strong drink, or for whatsoever thy soul desireth: and thou shalt eat there before the LORD thy God, and thou shalt rejoice, thou, and thine household"* (Deu 14:26 KJV). Wine and strong drink sounds like one heck of a party to me!

I can just imagine how offended holiness people will be in heaven, when Jesus himself serves them wine at the marriage of the Lamb. It is going to be a celebration par excellence. He has done it before. The last time He produced wine was at the wedding in Cana of Galilee, when He provided the best wine last. Anybody who knows anything about wine, understands the significance of always serving the best wine first. Obviously, you cannot impress your guests with the best vintage at the end of the party when people are not clear-headed enough to appreciate quality.

For holiness people, it is unthinkable to imagine that Jesus would make tipsy people tipsier. They have difficulty getting their minds around a Jesus who revels in the merriment of His friends. To the religious mind, even to think of a "merry making Jesus" would be blasphemous. But then again, that's religion for you!

Louis Pasture said, "There is more philosophy in one bottle of wine than in all the books of the world". Wine is not about good sense; it's about good company. There is nothing in life more precious than friendship, and there is no question about it—the fruit of the grape connects people in special ways—happy ways! Jesus made the equivalent of 980 bottles of it at a social occasion for social reasons.

Of course, holiness people will be quick to say that Paul instructed us to choose elders and deacons who are not given to drinking much wine. Please note that Paul had nothing to say about drinking wine; it was overindulgence that was of concern to him.

"But you don't understand Deon; the wine of that time was grape juice". Really! If that were the case, it would make utter nonsense of Paul's instruction. Why on earth would he instruct deacons not to drink too much of something as inconsequential as grape juice?

Immediately after grapes are pressed, the juice begins to ferment. The winemakers of that era were powerless to prevent it from producing alcohol. Fermentation was further accelerated by the sweltering heat of the deserts of the Middle East, and they had no way of preventing this natural process from running its course. The non-alcoholic version of grape juice available to us in our day and age, was not available during Jesus' or Paul's time. Non-alcoholic grape juice has only in recent times been made possible by modern processes that prevent fermentation from running its course.

Besides turning water into wine at the wedding, Jesus was not shy to use winemaking as a metaphor in His sermons. According to Jesus, the reason that old wineskins should not be reused for new wine, is that fermentation produces a gas that stretches wineskins to their breaking point—there is no elasticity left in them for a second vintage. And with fermentation we get alcohol. It certainly doesn't sound like Jesus had any reservations about merry making. Of course, abuse of something as precious as jollification, is an entirely different matter.

There are those who would counter this notion by saying that new wine was to be consumed before fermentation could take place. But that would make nonsense of Jesus' metaphor. If new wine is not going to be left to ferment, then it would be quite in order to put new wine into old wineskins. Quite obviously, the fermentation of the new wine is the whole reason why old wineskins are not suitable for reuse.

"So let no one judge you in food or in drink" (Col 2:16). Here Paul takes issue with those who would judge believers for their choice of consumption.

I have not mentioned the drinking of wine because it has anything to do with grace. We don't need permission from grace to do something as normal and every day as was the custom and way of life of the saints of the Bible. I have mentioned wine because religion cannot substantiate legalism. It uses distortions and misinformation to convince us to live by its many rules.

As active participants in the holiness movement, Susan and I felt obliged to live double lives, doing our best to shield the freedom we had from our teetotaling church friends. Thank God, we eventually found the courage to repent of religious charading, and were pleasantly surprised to discover that many of our church friends had also been shielding their freedom. But our celebration was sort lived—our honesty proved to be costlier than we could ever have imagined. Some of our teetotaling friends were so offended by our freedom that they reported us to church eldership. This resulted in the severing of long standing close friendships with elders, followed by the issuing of a stringent printed code of legalistic do's and don'ts headed "The Spiritual and Moral Qualifications for Church Membership". Our continued membership was conditional upon our endorsement of, and adherence to the code. Does the evil of legalism come any more blatant than that?

Ultimately the elders fired our pastor for the freedom he had found in Christ. This was more than the congregation could handle. Sadly, this vibrant church split down the middle and never recovered. Ultimately legalism won the day—it swallowed its own tail and ate itself up! Twenty nine years later, the hollow frame of the church building stands as a stark memorial to grace defeated by the dead works of legalism.

Jesus turned water into wine and the Evangelicals and Pentecostals have been trying to turn it back into water ever since!

"Oh my goodness Deon! There you go again! Do you mean to tell us that we are licensed to get drunk?" Certainly not! Grace is the process of being led by the Spirit, and the fruit of the Spirit includes *"self-control"*. But legalism would rather have its followers stay away from merriment, than risk them living by the Spirit's fruit of *"self-control"*.

Why are religious celebrations so dull, and sinners' celebrations so joyous? Are we really more miserable than people who don't know Jesus at all? Is the joy of the Lord that we profess to have, only a figment of our imagination? Are we seriously going to allow legalism to have the last say?

Legalism says, "Surely in the light of so much alcohol abuse taking place, it should be forbidden in Christian circles? How dare we risk the awful consequences that come with abuse?" Using that logic, legitimate sex should be forbidden, because there is so much sexual abuse taking place in the world. No! God's way is not to stop something good in order to prevent something bad from taking place, but rather to equip us to enjoy His generous gifts without abusing them.

In discussion with a church leader, he was quick to point out that Jesus, like Samson, was a Nasserite, and Nasserites were prohibited from drinking wine. I reminded him that Nasserites were also prohibited from eating grapes and raisins. If we are going to adopt the Nasserite sect's restrictive lifestyle, then we will be required to stop eating grapes, including hot cross buns, Christmas cakes and any other dishes that have raisins in their ingredients. Besides, we will never be permitted to visit a barbershop for the rest of our lives.

The bottom line is that Jesus was not a Nasserite; He was a Nazarene—two very different labels. The one was a member of a religious sect, while the other, a citizen of the village of Nazareth.

Interestingly, David enjoyed his wine so much that he remembered to thank God for the *"wine that makes glad the heart of man"* (Psa 104:15). Anybody who enjoys wine knows its heart gladdening effect—non-alcoholic grape juice just isn't the same—it lacks good cheer!

Jesus used the analogy of the wineskins to illustrate how difficult it is for a legalistic mind-set to grasp the concept of walking in the liberty of the Spirit of grace. A law mind-set simply cannot accommodate the thought of a life that is free of religion. It insists that grace must be balanced with laws—rejecting anything that doesn't fit neatly into religiously established paradigms. Of this we can be certain—legalistic wineskins cannot contain grace—they will burst! It takes a process of oiling our wineskins with the oil of the Holy Spirit of grace to restore their elasticity. We may need to put aside our "extreme grace" prejudices to allow God to have the last say on the matter!

When religion tries to make us become what grace has already made us to be, it makes itself complicit in reducing the completeness of who we are in Christ. The best that we can do is to flee legalism before it reduces our security in Christ to the level of our *"filth rags"*.

In our sincere endeavours to do what Christ would do in every situation, we end up doing Jesus' works in a less perfect way. It reduces divine perfection to the level of human imperfection. Far better to allow Him to live His perfect life through our actions—His holiness cannot be imitated! It would be presumptuous on our part to imagine that we can keep a promise to do what Jesus would do in every situation. The best we can do is to have the humility to submit to His Lordship, and to confess that "Jesus is Lord of me and my actions". Nothing can be more satisfying than yielding to His gracious Lordship in every respect.

HOLINESS BY EFFORT

What must I do to be Holy?

When our holiness is not a work of the Holy Spirit, it is a matter of our flesh pretending to be holy. But pretence is a far cry from holiness—in fact it is precisely opposite. Living up to what legalism requires of us may make us look good to some, but is it really worth the trouble if it leaves our hearts entangled in sin. On the other hand, living by the Spirit of grace, is living by a purifying process that is more than capable of dealing with our hang-ups. Hearts that have been filled with God's love are hearts that have little room to accommodate unwholesome living.

Holiness achieved by the Spirit of Grace is the closest that we will ever get to the real deal, yet it is not the kind of holiness that would impress the purveyors of the holiness message. They are more concerned with what they have figured holiness to be—nothing but legalistic conformity. They will insist on sideways hugging when it comes to opposite sexes—it is an endless list of religious trivialities—the mumbo jumbo of religious witchcraft. The focus on superficiality blinds holiness people to the real issues at hand—hidden feelings and animosities—unhealthy attitudes left to fester in hearts. But unchanged hearts make nonsense of holy appearances—unwholesome thoughts rubbishing piety.

Intimate relationships with these apparent "paragons of holy virtue" is nigh impossible—one seldom gets past their pious facades to discover if they are for real—so adept are they at concealing their true feelings. That is until they are provoked. That's when their hidden attitudes show up in the fury of their eyes—their acid reactions unveil their pious masks to reveal the ugliness of gracelessness.

The shock of discovering fragility in the holiness of a person that we have come to admire can be hurtful and deeply disappointing! I know this only too well, after all, I have been just as ungracious as the next man, and this despite having walked with God for most of my life. But then again, for the best part of my life, I had little appreciation for the sanctifying work of grace—religion had hidden this information from me—religion had exalted my state of "holiness" above God's "grace". By making my righteous making efforts seem important, religion had inadvertently made the grace of Jesus less important. In religion's effort to reform me, it had achieved the precise opposite. The grace that took Jesus to the cross had been reduced to fit our denomination's legalistically skewed thinking.

Wherever grace is lacking, be it from clergy or pew warmer, relationships suffer. A lack of grace speaks louder than words. Can that really be holiness? When "godliness" comes without grace, is there really any godliness in it? Can it really be holiness if it can flip over into un-holy offence taking at the drop of a hat? I don't think so! When God called for holiness, He had something very different in mind to what legalism has foisted upon its unsuspecting followers.

"Heresy!" I hear some cry, "How dare you refer to Pentecostal holiness as religious mumbo jumbo Deon? Don't you know that God requires us to be holy even as He is holy?" Agreed—there can be no quarrel with that. The question we should be asking ourselves is, "How do we attain such a noble ideal? By carnal effort, or by the leading of the Spirit? By law keeping, or by faith? By legalism, or by grace?"

"For to be carnally minded is death; but to be spiritually minded is life and peace" (Rom 8:6). As odd as it may seem—to strive for

holiness through law keeping is to be carnally minded, because fleshly restraint is required to control fleshly actions, and *"they that are in the flesh cannot please God"* (Rom 8:8). Strangely, the thing that holiness people try their darndest to achieve is something that comes naturally to those who *"Walk in the Spirit",* because in doing so, they do *"not fulfil the lust of the flesh"* (Gal 5:16). It is not a case of "must not" as though it were a matter of physical restraint; it is a case of *"shall not",* because according to Paul, it won't happen! When we submit to the Spirit, the flesh follows—there is no effort in that!

If we walk surrendered to the Holy Spirit, does it mean that we will never sin again? You have got to be kidding? Just because we are walking hand in hand with the Holy Spirit, it does not follow that Satan is going to lie down and play dead. Not even close! When we raise our game plan, he raises his game plan. If he wants to stay in the chase, he has to turn up the heat—temptations have to become all the more tempting.

Unlike redemption, justification and atonement which take place in a flash, even though sanctification is complete in Christ, its effect on our behaviour is on-going—an entire lifetime is not long enough to complete the process. As a result, all believers, including the saintliest of us, continue to miss the mark—our actions are never entirely transformed this side of the grave. Despite this work in progress, which is always incomplete, we are nevertheless invited to walk hand in hand with the Holy Spirit. In other words the Holy Spirit knows that He will not find sinless people to walk hand in hand with—such creatures do not exist. Fortunately, He has made a way that allows Him to overlook our sin.

Of course, walking hand in hand with the Holy Spirit is a step by step progression towards living more and more righteously—yet we never entirely reach our objective this side of eternity. Despite this always unfinished work, we notice that we are bearing fruit that only the Holy Spirit can produce. This does not happen because we have reached a certain state of holiness; it happens because we respond in faith to God's grace. Grace does not stand on its own; it is a three pronged endeavour. It is our faith responding to God's grace with the help and guidance of the Holy Spirit. It is not about what can be achieved in our strength; it's about what can be achieved in God's strength—all the glory belongs to Him alone!

Jesus said, *"It is the Spirit who gives eternal life. Human effort accomplishes nothing. And the very words I have spoken to you are spirit and life"* (Joh 6:63). Religion often has us chasing our tails in an endless *"human effort"* to deal with our sins, and then we wonder why we *"accomplish nothing"*. But then again, something is achieved, if defeat and despondency count as achievements. In our efforts to defend our spotless spiritual reputations, we are likely to put up a front to hide our weaknesses. But the sad thing about spiritual fronts is that ungodliness gets to flourish in hidden places. *"Human effort"* may look good to others, but in reality, as Jesus said, *"Human effort accomplishes nothing"*.

If we were required to be entirely pure before being permitted to walk with the Holy Spirit, there would be no need to walk with Him. Such thinking is absurd! No! We desperately need to walk hand in hand with Him, because among other things, He provides the means to overcome sin. His way is not to condemn us for our sin, but rather to lead us to better things. There is no behaviour that is more righteous than that of the Holy Spirit's. His fruit becomes more and more evident in our behaviour as we walk hand in hand with Him.

"For by grace you have been saved by faith, and that not of yourselves, it is the gift of God, not of work, lest anyone should boast." This verse is the anthem of grace—other than faith, there is no mention of any other required contribution from us—it is all God's work—all the glory belongs to Him alone! And when it is His work, it is grace! What about good works then? We do not work for salvation, but rather work our salvation out in the form of being gracious to the world around us (Phil 2:12).

Sin, an extreme problem, calls for an extreme solution! It simply cannot be fixed with anything less. "Extreme grace" provides an extreme solution. Legalism doesn't work—it is man's invention; how can it possibly compete with what Jesus accomplished with His blood?

Hearts that have been overwhelmed with God's extreme love lose their appetite for sin. Conversely, those who are fixated on holiness either become obsessed with their spiritual superiority, or with their sins and shortcomings. Neither obsession is commendable. Their spiritual superiority leads to pride, and their shortcomings, to a sense of unworthiness. Unworthiness leads to a poor self-image, which in turn, leads to self-destructive inferiority complexes. Lack of healthy God inspired self-esteem is fertile ground for the incubation of sin. And so without grace of the most extreme kind, the cycle of self-destruction continues.

Of course, many believers are convinced that they have sufficient resolve and determination to achieve holiness. Usually these believers display "older brother" mentality which is off-putting to fellow believers. Unbelievers are even less likely to be impressed with pharisaic holier than thou attitudes—it reinforces their opinions that Christians are hypocrites.

I greatly admired my grade eleven English teacher—like me, she was a devout Pentecostal Holiness believer. On the surface, she seemed pious enough—no makeup on her face or figure nails; no hairstyling; drably dressed—a perfect picture of "holiness"!

One day she asked each of us to name our favourite authors. When I mentioned Ian Fleming's name, she turned on me in "holy" indignation, and made my life miserable for the rest of the year. Quite obviously, she had not been exposed to true grace, and consequently had no grace within her to give to anybody who didn't measure up to her perceived level of "holiness". Her Christian snobbery was "older brother" mentality at its gutter-most best. Her so called "Christian" attitude influenced me to rebel against the brand of Christianity that was commonly displayed in this movement. I found it difficult to stomach the insincerity that comes with "holiness through legalism"—a pharisaic disease of pandemic proportions.

Why is it that meanness seems to accompany "holiness"? It seems that the "holier" they get, the meaner they get. One of the best holiness preachers I knew, was also one of the most unapproachable men I knew. If this is what holiness is, then count me out! I have a sneaky suspicion that if Jesus were asked, He would say the same. The Jesus that "holiness people" portray is certainly not the Jesus I have come to know and love.

One often hears legalists denying that they practice legalism. Their brand of religion doesn't seem legalistic to them, but once they sample the delights of God's grace, they get a completely new perspective—it becomes clear to them that legalism had only served to distort their Christianity.

Legalists may even defend their stand by saying that grace is okay as long as it is balanced. The problem with this thinking is that there is only one concept that grace can be balanced against, and that is legalism. And the moment that grace is balanced, grace is cancelled. Even if we embrace grace, but choose to keep a foot in legalism for safety sake, we are plain and simply practitioners of legalism. One ounce of legalism is enough to estrange us from Christ and disqualify us from grace (Gal 5:4). When Jesus encountered the legalism of the Jewish religious leaders, He warned his followers to beware of the yeast of the Pharisees. As with the tiniest quantity of yeast in dough, the tiniest quantity of legalism is all it takes to ruin the whole loaf of grace.

Jesus said, *"... only God is truly good"* (Luk 18:19). If Jesus' statement is to be taken seriously, then it follows that we are never truly good in a practical sense. We have to rely exclusively on the righteousness that was imputed to us. Any attempt to improve upon it is done in vain.

When one abandons legalism in order to embrace grace, it is enormously liberating. But, a person's liberation can be very revealing of their current spiritual condition. When they make the switch to grace, they often fall into sin. In this way, their hearts are exposed to reveal how ineffective their legalism had been.

If a person, upon discovering that there are no behavioural restraints in grace falls into sin, then that person's heart would be shown up for what it really is. Was his or her holiness a matter of conforming to legalistic obligations—a work of the flesh, or was it a work of grace—holiness by agape love—a Spirit led life? The truth soon becomes evident. Their fall into sin provides adequate proof that legalism had failed to accomplish its most essential task; namely the sanctification of his or her heart.

A Christian friend of mine was a very strict father. His children had to toe the line or answer to His wrath. As a result, his kids were obedient and well behaved—that is until they flew the coop. The moment they escaped his iron fisted "holy" discipline, they threw themselves wholeheartedly into all kinds of forbidden experimentations.

It was different for our children. We did our best to shield them from our church's legalism. Although we had set broad boundaries and principles, we allowed them freedom, with our guidance of course, to develop their own boundaries. Although we were not expert parents by any stretch of the imagination, nevertheless our children were not burdened with holier than thou parents. As such, we were often out of step with our denomination's legalistic expectations, and had to make peace with their criticism of our lifestyle. Their harsh words were never spoken to us directly; they were carried to us via the grapevine. Although, at that time, we had a very ropey understanding of grace, we knew enough to know that legalism is un-gracious—we were thoroughly convinced that God is good! Although our parenting skills were far from perfect, ultimately, un-legalistic parenting paid off handsomely.

Freedom is very telling—we only know the truth about a person when they have complete freedom to do as they please. Coming into grace reveals how effective, or for that matter, how ineffective our past brand of religion has been. Had we been living up to the religious rules imposed upon us, or living by the love that God inspires through grace? When the restraints are lifted, how do we use our liberty? Our actions can be very telling!

EXTREME SOLUTION

What is God's solution to sin?

I would like to suggest that "extreme grace" is not one option among many. God only provided one solution to the sin problem. That solution is the grace that took Jesus to the cross. We experience His solution in many ways. In one grand fell swoop, all sins, past present and future, were atoned for, for all time and eternity. The privilege of permanent justification is made available to whosoever chooses to receive it—it is a free gift!

Although this magnificent act of grace deals with the entire sin issue, it does not cause believers to stop sinning. In fact, we all know that everybody sins until the day they die. Fortunately, God has this issue in hand; He provides grace, not only to forgive and forget our sins, but also to empower us to deal with our innate penchant for sinning. Grace is sin's most terrifying foe! God does not have a plan B—grace is it!

Every other religious solution has failed to produce the lofty Christlike ideals to which believers aspire. The emptiness of any form of faith that is not rooted in grace is out of step with God—He relates to us through a covenant of grace. No grace, no covenant, and without a covenant, we are most miserable, having no connection to God!

Although legalism has much to say about sin that can be seen, it provides little help for what goes on deep within. Matters such as prejudice, bigotry, intolerance, unreliability, hidden anger, racism, prima donna-ism, touchiness and snobbishness, seem to stay under the radar while fingers are pointed at smoking and drinking. But Jesus was very clear on priorities. He said that it is not what goes into the mouth that defiles; it is what comes out (Mat 15:11).

We can excuse much of the Christian shallowness we see, and put it down to immaturity—the church is composed of members at various stages of development, ranging from the most immature to the most mature—a commendable sign of healthy church growth. None of us have arrived—we are all participating in the on-going cleansing process of sanctification. Immaturity is not the problem. But a problem arises when grace of the extreme kind is forbidden, leaving believers powerless to deal with inner struggles. Sadly, the only other option open to them is to portray an illusion of holiness for appearances sake.

In case you are wondering, I do not wear my halo too well—it keeps drifting off to the side. I am doing my apprenticeship for heaven and have a long way to go. Grace is my only claim to godliness—I am a blithering idiot without it. Some may say, "You are still a blithering idiot". They only say that because they didn't know me before I found grace!

The church is the precious blood bought body of Christ—Christ's visible presence upon the earth. But the best that "un-extreme grace" can produce is an un-extreme form of love that is out of step with the loving character of the One we represent.

Are the followers of "extreme grace" any different to those of the less extreme version? This is a good question. There are two answers to this question. Yes, they are different, and no, they are not different. Many "extreme grace" followers were previously devotees of "un-extreme grace". They have a lifetime of performance mentality to undo. Paradigm shifts can be difficult, especially when years of contrary indoctrination must be unwound. In many cases it involves, not only a process of learning grace, but also a process of unlearning religion. Our whole relationship with God needs to be redefined in terms of His works and not ours.

Although we buy into the liberty afforded by "extreme grace", the *"accuser of the brethren"* continues to target us—he plays the guilt and shame card from our previous legalistic indoctrinations. For as long as we have one foot in legalism, we remain susceptible to guilt, unable to fully embrace our new found freedom.

Interestingly, it is different for new believers who enter directly into "extreme grace" without religious baggage. They bring nothing from past indoctrinations to impede their progress. We witnessed this during a five year spiritual awakening that I was privileged to be a part of. Un-churched new converts fared decidedly better when it came to the realm of the supernatural than did those who came to us with any kind of church background. It is not easy to throw off the shackles of legalism when it has been drilled into one over a lifetime of devotion to it.

Religion is man's search for God, while grace is God's search for man. Religion says do; grace says done! Jesus said, *"It is finished!"*

When legalistic performance is demanded from sincere Christian folk, who can blame them for forgetting that the Gospel is supposed to be good news? But how can anyone be expected to see any good in it when all it does is reveal how bad we are? Shortcomings and inadequacies are not at all good news! It is not good news when we cannot be accepted for who we are. There is nothing good about being commissioned to fight a losing battle with our short-comings.

It is not the demands from Sunday sermons that change believers; only the good news of the Gospel can do that. It is not the bad news of hell and damnation; it is the good news of heaven in our hearts! It is not good news to have to live up to legalistic expectations; it is good news to be liberated from such onerous burdens. Yes, we must preach hell and damnation—the world needs to know what awaits them without the grace of a Saviour. But it all goes horribly wrong when hell and damnation are misused to frighten believers into living holier.

When we must dance to the beat of legalism, we are in danger of slipping into cultism. When Christianity evolves into a moral code, it devolves out of the glory. This is not the Gospel of Jesus—He has done everything necessary to bring us rest. Our part is to relax in what He has achieved for us. To not make good use of this most precious gift would be awfully ungracious on our part. But, sad as it is to say, in the commendable pursuit of "holiness", many will cringe at the thought of luxuriating in God's Sabbath rest—it sounds too easy to be godly—too much like extreme grace.

The gospel doesn't have to tell us how inferior and incomplete we are in the hope that it will motivate us to do better. No! The gospel tells us how whole and complete we are *"in Christ"*, reason enough to come up higher.

The gospel doesn't have to persuade us to love others. No! Just being loved by God is persuasive enough. The gospel is the story of God's goodness and love towards mankind—the cross is sufficient proof of His passion for us. Frankly, nothing could be more convincing. His love for us makes loving and obeying Him appealing. If He can accommodate us regardless of our shortcomings, then we can accommodate others regardless of their shortcomings. We are enormously loved, and that is enough!

There are so many unwritten church laws that are not necessarily broadcast over the church's P.A. They are hidden in the undercurrents and attitudes of the holier than thou's. But no amount of surreptitious pressure can change us; only the good news of the gospel can do that! For believers, the dread of hell, and the sense of not having done enough to get God's attention is not the gospel of Jesus. He did not give us the gospel to magnify our failings and tell us how bad we are; He gave it to magnify our Christlikeness and tell us how good we are in Christ.

When we are convinced of this, there is no need to persuade us to produce fruit of the Spirit. No amount of pressure from the pulpit can cause us to accomplish something that can only be accomplished by the Spirit Himself. After all, purity cannot come out of impurity, and without the Spirit of grace, we have nothing better to offer. When we are yielded to the Holy Spirit of grace, *"love, joy, peace, longsuffering, kindness, goodness, faithfulness, gentleness, self-control"* become the unforced rhythms of our lives. There is no need to persuade us to yield—unconditional love is persuasive enough.

Any attempt on our part to produce fruit of the Spirit is sufficient proof that we are not walking with the Spirit. His wonderful fruit can only be ours if we stop striving for it, and allow the Spirit room to produce it all by Himself. We are expected to love our neighbours without regard for their affability. For that we need a whole lot more than our fickle resolve. When it comes to loving loathsome individuals, it simply cannot be done without divine help! On our own, our love is often tinged with prejudice and selectivity.

If we are walking by the Spirit, we don't need to be persuaded to stop lusting after the flesh, because when we walk by the Spirit we do not fulfil the lusts of the flesh—sin simply loses its shine.

We don't need to be persuaded to be like Jesus when we are convinced that whatever goodness we see in Him is already vested in us. As we look at ourselves in God's mirror, we get a new perspective of ourselves—we are so much like Jesus.

We don't need to be persuaded to work for Jesus when we are walking by faith, because our faith is punctuated with works of faith. Nor do we need to be persuaded to do good when the Spirit of God is directing our actions. His fruit is never less than good.

We don't have to be persuaded to be humble when we have nothing to boast of—grace has nothing to do with what we have done; it is all about what He has done.

We don't have to be persuaded to hold our salvation together when Jesus has promised to do it for us.

We don't have to be persuaded to spread the gospel when there is such a good story to be told of His amazing love, mercy and grace.

We have a fine testimony—Jesus brought us out of a second-rate religious existence—we were going nowhere! Partnering with Him needs no laws, except the liberating law of life in Christ Jesus. But then again, His law is superlatively delightful to fulfil! Man-o-man! What a privilege to have connections in high places! He and us in partnership are a force to be reckoned with! It is not what we know; it's who we know that really counts! Or better still; it's by whom we are known!

Our witness is powerful—marked with signs and wonders. There is enough good news to get the attention of those who are travelling the road of life on empty. What does sin have to offer, other than empty promises? How can empty promises possibly compete with the appeal and contentment of a life flooded with Christ's divine life?

We don't need to be persuaded to fellowship with our Lord when we are already enjoying fullness of life and pleasures forevermore in the intimacy of His presence.

There is a sin to be on the lookout for. It is the one that reduces our redemption. We commit that sin when we underestimate what redemption is—confining its work to the beginning of our Christian walk—forgetting that redemption is not only what saved us, but it is also what keeps us healthy, protected, provided for and in good standing with God. How awful to insult Jesus. We do this when we minimise what took place on Calvary. And it seems that many believers are determined to reduce grace to something less than what Jesus established! We make small of our redemption when we have to do this, that and the other to complete what Christ "supposedly" left undone.

We don't have to be persuaded to stop sinning when we have grasped what we have become *"in Christ"*. We do not have to look for pleasures in sin when we have found supreme fulfilment in a divine romance.

As you read these final paragraphs, my prayer is that you have become just a tiny bit more aware of what God thinks of you. His love affair with you is not something that you must initiate; it is something He initiated long ago. He is not waiting for you to make the first move—He is waiting for you to respond to His affection. You cannot love more intensely, unless you have discovered the intensity of His love for you.

If your journey into His love has been cut short by religiously imposed constraints on grace, perhaps today is a good day to rekindle your romance. But be warned! His love for you is so big that you will never uncover all of it. But don't let that stop you trying!

Dear reader,

I will never leave you nor forsake you,

love,

Jesus

Deon and Susan Stevens

I believe that Deon is a strategic champion of a Glorious Grace revolution taking place throughout the earth. This is not a book of empty froth, bubbles and shadows but it has the substance of rich unveiled truth unfolding in a supernatural sequence of liberating revelation that will set your heart racing with joy and inspire a fresh love for Jesus. All things are possible to a people set free from uncertainty, confusion and condemnation. Thank you so much Deon for your courage and compassion. I honor you and salute you in His abundant Grace.

Rob Rufus, Pastor of City Church International Hong Kong.

How is it that eager new believers turn into dreary religious zombies? What is the process that destroys a new believer's free spirit?

Babes in Christ soon lose their individuality as they are pressed into the mould of religious conformity. Religion is a killer! If religion was a man, he ought to be strung up from the nearest tree.

What is the solution? Realising that we are loved in our present condition, without having to make any promises to change, is the greatest discovery that any believer can make. God would rather relate to weird and wonderful misfits, oddballs and characters, than to a whole army of terracotta soldiers. God's unconditional love gives us freedom to be ourselves. It is okay to live with childish wonderment!

Also by this author:

If you have inherited so much in Christ, why would you continue striving so hard to get it?

He left you wealth, health, peace, joy and much more—yet many live whole lifetimes without benefiting from any of it. Your inheritance did not come to you because of your good works or holiness, and therefore cannot be taken away because of your lack thereof.

If you insist on working for it, there aren't enough hours in the day to do enough to deserve it. You are already in receipt of an immense fortune. A bountiful inheritance was placed into your personal trust account—you are at liberty to make withdrawals at your leisure.

When you discover how highly God esteems you, exactly as you are right now, your self-esteem will get a shot in the arm. You are not highly favoured because you are holy; you are highly favoured because you are His dearly loved child.

Daily Reading:

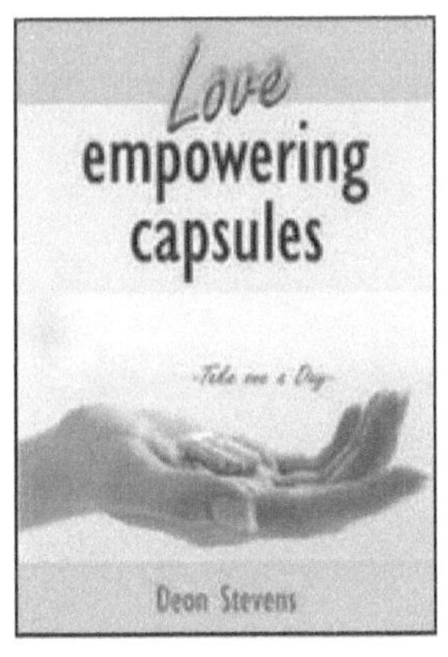

Believing in God's grace is one thing—a wonderful thought in theory, but how do we apply it to our daily living?

Where did we get the idea that God is a small-minded bookkeeper, tallying up our failures and successes on a score sheet? How we score in life has no bearing upon our entitlement of God's favour. We are the objects of His furious love pursuit, and we can luxuriate in this liberating knowledge.

If Christians are guilty of anything, it would be navel gazing. So much time is spent with self-introspection, self-recrimination and self-condemnation. Somehow we have lost sight of the fact that we are made right because of what Christ did, and not because of what we did. When we discover how highly God esteems us, exactly as we are right now, our self-esteem gets a shot in the arm. Our new sense of worthiness emboldens us to expect more from God. You are not highly favoured because you are holy; you are highly favoured because you are His dearly loved child.